Comic Practice/
Comic Response

Comic Practice/ Comic Response

Robert I. Williams

DELAWARE

Newark: University of Delaware Press
London and Toronto: Associated University Presses

Associated University Presses
440 Forsgate Drive
Cranbury, NJ 08512

Associated University Presses
25 Sicilian Avenue
London WC1A 2QH, England

Associated University Presses
P.O. Box 338, Port Credit
Mississauga, Ontario
Canada L5G 4L8

The paper used in this publication meets the requirements of the American National Standard for Permanence of Paper for Printed Library Materials Z39.48-1984.

Library of Congress Cataloging-in-Publication Data

Williams, Robert I., 1929–
    Comic practice/comic response / Robert I. Williams.
      p. cm.
    Includes bibliographical references and index.
    ISBN 0-87413-463-3 (alk. paper)
    1. Comic, The, in art. 2. Arts. I. Title.
NX650.C678W56   1993
700—dc20   92-50571
                                       CIP

Contents

Acknowledgments

True acknowledgments can never be credited sufficiently. In my case they range from Jonas Barish, who directed my doctoral work at Berkeley, to hundreds of students in comedy classes. But there is a special debt owed to Gregory Goekjian, a patient reviewer of drafts over the years, including key sections of this book.

Portions of what follows appeared in *The Journal of Aesthetic Education* (22:2, Summer 1988) and in *Philosophy and Literature* (12:1, Spring 1988). The following have kindly allowed use of materials:

- The British Museum, Hogarth's *The Bench*
- Hamburger Kunsthalle, Paul Klee's *Revolution of the Viaducts*
- Harcourt Brace and Jovanovich, and Faber and Faber Ltd., Richard Wilbur's "Death of a Toad"
- The Washington Post Writers Group, two cartoon strips from *Bloom County*

Comic Practice/
Comic Response

1
Groundings, Groundlings

Relative to the bulk of commentary on the arts in general, there has been very little written on what comedy is and how it actually works as an aesthetic mode. What follows is an account of comedy's basic operations and its peculiar forms as well as our equally peculiar involvement in the comic experience. As my title suggests, comic practice and response are highly interactive. Understanding their interaction is what this book is about. Necessarily, conclusions reached are provisional. Comedy is complex, and so are our mental processes. Hence, this brief treatment can only be a groundwork for further study. The intent is not to exhaust all genres and types, nor to cover the "canon" of masters—Aristophanes, Cervantes, etc.—but only to examine major forms and the thorniest problems comedy presents.

Even that modest aim is impertinently ambitious. To ask what the art of comedy is unclosets a jumble of phenomena, concepts, contending assumptions, and dubious methodologies such that the question itself seems hopeless. Concerning humor alone Patricia Keith-Spiegel has identified eight theories and twenty-two unresolved issues arising from them, ranging from "the briar patch of terminology" to "the confidence level of theorists," which has steadily declined in our century.[1] More recent discussions have only added to the multiplicity of views on humor and laughter.[2] Nor is the situation much better with theories of comedy per se. Ultimately, however, there is a dispensation. One could subscribe to virtually any theory of the *comic* and doing so need not determine what *comedy* is as an art—what it is as a social or psychological phenomenon, perhaps, but not as something engaging us in an aesthetic response.

The difference in theoretical position is crucial because it determines the scope and nature of this discussion. For instance, theories of comedy have traditionally situated it in theater, historically a reasonable choice but aesthetically a needless reduction of an art that is expressed in a variety of forms and media. What is one to do, ignore these manifold ways comic artists work? Far better to acknowledge the evidence, delight in the multiplicity, and set the comic painting or sculpture alongside the stage play, the novel alongside the film to see what properties they share and how they differ. Not that one can speak with assurance on media outside one's own discipline, but an overall understanding of how comedy works as its own art is entirely possible.

It is also possible to conceive of comedy in a way that allows for concentration on its nature as an aesthetic mode, although one might never know it from the general drift of theory. I must risk sounding like an ingrate (truly, anyone's understanding of comedy would be impoverished without the work of Bergson, Langer, Barber, and Gurewitch, to mention only a few) and point out that there has been hardly more than passing discussion of the art of comedy. What is missing is detailed consideration of not only local effects, such as Bergson provides for a special kind of theater, but of response, the active involvement of an audience in experiencing the whole work and deriving aesthetic as well as other pleasures from it. All in all the subject has been avoided either through lack of interest, out of prudence, or, I suspect, because it has been approached with a certain mindset.

There is no dearth of explanations as to what comedy is, beginning with Aristotle's, of course. The examination of comedy he promised in *The Poetics* has not survived. That has caused lament. Actually we may have been blessed without knowing it. *Mimesis*, in fact *any* teleological explanation of comedy as an art, is suspect from the beginning. As long as one considers comedy a social phenomenon, assigning ultimate purposes and ends to it makes perfect sense: comedy *is* social, symbolic, ritualistic, and so on. But when comedy as an aesthetic mode is so treated, its distinctive nature and operations tend to assume a secondary, transient, quasi validity. One looks through comedy on the way to some authentic thing, over there, that reality the theorist perceives to be true purpose. Here I begin from quite a different assumption. Comedy is not ontologically "on hold." It does not need some final end or purpose homogenizing its multiplicity of forms, reducing its amplitude, and making its achievements referable to something outside its own peculiar aesthetic being.

Given that somewhat high-handed position, a survey of major theories of comedy would amount to plodding rejection of any that are teleological: Aristotle's *mimesis*, Horace's *utile et dulce*, Bergson's comedy as *élan-vital*, Langer's comedy as biological determinism and the life force, Frye's (or Cornford's) comedy as myth-ritual and literary archetype, even comedy as folk ritual, which in C. L. Barber's application to Shakespeare's comedies is most responsive to artistry.[3] However reluctantly, one would also have to reject Morton Gurewitch's fine, broad survey of comedy as a manifestation of the irrational in man,[4] Robert Heilman's study of comedy as expression of attitudes of flight, challenge, and so on,[5] and Alice Rayner's comedy-as-persuasion.[6] But, one might ask, what theory of comedy does not deal with its art to some extent? It is a matter of emphasis, often, and worth considering some theorists in more detail to see how comedy as an aesthetic mode is glided over.

The difficulties with Aristotle's treatment of comedy in *The Poetics* are well known: an assumption that it is essentially another form of serious theater, representational in nature (the imitation of an action), and divisible into constituent parts of plot, character, and the like. That comedy transcends one medium of expression is not considered; it is taken to be a species of dramatic poetry. Furthermore, the stage comedy on which Aristotle based his scant observations was, roughly, Middle Comedy on the way to being Menandrine New Comedy, a later development that was to be the dominant form of western comic theater up to the present. What he had in mind had a heavy element of clownery and slapstick—none the worse for that, but hardly "comedy" as we think of it. Even with admirable extrapolations of Aristotle's theories such as Richard Janko's,[7] it is pointless to take up what the philosopher might have said. Rather, one can look at neo-Aristotelians such as Elder Olson to see the spirit of *The Poetics* carried on.

The Theory of Comedy[8] embodies Aristotle's assumptions and extends them in curious, limiting ways. Olson explains comic "catharsis" as *kastasis* of concern, and defines plot, character, thought, diction, etc., as they apply to stage comedy in general (pp. 25–44, 46–65). His focus is on ultimate explanation of response and on the constituent elements of drama, rather than on emotional, judgmental, and perceptual factors which supply "meaning" and help explain comedy's operations. Aristotle's analytic categories do little for understanding comic effect as it is experienced, and next to nothing for describing comedy as a mode transcending use of a particular medium. For instance, Olson's "four basic plots of comedy" (p. 52) set up categories like the ill- or well-intentioned fool, which rest upon an unspecified a priori assumption. Hence one has little way of knowing how Olson arrives at some of his pronouncements or exactly why he includes some works and excludes others from comedy.

An important omission is farcical effect, one way or another a substantial element of the art: "Except for sheer slapstick and froth and buffoonery, there is always a serious element in comedy" (p. 40). In fact, joy, clowning, and flippancy seem to bother Olson. He finds Wilde's *Importance of Being Earnest* "involves no great amount of comic art; it is not comedy so much as theatrical *badinage*" (p. 112). Without detailed consideration of response, what such determinations show are the hazards of applying Aristotle's thinking on tragedy to another mode—risks the philosopher recognized when he refused to discuss comedy at length in *The Poetics*.

With other theorists avoidance of detailed discussion of the actual operations of comedy is less obvious. More often than not the workings of comedy, and the equally important matter of audience response, are merely left buried. For instance, there is Northrop Frye's description of the endings of *Volpone* and *The Alchemist* in his 1948 "Argument of Comedy," later incorporated into *The Anatomy of Criticism*:

> The final assertion of the moral norm takes the form of a social revenge on Volpone, and the play ends with a great bustle of sentences to penal servitude and the galleys. One feels perhaps that the audience's sense of the moral norm does not need so much hard labor. In *The Alchemist*, when Lovewit returns to his house, the virtuous characters have proved so weak and the rascals so ingenious that the action dissolves in laughter.[9]

A vague sense of audience appears in "moral norm," an important element of response, and one laden with problems. But concerning *The Alchemist*, audience response is left cloudy. *Which* virtuous characters, which rascals, and what happens, specifically, when "action dissolves in laughter"? The tendency to displace audience and its involvement in events on stage with the critic's own "work out there," embodied in the interpretational essay, characterizes modern theorizing on comedy.

Evidently, there is another displacement operating as well, the assumption that if there is an art to comedy, it is of little significance. The position taken here is just the opposite: discussion of comedy in a critical, social, cultural, or other context is all but irrelevant. Ironically, the best example of irrelevance is comedy filtered through Freudian psychology. After all, one would think an account of our motivations would illuminate how we respond to comedy.

Not so. Freud's *Jokes and Their Relation to the Unconscious* has to do with wit or humor, not comedy, and certainly not comedy as an art. Like Freud's followers Kris and Jekels,[10] Eric Bentley applies Freud's thinking to farce.[11] Bentley's "we" of critical discussion have forbidden desires which we cannot get at because we are repressed, but, through jokes and humor, gratification can be slipped past the censors of the mind. Unfortunately, Bentley does not give our responses to a whole, specific play in detail. Response is limited to particular effects that happen to show Freudian impulse fulfillment which becomes, by default, the implied totality of our psychic being. Our full, immediate involvement in a stage play and a whole play is reduced to the system of Freudian psychodynamics—quite all right if one is predisposed to view man in that way but limiting if one is not.

In quite another way Morton Gurewitch avoids direct confrontation of audience response by applying Freud to a span of comic works, showing a general element of the irrational in man.[12] His considerably expanded Freudian categories provide a framework for displays of "wackiness" or "lunatic" effects registering upon an assumed audience-reader, but actual registering seldom appears. For instance, discussing forms of non sequitur in Wilde's *Importance*, Gurewitch cites the scene in which Jack announces the "death" of his brother Ernest. "Miss Prism is particularly deranged here since she hopes that cadavers may learn to reform" (p. 119). From the standpoint of reception—of the text as an interaction between stage event and audience—the question is, how does an audience respond to this illogic? What is made of it *by us?* There are generalized Freudian explanations in abundance (e.g., pp. 53–59, 108–11), but comic effect, the actual *happening* of the comic moment, remains "out there," another case of the general phenomenon of irrationality.

It may seem an unreasonable, quixotic demand that we get right down to audience response, considering how little we know about it.[13] But it is hard to see how comedy as an art can be discussed without it. When we look to explanations of how comedy works, theorists become evasive at just that point. For example, there is Maurice Charney's admirable survey of comic forms and types, *Comedy High and Low.*[14] But what transpires at the moment of our engaging in a comic happening?—a ritual release, a comic catharsis to be sure (pp. 177–78), but what exactly is involved in that? Sooner or later it has to be asked, just who, what kind of sentience is interacting with comedy?

The question is still receiving waffling replies, if it is posed in the first place. For instance, Robert B. Heilman establishes a rough typology of comedy based on flight, challenge, reconciliation, etc., embodied in the work. But he demurs on response itself, passing over "the impact of art on individuals and society."[15] On the other hand, more recent discussions of comedy have confronted in various ways just how an audience contributes to the comic happening, e.g., Alice Rayner and William F. Gruber. Rayner touches upon an important point, that is, audience values brought to bear upon the comic experience, but the interplay between text and audience is subsumed in the overall categories of *utile et dulce* she is concerned to show.[16] Gruber traces the interaction between playwright and audience, e.g., in Ben Jonson's *Bartholomew Fair* the audience is "forced to sympathize, to judge, to plot sequences of action, and then is mocked for its folly."[17] The difference between Gruber's responsiveness to involvement of audience and the close attention I will be engaged in is context. Gruber takes comedy as one kind of theater, whereas I take theater as one kind of comedy. With Rayner the difference is that audience response is referable to persuasion as the purpose of comedy, whereas I will try to keep my position as free as possible of predetermined ends in order to focus on the ultimate goal: understanding the operations of an aesthetic mode.

Why? Any approach to comedy is bound to be teleological to some extent. Recognizing that no investigation is innocent of assumptions about the nature of the thing studied, I suggest that comedy is play—*paidiá*, or nonsensical, pointless frippery, looniness. And the reference is to play not just as a part of our psychological makeup, but as an aspect of being. Play is what comedy *does*, and essentially what it is. Seeing comedy as play does not preclude other interpretations (one of my favorites is Susan Langer's in *Feeling and Form*[18]). It is only that play is singularly free of ends and purposes, otherwise it would not be play.

That is not as tautological as it may sound. The best known study of the subject, *Homo Ludens*,[19] examines play as ethnography, whereas the play meant here is philosophic, both a deep impulse in us and a principle of existence. Huizinga's overall view of play—its removal from ordinary life, involvement in and only for itself, and so on—is in general accord with philosophic treatment of the matter. Yet from the very first Huizinga sees play as having meaning: It is "a *significant* function—that is to say, there is some sense to it. . . . All play means something" (p. 1). Ethnographically speaking play is indeed manifest in meaningful activities, from ritual to war, children's games to poetry and art. But can play formulated into a structured activity and assigned purpose remain play at all? Does it not then become *ludus?* The line between the two is not always clear, but when one assigns to play the sense, meaning, and function of game he puts play in an ontological framework that has no way to accommodate it in its pristine formlessness. Play and structure-purpose are incompatible by their very natures. Thus we tend to reject play as a legitimate form of existence but still feel the need to incorporate it into an overall scheme of things, to place or fix it.

It has been the fate of play in Western thought to occupy this untenable position, to be an enigmatic, equivocal phenomenon that keeps appearing as a philosophical puzzle. Any statement on the subject is likely to require a separate study of considerable size. Yet it is imperative that one senses the depth of play before engaging Huizinga's or some other concept as the basis for understanding. While my focus will be on how play "means" anything, to the extent it does, its ontology has been a major concern of philosophers from pre-Socratic thinkers to the present.

Mihai Spariosu gives a useful summary of play as a concept, to which I am most indebted; he has recently expanded it into a full-length study.[20] He finds that in pre-Socratic philosophers play is associated with war, chance, and the spontaneous flux of existence. Or, more generally, it becomes part of a dialectic of the rational/irrational and necessity/chance. In Plato's well-ordered world, play is subsumed and transformed; it is meaningless but admissible as art "playing at the noblest pastimes" (*Laws* VII.803). Though subordinated to philosophy always, through its pleasures the play of poetry as *mimesis* can help men attain higher understanding. The same holds for Aristotle. It was to be a good while before this subordination of literature and play would be undone. The process, still going on, occurred by way of Kant and German idealism, emerging in Schiller's privileging play as an important impulse manifest in art, through which man's spirit is freed.

Schiller brought about a far-reaching epistemological shift by seeing reason in its "as if" mode as play.[21] He conceived of a three-part scheme in aesthetic production: the sensuous drive, the formal drive, and the play drive or *Speiltraub*. Play allows man's sensuous and formal instincts to interact harmoniously; it thus becomes form shaping life in art, "living form." Hence, a man is completely a man only when he plays. Still, play is finally subject to reason. Schiller's important contributions were seeing rationality as a form of play and granting play ontological status, both of which Nietzsche furthered.

The problems of Nietzsche's philosophy—e.g., a proliferation of ideas expressed in a highly aphoristic style—tend to obscure it, but the idea of play kept recurring in his thinking. Lawrence Hinman goes so far as to see play underlying and tying together three major Nietzschean doctrines: the will to power, the eternal recurrence of the same, and the concept of the Overman.[22] Roughly, the will to power is the highest expression of man's being in confrontation with a nihilistic void; it is creative play. The eternal recurrence of the same is the world-as-play, in its terrifying and chaotic as well as its joyful aspects. The Overman expresses his will to power as creative play, and in doing so constructs a coherent imaginary world that both reflects the world-as-play and transcends it. This description greatly oversimplifies the relationship between the three concepts, but the importance of play in Nietzsche's thought is nonetheless clear. For Nietzsche play is both powerfully creative and meaninglessly chaotic, but it has ontological autonomy; it is a primary element of existence.[23]

What is implied, we are later to learn from Jacques Derrida, is a displacement of the center of Platonic and Kantean metaphysics, a reversal of the positions of reason and play and the qualities attributed to them. As Spariosu puts it, "appearance, falsehood, copy, representation, fiction, irreality, irrationality become privileged over essence, presence (*ousia*), model, truth, reality, and rationality" (*Literature*, p. 25). And, as he sees it, each term of these oppositions becomes "the other's condition of possibility, both being a manifestation of the power-principle in its rational and irrational guise" (ibid.). Whether or not the irrational play of being is accounted for by the power-principle, its chaos can be shaped by man through art. Only now man is the player *and* is being played with.

This position is extended further in the thinking of Heidegger (*Sein und Zeit* and late work such as *Unterwegs zur Sprache*; see Spariosu, *Literature*, pp. 26–29, *Dionysus*, pp. 99–124). Heidegger rejects the Nietzschean ideal of a Dionysian impulse but retains the concept of play as being. Indeed, being derives from play, so that rather than man being the cosmic gameplayer, the Overman, he is what is being played upon. World-play shows as risk, as a game between danger and death, and is a metaphysical first principle, grounding but groundless. Hence there can be no correspondence between language and a referent truth, only play of meaning. Language is play or chance, and as play defines man so does language; man does not control either.

Heidegger's thinking has had considerable influence, for instance on Hans-Georg Gadamer,[24] Eugen Fink, and Derrida. Synthesizing Heidegger's views was undertaken by Fink, on whom more below. In an early, seminal essay, "Structure, Sign, and Play in the Discourse of the Human Sciences," Derrida rejects the sad, negative Rousseauist version of play—"freeplay" is the interchangeable term for him—to embrace the Nietzschean positive view, the "joyous affirmation of the freeplay of the world and without truth, without origin, offered to an active interpretation."[25] Freeplay (play) is,

> the disruption of presence. The presence of an element is always a signifying and substitutive reference inscribed in a system of differences and the movement of a chain. Freeplay is always an interplay of absence and presence, but if it is to be radically conceived, freeplay must be conceived of before the alternative of presence and absence; being must be conceived of as presence or absence beginning with the possibility of freeplay and not the other way around. (pp. 263–64)

Thus, under the influence of Heidegger and Lavinas, and with a Talmudic perspective, Derrida's play or freeplay becomes *écriture*, the seminal adventure of the trace, the eternal signifier never becoming the signified. (See also "The Double Session" in *Disseminations*, 1972.)

This sketch of concepts of play (primarily a summary of Spariosu's summary in *Literature*, later expanded in *Dionysus*) is meant only to suggest the great variety of views on the subject and its current uncertain status in philosophy. Concepts range from seeing play as an innocent, violent movement of "cosmic becoming or cosmic power" to play as natural activity, or a relentless contest of forces, or risk-taking and chance, to "an infinite, aleatory permutation of interchangeable elements, within a decentered structure or limitless series of events," the elements being linguistic and nonlinguistic signs (*Dionysus*, p. 158). Overall, from Nietzsche to the present, there has been a seismic shift away from a metaphysics that eschewed play to one that gives priority to it. Spariosu sees this shift as a reassertion and valuation of prerational thought (roughly that of the Homeric epics and the pre-Socratic philosophers) in which art and play are aspects of power, not subordinate to the moral truths of philosophy but privileged over them.[26]

Meanwhile, stimulated by Huizinga's *Homo Ludens* and the codifications of Roger Callois,[27] the notion of play and game was to spread through many disciplines, from child development to the sciences.[28] The same development in philosophy, reversal of play's subordination to reason, has been felt in aesthetics, especially in the study of postmodernism and in its practice.[29] This profound shift has influenced literary and dramatic criticism, most obviously in poststructuralism or Derridean deconstruction, but has not been seen in its historical context as part of a continuing exploration of play.

On the other hand, the notion of comedy-as-play has appeared now and then in literary criticism, for instance in Harold C. Goddard's conception of Falstaff.[30] There is even a study based on play of Shakespeare's early comedies.[31] Dennis Huston has Shakespeare finding a world of play with the reality of actors, stage, and audience (pp. 8–9). This conception relies upon Huizinga's *Homo Ludens* extended into Jean Piaget's theories. Play is "an attempt to mediate between the self and the outside world by exercise of control" (p. 6). Unfortunately, play is thereby narrowed to equation between child and artist, which may account for Huston's excluding *The Two Gentlemen of Verona* because it brings into the charmed world of play "the problem of evil intention" that appears regularly in the later comedies (p. 11). There go Touchstone and Falstaff, and there goes the wider accountability of a theory proposing to illuminate comedy—not exactly Huston's aims, but fair criteria to apply. Yet Huston only engages in current practice, which tends to ignore ontological and epistemological problems and, instead, seizes upon parts of concepts.

Unfortunately, play is not packaged ready for transport over to literary criticism, and may well never be. That being so, just what version of play is to be applied here? With a few misgivings, the conception that comes closest to my own is Eugen Fink's, possibly because he emphasizes play's creative aspects; I shall paraphrase some of his views.[32] For Fink play is essentially creative impulse. It has the capacity to free us from our individuality, to dispel the subject-object dichotomy of existence in the absorption of activity. We tend to see play in relation to the serious. It "remains in the shadow of phenomena seemingly opposed to it, which obscure and deform it," Fink observes, and as "'non-serious,' non-obligatory, as mere idleness" play is a kind of peripheral counterbalance, an "ingredient adding flavor to the insipidity of existence" (p. 149). "But play is not a contingent phenomenon that emerges upon occasion. In essence, it comes under the ontological dispositions of human existence. It is a fundamentally existential phenomenon. It is not derived from any other manifestation of life" (p. 150).

Thus play is intimately bound up with death, work, domination, and love, yet autonomous (ibid.). In our understanding, our other modes of existence are characterized by purpose and imply futurity and struggle toward an end. Play has only its own "internal finalities" (p. 152), exists in the present, and is an active, creative force confronting the other phenomena of life to use them representationally. "We play with the serious, the authentic, the real. We play with work and struggle, with love and death. We even play with play" (p. 153). Thus play can include profound sadness and tragic suffering. Paradoxically joyful-sad, embracing striking contraries, play is a creative, spontaneous entry into life, into a new world of experience. It can have meaning, the "meaning" of the activity itself and the meaning ascribed by those involved in it.[33] Other attributes of play, according to Fink, are its nature as a communal activity, even when the player is alone; its operating by rules of the community of play; and its need for a play*thing*, which includes man himself. This plaything symbolizes the whole, the totality of real things (p. 155). The symbolic and representational aspects of play are important in Fink's conception. Play is always characterized by an element of representation, which is dialectical but "much concerned with not reducing paradoxes to a dead level"; rather, it would let us experience "the tantalizing ambiguity of dialectic" (p. 157).

Fink's concept of play emphasizes its boundless, creative, symbolic, and representational nature while insisting upon its autonomy in the scheme of things. Though my own position acknowledges these characteristics of play, and, in other circumstances would stress the connection between play and creativity, here it is ontological status that is important. That play *exists* is perhaps the most difficult aspect of it for us to accept. To say that play, and by implication one of its expressions, comedy, has ontological independence is to say that being itself is not the stable, monadic, containable phenomenon we once believed it was. Terms that appear increasingly in critical discussion—instability, indeterminateness, open-endedness, ambiguity, undecidability, ambivalence, displacement, and so on—express a profound shift away from a rational order that excluded play as an anomaly, and devalued it. The radical overhaul of our metaphysics now underway has not really altered our habits of thinking. In our day-to-day lives play has a designated place which both contains and negates. We have little game preserves, so to speak, where erratic, spontaneous play is given provisional exemption from the normal, rational world we believe to exist, or else we explain it away as having a function.[34]

Carefree, capricious bodily play is channeled into athletics as soon as school and parental pressures allow. Play is turned into game. Games we understand. Sports encourage health, a competitive spirit, aggression, and self-reliance balanced off with team playing, all of which prepare us for success in the bureaucracy, the world of business, or, with luck, the ferocity of war. Such control of the play impulse exhibits fear as well as our need to sustain our prevailingly serious outlook, for there *is* something unpredictable and chaotic about play, and we feel the threat of it. Hence the condoning, and containment, of play in social rituals which allow for spontaneous, loony expression within specified limits, including comedy. Comedy is play so contained, yet it remains at its heart "the tantalizing ambiguity of dialectic" and thus a way of knowing through experience—"knowing," that is, in the viscera more than the head.

Articulating this "tantalizing ambiguity" and "knowing" requires, among other things, a clear sense of the difference between play and game—not always easy to establish but most important.[35] By way of clarification, consider Peter Hutchinson's analysis of the games of narrative fiction.[36] Hutchinson says there is a distinction to be made between play and game, albeit one largely of degree:

> "Play" operates at a more superficial level, it is often ostentatious, it is incidental. "Game," on the other hand, suggests a more developed structure, it represents more of a challenge to the reader, involves greater, more prolonged intellectual effort. It is not as "obvious," as fleeting, as the playful indulgence. . . . It is more than the mere decoration which play can be, more fundamental to the work in which it is employed, it involves a *goal*. (pp. 13–14)

Though Hutchinson is sensitive to the continuum along which play and game can be situated, and to the structuring and purpose that distinguish one from the other, there is a built-in hierarchy of value that is questionable. Play is superficial, incidental, "obvious," fleeting, indulgent, etc. Game "suggests" more of everything—developed structure, challenge, and intellectual effort—and is more than "mere decoration"; it is "more fundamental to the work" than play, and, most of all, it has a *goal*. What is involved is not only the privileging of goal, but a certain concept of text and reader.

As regards comedy overall, Hutchinson's hierarchy is best reversed: play is the basic stuff of comedy and can well *be* the essential mode of a work's existence; games are instrumental, secondary, and derivative manifestations of the play impulse. Hutchinson assumes a primacy of artifact, of "the work." That is my bent, too, but with a difference. The comic work is experiential, an interaction between the text and ourselves as audience, readers, or viewers. Comedy *happens*, first of all. Looked at that way, play is the common feature of comedy in all its range, expressed in various media and forms within a medium, while games are local configurations or structurings of play each kind of communication necessitates. This is not to deny Hutchinson his preferences, especially since he is aware of the cultural bias they reflect, but only to establish an important distinction.

Considering the shaky status of the concept of play in philosophy, there is much to disagree with in the views given above. But it is hard to discount the play aspect of comic expression. Comedy relies on sleight-of-hand as its fundamental mode of signification. Much of the trickery of comedy, as of humor and other risible expression, is cognitive, a switch in frameworks of thinking. However, there is more involved in a joke or pun or comic episode. Almost by definition comic effect cannot occur without embodying values, judgments, and emotions as well as thought. (Otherwise, jokes would be fully exportable from culture to culture, social group to social group, across lines of age, sex, and intellectual difference, which they are not.) Hence "perceptual play" seems an apt general term for what occurs in comedy.

On the other hand, "perception" needs to be specified to be of any use. As I use the term here, perception includes both the act of responding to stimuli—the very split second of recognition—and apprehension of significance; it involves a substantial element of judgment and emotion, and often snap judgment in a rush of sensation.[37] In its representational mode play is not only with words, structures, codes, and conceptual frameworks; it is with states of awareness and some deeply held convictions. The latter are not necessarily matters of reason. They often boil down to prejudices, and, in satire, some ugly impulses we would rather not acknowledge. Comic response embodies no less than our whole psychic being: love, hate, sympathy, and desires of all kinds. Only, these are not the elements of perception I will be pursuing. Rather, emphasis will be on the act of perceiving, as much as possible on the grasping of phenomena before their assimilation into reflective thought and while they are still in a state of playful indeterminacy.

This state of immediate sensation has an infinite range of possible "meanings." But then, play in its representational mode is wide-ranging and adaptable to light or dark subject matter. This may be so because play is in itself Janus-faced: cheerfully benign at one moment, terrifyingly chaotic the next. Other than its own peculiar unstable, flippant, reckless condition of existence, it has no structure, substance, or given content. True, once expressed in verbal humor, theater, novel, painting, and so on, play assumes the configurations of game, the rules and strategies dictated by the semiotic "language" of the particular medium the artist uses —configurations, I might add, that are not inherently comic.[38] Yet, as Fink puts it, play refuses to flatten "the tantalizing ambiguity of dialectic" into certainties of the serious. It is also the case that there are overall, reiterative patterns or "macro-messages" that emerge from any aggregate of works, e.g., love conquers all, youth will be served, the good of heart can prevail. But these have little to do with play. In fact, the clearer the "meaning" of a work, the more likely it is that its playfulness has been curbed, its power bent to serve content.

While most of these assumptions may be provisionally acceptable (all cannot be said at once), those concerning response to comedy are contentious indeed. For rather than the cultivated, sensitive critic responding to a text, the "we" of critical discourse no matter what its guise, I envision the ordinary person, the groundling, rather mindlessly engaged in what he or she considers entertainment, and for laughs, a smile—anything but thinking. Comedy is a communal art. While it can be directed at the *cognoscenti*, the privileged insiders of a social class or circle, all in all comedy is egalitarian, broad in appeal, available to the many as serious art or literature seldom are. This does not mean all engaged in the comic moment will respond the same way. It only means that a certain primary range of effect is available to virtually anyone.

Insistence on this point comes from conceiving comedy as a happening, an interaction between text and audience or reader or viewer that requires accessibility and apparent innocence for comedy's sleight-of-hand to work in the first place. Comic effectiveness depends upon an audience, or readers or viewers, giving themselves over to the experience in good faith, without guile or suspicion either of the artist's intent or serious implications. And while a comic moment can be recalled again and again, savored for its artistry more than for its content, immediateness of response, genuine laughter, is diminished. Rarer tastes may be satisfied and exquisite effects noticed for the first time. But as with a past love affair, seldom is the original, full phenomenological moment of response retrievable. Yet one has to choose where one's emphasis is to be: on comedy experienced in the flesh or in reflection, or on comedy seen or read, as event in the world or in the imagination. The implied choices are not mutually exclusive, of course, but it is the rare sensibility that can be aware of all the nuances of a gag while seized with laughter.

One *can* take comedy as just another text, a repository of meanings and concepts awaiting exhumation by a knowledgeable, perceptive critic. A great deal can be lost thereby. The very playful nature of comedy, its immediacy, tends to get abstracted into serious statement. That is, comedy can be the beginning of a new "text," that of theory embodied in the critical essay. But for present purposes the only practical choice appears to be between the critically aware reader—he or she versed in genres, responding in a magnetic field of intertextuality, etc.—and the groundling. In point of fact, the more one considers actualities of response, the less authentic the difference is. *At the moment of laughter,* and discounting specialized knowledge, for instance of Shakespeare, the responses of the sophisticated and ordinary person are much alike.

That is so because of our mental state at the moment we respond to, say, a stage comedy. While we like to think of ourselves as gimlet-eyed and alert, there is little in audiences that suggests anything like such readiness, such intellectual receptivity. An audience's stake in comedy in the first place is the liberation of laughter, and it carries to the experience the very same mental habits manifest in daily living. (Why should it be otherwise?) Only, it is precisely this habitual mental set that neither cognitive nor motivational psychology fully explains. Crises, fantasies, dark impulses, perversions, psychoneuroses of all kinds: *these* we know about. How a person's consciousness operates in getting through a day of business, family, and whatever else—actually how our minds work, or avoid work, and how our judgments and emotions influence daily decisions—has hardly seemed worthy of study.

Perhaps the most substantial thinking on the matter has arisen out of phenomenology because of its recognition of the importance of states of consciousness, its interest in what Husserl called the "mundane" or "natural attitude," the immediate impact of ordinary experience. An interesting thinker in this respect (a follower of Husserl and student of cognitive psychology) is Aaron Gurwitsch. What is unusual about Gurwitsch among phenomenologists is his bent toward systematic formulation, most pertinently in his notion of a "field of consciousness."[39]

Roughly, Gurwitsch finds our minds operate by a nucleus of attention, a halo of potentially relevant phenomena, and a largely unconscious fringe of vague awareness, "marginal consciousness." It is hardly surprising that we focus on certain scraps, bits of information, sensations, etc., according to activated interest, nor, even, that we have a halo or "encyclopedia" of related things surrounding our nucleus of attention. (When we work out a mathematical problem, there is a whole repertoire of possibly related formulae hovering about.) The most interesting aspect of the paradigm is Gurwitsch's notion of a conceptual unconscious. It is at the fringe of consciousness precisely because its vast contents are not germane to thought, nor, necessarily, to psychic operations. Unlike Freud's realm of the libido this unconsciousness (or semiconsciousness) is a surplus of mental quanta. It can be drawn upon should our nuclei of attention so require; otherwise it is merely there.

One could apply Gurwitsch's paradigm literally, except that new nuclei of attention replace prior ones with astonishing speed, the more so in comedy in performance, where pace is kept up. Following that line we would end up with something like a model for computer simulation of thought. Furthermore, the conception is based on cognition and perception as if they were somehow detached from motivational factors, which they seldom are. Yet the notion of a cognitive-based semiconsciousness is most useful. It accords with what we observe of ourselves and is far more descriptive of day-to-day thinking than the paradigms of motivational psychology. The proposition is this: By and large we grasp stimuli in much the same way; what we make of the sensation is dependent upon mood, disposition, past experience, desires, and other variables that make up our psychic being and that virtually defy formulation.

In any event, what is important in grasping comedy's operations is not to account for all the primal impulses with which man seems to be victimized, but rather to acknowledge that this *is* our feeling, that *is* our judgment, then to focus attention on our general state of consciousness and its peculiarities. Our habitual mode of thought operates far short of the mind's potential. Much of our day is made up of waiting to cross streets, pushing papers from one bin to another, and fulfilling obligatory rituals ("good morning"). We are impatient with such things and spend as little effort on them as possible. We wait at a bus stop convinced a bus will arrive; it always has, hasn't it? We deal with people according to an expected pattern of behavior; they've always acted that way, haven't they? Effects have causes; probability is a good guide because it is frequently affirmed, and so on, out to the very feathered edges of our mental worlds.

Though at any moment we can bring intense awareness to bear on this habitual half thinking—"I mean it: *good morning,*" or, "the bus need not come; we are to the gods as flies to wanton boys"— there is ordinarily no need to do so. Without necessity, who spends effort on what is usually, dully confirmed by experience? We are creatures of habit only partly to allocate energy judiciously. Sheer monotony influences. Repetition and lack of challenge erode an otherwise alert mind, and the geometry of consciousness is not easily altered, even when we are thinking intensely about it.

The suggestion, then, is that for purposes here we conceive of our minds as in a condition of near somnambulence, or as Ellen J. Langer calls it, mindlessness.[40] That is the condition on which the comic artist relies. If it is generally true that comedy is a turn on expectation, of what does expectation consist? Precisely those things we least think about, including the rickety scaffolding of thought itself. No pun will work without a strong, widely accepted usual meaning brought into play. No play on conventional phrasing will work unless the phrasing *is* conventional ("he has the uncanny ability to snatch defeat from the jaws of victory"). So with the larger turns, flips, and flippancies of comedy; all require a certain fixity of mind, a predictable lean of consciousness, not to mention a bundle of assumptions, judgments, and prejudices.

Given that comic response rests on inattention, a casual, unthinking acceptance of what is, the attitude is reinforced in two ways. First, there is the overall ambience, the holiday spirit of the event. We are not at a comic play or film, or reading a comic novel, to *think* but to enjoy. Second, there is the nature of the response itself. Whatever laughter may be, it debilitates thought, draws upon those nerve centers and energies we might otherwise devote to thinking. And in the performing arts there are pace and timing. In a good stage comedy action goes on as rapidly as subsidence of laughter allows. As with the stand-up comic's routine, the show must not drag. Where timing is not crucial, as in the visual arts, more duplicitous means have to be found, but the net effect is the same: what we first thought to be the case proves not to be so. *Trompe l'oeil* is merely a petrified joke.

In all of this there are bound to be exceptions. There are those gifted or cursed few who can respond to comedy while a part of their response remains critically aloof. Or, what is more frequently the case, one declines full participation because he or she disagrees with the attitudes built into the comic moment. One person's exuberance comes out as a guffaw, another's as a wheeze. We differ as human beings. Yet there are common factors running through these variables, chiefly the values we share as an audience, our cognitive habits, our mindlessness, and our acceptance of the protocols of a social ritual to which, oddly, we keep returning for more trickery to be played on us.

What, then, of laughter, since that is where theories of comedy often begin? One can subscribe to any of a number of explanations as to why we laugh.[41] By and large the choice would make no difference. Laughter is both raw material and a product of the ludic arts. It is what is *done* with laughter that counts aesthetically. At the same time, there is this to note: whether one guffaws, chuckles, or snickers, the *intensity and nature* of the response express a wide range of feelings, the whole of our personalities. The shades of feeling are infinite and cannot be described in terms of a physical reaction. Expressions like "free and open laughter" or "malicious chuckling" can be used only adjectivally to express underlying attitudes of joyful acceptance and vindictive glee.

Given this general description of response, to be fleshed out later, exactly how is it to be formulated in relation to the comic work? Any comic work is problematic if we take comedy as a happening, a phenomenal event with which response is inextricably entwined. The event is immediate and palpable, ourselves wholly involved in the moment and careless of subtleties of critical interpretation. That is especially true of the performing arts, but applies only to a lesser degree in reading a novel or viewing a painting. Compared to the experiencing of comedy, critical discussions by and large embalm a readerly, "theatrical" text in an essay. On the other hand, discussing lived experience is never easy. The theatrical text as a happening remains a tantalizing enigma, if not something of a methodological black hole, and the reading text is scarcely better off. Both reception esthetics and reader response theory have attacked the problem, reaching a virtual impasse. In general, neither has taken on comedy as a discrete mode or art form in itself.

To the extent it is indicative of *Rezeptionsästhetik,* and representative of the Konstanz school, Hans Robert Jauss's discussion of comedy suggests reception theory offers little. His comments on the ridiculous and the comic, and "On Why the Comic Hero Amuses," disappointingly register effects as abstract qualities, such as innocence (Dickens's heroes) or grotesquerie (the Rabelaisian hero).[42] These qualities reflect our laughing at or with a character, a concept derived from Freud's humor as expenditure of psychic energy. A more interesting figure from the same school is Wolfgang Iser, whose roots are in phenomenology, e.g., the work of Roman Ingarten, but who is better known in Anglo-American circles as a reader response theorist.

Reader response theory has had a short, contentious history.[43] Though its contribution to literary criticism has been valuable— chiefly emphasis on the "transactional" nature of the text, to use Norman Holland's term[44]—in actual practice concepts of text and reader vary widely, and, in relation to comedy, offer no ready solutions. For instance, Holland's motivational psychology may offer, like Freud's, a teleological explanation of comic response, but does little to illuminate comedy as an art. Similarly, David Bleich's advocacy of subjective response does not work with an art that is communal, as I take comedy to be.[45] The most useful theorist would seem to be Wolfgang Iser. In spite of Stanley Fish's objections, Iser's notion of the "phenomenological reader" has strong appeal for the study of comedy.[46]

Unfortunately, in addition to circularity of argument, there is the danger of Iser's phenomenological, dyadic reader, existent in and out of the text, becoming located in the structurings and strategies of the text itself.[47] Whatever Iser's own practice, it is possible to give reader or audience response more weight than he does. The more one conceives of comedy as a field on which games of authorial involvement and audience participation are played, the more the text is genuinely transactional. Only, one returns again to the nature of audience or reader.

Given Iser's overall concept of response, much depends not only upon the reader assumed but on the phenomenology incorporated into the conception. In turn, that implies a certain kind of sentience, and, further, the cognitive and emotional nature of man. If one inclines toward, say, Merleau-Ponty, this is likely to include a strong element of our corporal being;[48] if one favors Heidegger, phenomena themselves dominate. Heidegger's dictum "art is the setting-into-work of truth" emphasizes the active, almost autonomous nature of phenomenal existence.[49] Whatever emphasis one gives, for the phenomenologist perception is never passive. It is alive in our interaction with the world, most vividly with the work of art.

Hence Bert O. States prefaces discussion of the phenomenology of theater with Victor Shklovsky's well-known statements, "art exists that one may recover the sensation of life; it exists to make one feel things, to make the stone *stony*" and "the purpose of art is to impart the sensation of things as they are perceived and not as they are known."[50] The privileging of perception over knowing is a basic tenet of existential phenomenology; hence States goes on to argue that our response to phenomena is direct, not mediated by or the product of our search for meanings (pp. 21–29f). True, but our cognitive-emotional makeup is always implied; there are always elements of ourselves we bring to the experience of theater, including comedy. States sidesteps the matter of audience response by collapsing it into theater as ritual (p. 157).

No wonder. Thus far performance theory has offered only tentative suggestions about who and how we respond as we do. For instance, Bernard Beckerman sees an explanation in Gestaltist "field and ground" and "empathic parallelism," or carrying over into ourselves patterns embodied in performance (an effect now disproved in psychological study).[51] Sondra H. Fraleigh takes a firm existential-phenomenological stand and discusses dance from the performer's point of view or out-on-stage as autonomous movement, e.g., the angular style of Doris Humphrey's *Passacaglia*, without specifying what Humphrey's departures from balletic line do *to* or *with* an audience.[52]

On the other hand, Bruce Wilshire provides a useful concept in the transactions between self in the members of a theatrical audience and surrogate beings on stage; these transactions are a complex set of understood relationships or "authorizations."[53] While comedy does involve us in the general phenomenon of theatrical experience, we need a way to articulate response in detail, to grasp what occurs with each turn of a gag, each stitch of development as the play unfolds in the peculiar way comedies operate. At a macrolevel of discussion, comedy is like any other theater (or novel reading, etc.). Like serious theater in general, it, too, engages us in an act of ritual substitution for the "real" and authentic.

In general, for comedy differs from serious theater in the nature of the response each evokes. Whereas most of what transpires, say, in *Hamlet* is known to us at the moment of performance, give or take a few quibbles on word meanings, very little of what we experience in stage comedy registers on our consciousness at the time. Much of the "meaning" of comedy occurs in the basement of our response, only partly accessible to us until after the experience is over. Then we feel a glow, an emotional "high" (if comedy has really done its work) that often needs sorting out by reflection or discussion. Furthermore, the essential traffic of comedy is less with ideas, concepts, constructs, and so on than with emotions and the value judgments brought into play. One knows exactly why Hamlet decides not to kill Claudius in the chapel, and precisely how his decision fits into the overall fabric of the drama up to that point. One *feels* the absurdity of Lady Bracknell's approving Jack Worthing's smoking because a man should have an occupation of some kind, or Elmire's rapping on the table to bring Orgon out from hiding under it while she fends off the ardent Tartuffe. And though there may be dim awareness of how each comic episode fits into action and theme, for most of us not critical consciousness but enjoyment and laughter absorb our being.

The very mention of an "us," an assumed communal sentience, goes against the current objections of critics that we cannot reify an audience, say of Elizabethan playgoers. I doubt we can do anything else unless we elect ourselves an audience of one. "Reification" is pejorative, implying that since we cannot know what Shakespeare's audience truly felt but only what a critic writing feels, the only reliable, authentic response is the critic's. If the reasoning holds, what do we have in this authentic, reliable response? We have a vast network of abstractions underlying interpretation: in *Hamlet* concepts of rule, kingdom, love, ghosts, of filial ties, of friendship, of providence and sparrows. Not only are such things as these reified, the critic's "I" attempts to give substance to something that does not exist, an entity we call *Hamlet*, but not the theatrical one; a play script, masquerading as performance, is given "reality" in the act of interpretation.

The interpretation of an "I" may be valuable by appeal to its efficacy as theory and wit of style (sometimes the same thing), but it cannot claim superior status as a way of knowing. We come down not to a logical argument about epistemology, but to the assertion that my reification beats yours. In fact any discussion which assumes there is an audience responding must settle for an approximation, a generalized concept of a collective sentience. In this case, seeing comedy as play entails the question, play *with* whom and what?

The evidence is overwhelming: there are values and perceptual habits shared by a broad spectrum of people in a given culture. Comic films, even low budget ones costing one or two million dollars, are not made for audiences in Omaha, Nebraska alone, or, if produced in England, tailored to the humor of Coventry or Exeter. Stage comedies have gone on season after season appealing to a wide span of people of different gender and socioeconomic background. (*No Sex, Please, We're British* lasted almost as long as *The Mousetrap*; *The Odd Couple* had long runs, spawned a television series, and is still played in small theaters.) Nor do novels like *Catch-22* appeal only to the *litterati*. In any fully achieved comic work there are, of course, levels and levels, but before the richness of comedy can be appreciated, its basic nature and operations should be understood, its quality as experience articulated. Hence my choice of the groundling, the ordinary person of unremarkable critical awareness, as the "representative" of a generalized audience or reader, a common sentience whose perceptual habits are shared by virtually everyone in a given culture.

What, then, of the "language" of comedy? Comedy is not to be limited to theater or the novel, or film or painting; obviously there are a number of semiotic "languages" the comic artist can use. In one sense there *is* a transcendent, "supra-language" of comedy, a fairly systematic repertoire of patterns, structurings, and configurations of experience that keep appearing as one moves from, say, theater to the novel, or fiction to sculpting. The semiotic nature of a medium determines the specific shapes these take. What is remarkable is the recurrence of these configurations across media, across periods of time and changes in culture. Their morphology in the various semiotic "dialects" of the ludic arts could be charted. In another sense, there are an almost infinite number of particular forms the comic artist can use, and it would seem formal analysis of signification and its processes would be helpful in describing these.

The difficulty with formal study of semiosis is that its practitioners, by and large, have concentrated on process and result, on signs and sign systems, at the expense of ordinary experience and day-to-day mental states, or, in other words, at the expense of the responding subject. The Heideggerean primal presencing, the imminency of the moment, is reduced to participation in a vast network of sign production. It is in this sense that Paul Ricoeur said semiotics asks not a reduction *to* consciousness, but a reduction *of* consciousness.[54] In practice the responding subject is shunted off, assumed to have certain perceptual competencies, as the linguist speaks of "language competence." Thus Umberto Eco takes pains to distinguish between the Peircean interpretant and the ordinary person: the interpretant is a purely semiotic construct determined by culture, not by human beings or a collective psychological entity.[55] A. J. Greimas and J. Courtés define "Reader" not as a person or sentience but as designating "the domain of message or discourse reception," and "Reading" as a process in which "the receptive and interpretive doing of the enunciatee-reader remains implicit," or outside the pale of study.[56]

This tendency to displace the perceiving subject with process and to dispense with reception of the work as a matter of aesthetics limits the usefulness of semiotic analysis, or at least analysis which bases itself on linguistics. True, there are those who have not been obliged to follow the methodology of linguistics. The early Roland Barthes used an approach more indebted to Lévi-Strauss than Saussure to show various codes operating in response, i.e., hermeneutic, sememic, or semantic, proairetic or actional, and cultural codes.[57] But what he gained by inclusion of response he lost in clarity and defensibility of method.

By contrast, Keir Elam is less ambiguous in suppositions about audience/reader than Barthes, and less bound by linguistic methods than, say, Umberto Eco in his *Theory*.[58] Elam draws upon the Prague School theorist Bogatyrev for theater as sign, Gregory Bateson's and Erving Goffman's concept of the frame, and Urmson and others for spatial effect, e.g., "blocking" or positioning action on stage. Still, he has little to say about the nature of our cognition, emotions, judgment, and reception per se. His focus is on the process of semiosis, a confluence of cultural and theatrical or dramatic codes. To judge from Eco's attempt to include reception in semiotic analysis—sixty pages spent analyzing Alphonse Allais's four-page *Un drama bien parisien*[59]—there is probably no way to extend semiotics into response without sacrificing the field's methodological rigor. Again one returns to assumptions about our psychological and cognitive makeup.

The fact is our ignorance of the psychology of everyday consciousness is a formidable obstacle to study of semiosis as it actually affects response. In 1972 Harold Garfinkel described just the kind of "expectancies" operating in everyday living that I have portrayed when we experience comedy, yet admitted it is "disconcerting to find how little we know about these."[60] Nor has our knowledge increased much in the last decade or two, to judge

from recent work by Norman and Langer.[61] The exception would
seem to be visual semiosis, but it has its problems, too. Visual
perception has long been studied, by Rudolf Arnheim in his considerable work on visual thinking and by Ernst Gombrich.[62] And
the study is supported by scientific research.[63] However, in the
case of comedy, it is not the cognitive aspect of visual and other
perception that raises difficulties. It is the emotional and judgmental element of response that defies formulation, the very aspect avoided by research.

All in all, then, I can only offer a tentative, "experiential" conception of a responding sentience, one not very flattering to our
self-esteem. How this habitual state of mindlessness, or semisom-
nambulence, finally produces some acute insights can only be
shown in particular cases. If Shklovsky is right, that "the purpose
of art is to impart the sensation of things as they are perceived
and not as they are known," then it is reasonable to begin with
sensation and perception of a low, primal kind. Their transformations in the play of comedy are as exciting in their way as the
creation of any art from raw materials.

Finally, what of the scope of this discussion? It is quite impossible to take in the full province of comedy, all of its forms, shades,
favorite devices, and so on. I will focus on the mainstream of our
comic tradition, theater and Menandrine or New Comedy because they are familiar to most readers and because they are a
force in popular entertainment to this day. Meanwhile, although
I will use theater to establish major forms and structures—the
"supra-language" of comedy mentioned earlier—I will show their
operations in a variety of media, from painting and sculpting to
novels and poetry, with at least a glimpse of them in music and
dance. This inclusiveness is not profligate eclecticism on my part.
Comedy is an aesthetic mode, not an art form like genre painting.

Nor will I set up a clear demarcation between humor and comedy. The two blend into one another as building does into architecture, mimicry and playacting into theater. Mainly from
exigencies of communication, I take separation between the skill
or "folk art" of humor and the art of comedy to be embodiment
in what we normally consider a work: a play, a painting, novel,
piece of sculpture. Not that our concept of what constitutes a
"work" is without question, but that is only one of the duckings
and silences that I will have to address as I proceed. In any event,
such are the groundings of what is to follow.

2
Operations of the Art of Comedy

Comedy is an art, or mega-art, transcending skillful use of a medium. It can express an astonishing range of feeling on virtually any subject, profane or sacred. Why not? It has its own power increased by whatever a particular medium of expression offers, a considerable armory. We tend to associate comedy with representational modes such as drama and fiction in which some meaning can be found, yet it works as well in abstract painting and nonrepresentational art. That is so because while comedy can deal with meanings, or, more often, play with them, it is essentially a significational "language" embodying statement in its own presence, as indeed any art does. We know this presence through experiencing it, and find it difficult to articulate just what our experience means. (What does a Calder mobile "mean"?) We are better off to speak of what art *signifies*, and often at a deep level of response where cognition and emotion are entwined.

Yet in spite of this considerable aesthetic power available to it, comedy appears a fairly simple activity at heart, a grab bag of paltry devices, conventions, tricks, stock characters and situations such that it seems anyone can master its skills. Paltry or not, the devices are capable of exquisite effect, both in virtuosity of execution and in the reverberations set off in us that we savor long after laughter has ceased. Just how do these shopworn, vacuous formulae of jokes, gags, and the like become art? What do they have to do with one another and with the kind of experience we associate with our response to serious aesthetic works?

Seeing comedy as play helps answer such questions. Comedy's devices, techniques, and forms are different versions of an essential sleight of hand: now you see it, now you don't. What is the difference, then, between a lady in a glittering cabinet apparently sawed in half and even the sleaziest one-liner? The magician involves us in perceptual peek-a-boo, while the comedian's one-liner engages us both in that game *and* in play with meaning. (Again, while we think of the one-liner as humor, not artistry, from the perspective of play comedy is only an extension of humor, a refinement of its techniques, and none the worse for that since humor, too, has considerable power.) In both humor and comedy, the essential play appears to consist of misleading us, but in such a way that we are unaware of being misled. Or, as is frequently observed, comedy is a turn on expectation; the term I shall use for that is perceptual play.

Insistence that the fundamental play of comedy is *perceptual* comes from the fact that "expectation" includes far more than word meanings and symbolic associations; it involves our whole mental state and working of mind. Roughly, in the nonrepresentational work that mental state is what is being played *with*, while meaning is what is being played with in the representational work. Yet even in stage comedy, which attempts to mimic reality to some extent, and where issues of love, youth versus age, restraint versus freedom, and so on are the main concern, there is always an element of play with perception, a turning over of our habits of thinking. In farce the element of perceptual play is stronger yet, tending to become the "message" of the work, its signification embodied in nonsensical, pointless jolts and bursts of action. Furthermore, the term "perceptual play" is divorced from the nomenclatures of study of drama, literature, and the visual arts, which helps remind us that the focus is *not* on skill in the medium but on operations of comedy as its own art. If comedy is perceptual play, what specific forms does play take?

It is tempting to seize upon a common action and have it stand for the essential operation of comedy: Bergson's man slipping on a banana peel, a pie in the face, or the joke as a form of cognitive switching. But none of these capture how comedy signifies in many and complex ways. Some of the ways are much influenced by the capacities of a medium of expression; for instance, the painter's *trompe l'oeil* does not work well on stage. For the sake of clarity let these influences be deferred for now. Let concentration be on the range of experience lying beneath kicks in the pants, double takes, puns, jokes, and the rest of the comedian's repertoire of tricks.

If one goes deeply enough, play is pointless, chaotic. Comedy formulates this profound looniness into game; it has to in order to communicate. Moreover, the play of comedy occurs in the context of our mental state, a largely habitual bundle of assumptions about the world, and a largely communal set of meanings and values. Thus play, meaning nothing in itself, can take on significance in the hands of the comic artist, that is, it becomes signification. For instance, it is often said that comedy rests on incongruity. Incongruous with or between what? Without some base in meaning incongruity is merely difference. Difference takes on significance—as disparateness, incompatibility, opposition, etc.—to the extent that it has substance. In comedy we, its respondents and participants, supply the substance. Hence the notion of comedy springing *from* incongruity is vacuous, not to mention the fact that neither incongruity nor any other quality of comedy or humor is ipso facto funny. Comedy uses incongruity, not the other way around. So to speak, comedy overall translates the inexplicabilities, the play of existence, into a form we can apprehend.

When in comedy play is formulated as game, it takes on the characteristics of a language. (There is part of play that is never formulated, however, a point of importance to be taken up later.) The language of comedy is semiotic, a trafficking more in signs and significations than in meanings. For instance, we respond to semiosis when, in a family argument, we note not just words but facial expressions, gestures, the lean of the body, the silences and inferences, just the sort of thing we can never quite explain—"I know you said you agreed, but it was the *way* you said it." The characteristic structures of comedy's semiotic language appear to have risen through trial and error to become conventions of use primarily because of their efficacy as tricks. Virtually any trick form will do if it fits the protocols of the game, which are, usually, that no one present gets hurt, that the participants accept their understood roles in the play, and that the net result is pleasurable, meaning more than being amused and implying some aesthetic quality.

Two primary structures of the language of comedy are juxtaposition of things usually not associated with each other and the joke. What makes them important beyond their propensity to deceive is their capacity to be transformed into numerous, larger structures of comedy's discourse while retaining their essential configurations. Like the subject-verb-object structure in English, comedy's language has its primal patterns capable of almost limitless expansion within the work of art. Both juxtaposition and the joke appear in different guises but are recognizable as structures of perceptual play. Like speech and writing, comedy's language has its deep and surface structures. Surface structures are most influenced by demands of a medium. The verbal joke becomes the five panel cartoon strip, which in turn takes the form of the comic episode in the novel because the joke structure works best in these particular forms. It is the underlying structure that is most important, however; that is where the real business of comedy goes on.

Juxtaposition is a primary deep configuration in the visual arts, the joke its counterpart in theater, literature, and related modes such as film. The two structures are closely related as play. One could say that juxtaposition's inclusion of two things not usually associated with each other in a single image or event is the joke's lead-in and punch line collapsed into one another, made static. In both cases we as participants supply the "lead-in." In its simplest forms juxtaposition merely clashes together things that conflict in connotational or symbolic value, e.g., in a collage an image of a doll's head placed alongside one of a guillotine, or expressions like, "She's a saint, a goddamned saint." The higher the symbolic value, the richer the effect; the more inherently remote the two elements' associations, the more powerful and striking their clash.

In theater or film juxtaposition can be quiet, a passing whimsical effect, as in Groucho Marx's expression of anticipatory bliss and his plebian cigar as he leans his head against the ample, bepearled bosom of the society lady, Margaret Dumont. The Monty Python group, by contrast, uses violent, bizarre effects in its prelude to episodes of its television series: figures of authority and empire juxtaposed with plumbing, heads whose tops come off with flowers, and so on. The more bizarre the juxtaposition, however, the more its play can be threatening, symbolized in the Monty Python preludes by the sudden descent of a huge foot from the upper part of the frame. Though on reflection we may be shaken, in the ambience of comedy our first impulse is to smile at the surprise.

(Why that is our first impulse no one has discovered. The inclination may go back to early perceptual experience. There one is in his or her crib, looking up at a clearly defined, stable world of wooden bars, playthings suspended from a railing, a ceiling, a light. Suddenly this perceptual world is intruded upon. A face appears, smiles, makes cooing noises accompanied by odd gestures. The intrusion is a pleasant one. What was inert is now animated. There is a whole new relationship between forms, distances, lines, colors; our perceptual framework is enlivened. And where there was our own gurgling, now there is a tumble of voice in interesting ups and downs of volume and pitch. Possibly because all this interesting reshuffling is often accompanied by peek-a-boo, tickling, or being held or fed, this elemental pleasure remains with us throughout our lives.)

Whether response is caused by infant experience or innate capacity, any excitation of our perceptual field that is not threatening is a source of pleasure, from tumblers putting the body in postures we hardly think it capable of to the skittering of a kitten on a slick floor. It is some distance, though, from merely shaking up our perceptual field to dislocating, or reallocating, expected patterns. On the whole, comedy traffics in the latter, and in deep associations, implications, and meanings because these generate signification. The signification that results is rather complex, no less so than serious use of juxtaposition in, say, Donne's image of the drawing compass conveying the nature of love (*Valediction: Forbidding Mourning*). Or, of course, shaking up, bizarre effect with little or no inherent signification beyond the act itself may be the point, as in much farce or postmodernist art, e.g., Duchamp's *The Fountain,* a urinal turned flatways, or in music John Cage's 4'33", a "musical piece" consisting of silence.

Either way, what makes juxtaposition a fundamental form of play, or trickery, is that we provide the grounds of its operations. It is played in *our* consciousness, although we are scarcely aware of it at the moment of apprehension.[1] Art critics may be exempt from this, as from other human propensities, but for most of us juxtaposition in the painting or piece of sculpture comes upon us as a surprise. Few of us view art, even proclaimedly comic art, with a split-level sensibility, an awareness fluttering angelically above us observing how we observe. The whole phenomenology of reception balks at such a possibility, though certainly *after* first sensations critical awareness can begin as we stand back, squint, or otherwise absorb the work. Consider this, too: although we know very well that we are going to be duped by the single panel cartoon of the *The New Yorker* or *Punch,* we devour each and every one in search of comic effect.

It is in this spirit that it was said earlier that comedy is sleight-of-hand. For what we have to conclude about a structuring of experience like juxtaposition, or its kin, the joke, is that the structuring itself is not inherently amusing, any more than surprise, incongruity, or turns on expectation are indigenously comic. What can make the bland, simple structure of juxtaposition exciting is the total situation of accepted trickery (Searle's "speech act") in which it occurs. The requisite condition of that trickery is our state of *un*awareness as we first respond. Other than inherent dullness of being, there is probably no greater threat to the vital experiencing of comic effect than awareness.

Exactly why it is that we consent to play a game in which we are the inevitable losers I am not entirely sure, but we keep engaging ourselves in it with utter naiveté and faith, and, probably more to the point, out of habit. But let practice determine, first with a look at the visual arts and with focus on juxtaposition and its mutations throughout a work. The concept of surface and deep structures will be useful. And, as suggested earlier, while the configurations of perceptual play are important for achieving comic effect, the artist uses the power of the medium, its "serious" capacities, to reinforce the gag at hand.

Cioli, *Little Bacchus* **(or** *Statue of Morgante***). Florence, Italy, Biboli Gardens. Photograph by author.**

There is, for instance, Cioli's *Little Bacchus,* or statue of Morgante the dwarf-jester of the Medicis, in the Biboli Gardens outside Florence. Morgante has an overall attitude of authority vaguely suggesting the *condottiere* or warrior and echoing Aristotle in Raphael's *The School of Athens.* Juxtaposed to this suggestion is the actuality of a pudgy, babylike body mounted on a most unimpressive steed, a tortoise.

Juxtaposition is mainly by fairly obvious symbols and symbolic suggestion, or surface effect. Morgante's right arm extends out forcefully, a gesture that lasted as late as the Fascist salute of Mussolini; the left reposes on the hip insouciantly, a quality of *sprezzatura,* or the confident ease of command-nobility. Equally obvious are the associations of the potbellied, fat little body: softness and ineffectuality. The rather small penis does not help either, but that is not only part of the juxtaposition of images of warrior and dwarf, it is part of the incongruity of nudity itself, usually accorded classical or idealized subjects.

Further, the effect of interplay between masculine power and babylike softness, the essential joke of the piece, is enhanced by play with our visual field quite in the manner of serious art. The lines of the breast circumscribe and contain the focal point of the joke, the penis. Likewise, the major lines, the infolding of planes where dwarf and tortoise meet and where legs and torso meet, create an "X" at whose center is the penis. There is a certain gratuitous scatology involved in the penis (play tends to get carried away with itself), but it becomes the focal point of the whole piece and by its unimposing presence works against the overall message of masculine power and authority.

Thus perceptual play, primarily the structure of juxtaposition, operates at the level of fairly obvious semantic content and also at the level of deep, unconscious structures of visual response. One might go on with the latter (the effects of the roundedness of flesh, particularly the belly, and the complementary rotundity of the tortoise's shell, etc.) but the point is better made by the perceptually less complicated operations of our response to a two-dimensional visual image.

In his satiric engraving *The Bench,* perhaps because it was "address'd to the Honourable College" of fellow artists, Hogarth gives more than usual attention to serious composition as he pulls off his ridicule of the High Court. The satiric point is conveyed quickly by surface effects like the superimposition on the royal coat of arms of "semper eadem," always the same, a juxtaposition by way of a verbal gag. Juxtaposition lies behind the other immediate effect, what we generally conceive a court in session to be and the actuality of the figures of the judges, especially the one

William Hogarth, *The Bench*. Reproduction courtesy of British Museum.

dozing off at the far right (Lord Bathurst). Then there is the mysterious, dark person to the left of the central figure, Chief Justice Wills. The juxtaposition is between light and dark, and though the dark figure may be a clerk or functionary normally in that particular position, the suggestion is literally something going on behind, in the shadow. Other surface details include the stilettolike quill pen, lower left, held by exaggeratedly slim fingers. And for Hogarth's viewers, if not for most of us, there is caricature, the immediate recognition of the actual Chief Justice Wills and the rake Bathurst, at far right. Both surface and deep in their suggestion are the coat of arms placed directly over the head of Wills and the solid, round bulk of the Palladian column to the left of it—not an elegant, fluted Ionic one, but sheer mass.

At that stage of things we are into Hogarth's use of some unconscious registerings of visual effect. The slant of shadow upper right not only draws our attention to its apex, the coat of arms, it suggests light and power descending from on high, from the crown. The figures of the justices form a declining line to the right, augmenting the decline of attention in the chief justice to the deep thought of the middle justice (who, however, is not looking at the plaintiff or even consulting his rolled document) to the cuddled figure of Bathurst. At the light and compositional center is the figure of the chief justice. His very shape—that of a truncated cone or pyramid—suggests unmovable firmness, corpulent self-complacency, touched off with his grim, downturned mouth. Everything moves us away from a sense of humanity, concern, and the possibility of leniency, toward firmness, inflexibility, and authority, including Hogarth's positioning of the viewer in relation to the image. We are not above looking down, or on the side in strong perspective as an onlooker, but are in the position of the plaintiff.

On the whole, however, these compositional strategies are both perceptual play and reinforcements of the primary visual gag occurring on the surface of response, obvious ridicule of the High Court. Play with structures of visual perception is clearer in works having little semantic "meaning." In *The Revolution of the Viaducts*, Paul Klee does not rely to any great extent on symbols or symbolic association. (See next page.) Though viaduct arches may suggest something to each of us (triumphs of engineering, the bearers of water and life, etc.), collectively we draw something of a blank when confronted with them. We *do* think of arches generically, however, as existing in a single plane, as inert, as supporting something, as things we can see through. Klee adds the obvious, surface effects of the "feet" and the warping of the arches to make one foot "advance," thus turning static shapes into humanoid figures. In one sense, that is the gag of the painting, taken in conjunction with Klee's title: surface effect is immediately apprehended. But it is not where the real perceptual play goes on.

Klee uses the abstract pattern of the arches' placement to suggest movement, bustle. He uses a suggestion of depth perception (one arch before another) but breaks off the suggestion in upper center, achieving a sense of a crowd with one or two stragglers but in any event not an organized group. Less obvious is his play with an implied grid of horizontal and vertical lines. Each line— e.g., that along the top of the farthest row—is varied; each arch top is a little off horizontal. So with verticality. The arches deviate from plumb. This interplay between implied grid, a pattern we gravitate toward if given the chance, and slightly skewed alignment gives the arches movement. What with the other sugges-

Paul Klee, *Revolution of the Viaducts.* **Hamburg, Germany, Hamburger Kunsthalle. Reproduced with permission.**

tions of a disorganized group, and the added effect of a motley collection from different viaducts, we end up with a comically menacing "crowd" advancing toward us.

In other words, our overall comic response can be, and in Klee's case most powerfully is, influenced by play with underlying perceptual structures. So with Cioli and Hogarth, only their deep play is obscured by fairly obvious surface meanings. In fact, later on there will be cause to question whether any comic work can achieve full aesthetic potential if it relies wholly or mainly on surface effect.

Because of its importance, and problems, the difference between surface and deep effect is worth some elaboration. The distinction rests primarily on consciousness.[2] But not only is there no membrane separating conscious apprehension from unconscious registering, there is often nothing in the work per se that distinguishes surface from deep effect. What is "surface" in one artist's work may not be in another's, or even in a later work by the same person. Much depends upon reception, upon the viewer's "semiotic equipment." For instance, known in America as *Sinbad the Sailor*, Klee's popular print has nothing at all to do with Sinbad. Its original title is *Kampfscene aus der komisch phantastischen Oper "Der Seefahrer"* (battle scene from the comic operatic fantasy, "The Seafarer"). To the left, and mostly in ultramarine blue background, is a man in a small boat holding a large spear, off the end of which hangs a large drop of blood. In the center and to the right there is a swath of white light, fading off into the blue background. In the light, and moving threateningly toward the man, are three large fish, incongruously patterned as if in South Sea island cloth. To the average American viewer the scene is amusing: what is that little man, with his absurdly large spear and small boat, doing fending off the belligerent fishes? The whole is playfully enigmatic, the blue background and swath of light a meaningless pattern of "abstract art," or what I have called deep effect.

Not so for the German viewer, who would immediately associate the swath of white with stage lighting, immediately recognize the Lohengrin-like figure in the boat, with helmet fallen down over his head, and would take the frond on top of his helmet, and the large spear, as parodic too. That these elements have high symbolic value for the German, who brings to the experience prior knowledge of heroic opera, and for the American viewer are merely amusingly incongruous, vaguely suggestive forms and shapes, means that they are surface effects for the German, and deeper, compositional registerings for the American. Well and good, except, cannot these responses, one surface, one deep, be both at once, in this case for the German viewer? Does awareness preclude the possibility of, say, the swath of white being both representational of stage lighting *and* a compositional element?

Not at all, and there is always a range of effect which is indeterminately surface and deep. On the other hand, the smallness of the boat, the "heroic" figure, the little frond on his helmet, the huge drop of blood off the end of the spear, and the savage mein of the fishes he confronts are more recognizable symbols than elements of line and composition. They *are* those to some extent, of course (what in a painting is not?) but would have been more so had Klee chosen to make them blobs of color, hazy in outline, or only vaguely "representational." Acknowledging that gradation is involved, I would still call these elements surface effect. They are quickly recognized as man, boat, fish, spear, and blood, and their collective lampooning (of some vague "heroic" effort for the American viewer, for the German a more precise referent) registers consciously, like Hogarth's "semper eadem" on the coat of arms and his judge nodding off to sleep. Furthermore, the notion of deep/surface is to be conceived for *all* comedy, and in the performing arts timing is a crucial factor: effects come rapidly and leave us little time to mull over their deeper implications. That does not mean the implications do not register in a shadowy way, only that we are likely to be aware of the superficial, obvious "message" of comic effect. This registering can be diagrammed.

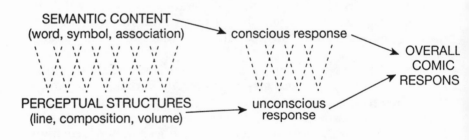

Diagram of Perceptual Play

The two strata of play with semantic content and with perceptual structures, are hardly separable other than for conceptual convenience. In actual operation they are interactive, one permeating the other, and, like the split between conscious and unconscious responses with which I have associated them, have no clear line of demarcation. Necessarily an oversimplification, the diagram is well kept in mind as I move on to the other major primary, almost archetypal, structuring of response, the joke.

What was remarked on juxtaposition as a structure of perceptual play applies even more fully to the joke; it works by surface and deep significations, is transformational, and operates within the overall social conventions of comedy. From experience we know a great deal about jokes, have heard hundreds of them, and have a highly developed, sensitive response to them. That does not mean we understand them, necessarily, but it does give us a common grounding in their operation. Our immediate reaction is to content. We know when a joke is in poor taste, when its meaning offends. Yet we also know when a joke is poorly delivered, when the snap of the punch line is missing, or when the joke itself lacks depth. That is, we respond to surface *and* deep effects. We like a joke we can feel down to our toes.

Transformations of the joke structure are not readily apparent, but we are at least dimly aware that the comic scene in theater or episode in the novel is patterned along the lines of a joke. And we recognize when a work is a joke on its own form, when an author like Sterne in *Tristram Shandy* gives us a "novel" that is about the writing of, or not writing, a novel rather than an ordinary narrative. It is just that we have not given much thought to how the childish, simple pattern of lead-in and punch line keeps reappearing in various semiotic guises, and seldom if ever do we reflect upon the global setting, the "speech act" in which it occurs, the actual protocols of our participation in a rather vacuous social ritual.

It is just as well we do not think about how jokes truly operate. *We* are the ones being made to look foolish. We are protected from our stupidity by two powerful defenses. One is the holiday spirit of the comic moment: if we are caught being foolish, that is allowable. The second line of defense is even more assuring, if not impregnable, which is that our egos do not accept ridicule. By psychological transference (a combination of denial and substitution) we put ridicule off onto a figure in the joke, or on stage. Who among us, hearing a good joke, exclaims, "You got me! What a fool I've been!" No one. We find it next to impossible to be laughed at unless it is in special situations and by *very* close friends or relatives. Whatever the psychological and social factors involved, our habitual transfer of ridicule away from ourselves is a blessing for the comic artist. Without it the sleight-of-hand of comedy could not occur, or not for long.

In this context, then, the joke appears as something like juxtaposition set into motion. As with juxtaposition we ourselves provide the lead-in, but that function is objectified, speeded up, and intensely focused by the (usually) carefully chosen bits of information divulged to us by openings such as, "Two nuns, a midget, and a TV evangelist went into this bar for a drink, see?" We respond with clusters of associations haloed around each stereotypical figure, the very typing itself easing communication and more or less assuring a predictable response—the primary function of stereotyping in comedy. There will always be the occasional spoilsport joke listener, such as a nun or midget or evangelist, but popular humor relies on a bulk, majority reaction. It is usually finicky where it counts, which is with the quality of the lead-in and the punch line. In fact, while the punch line indeed must be compressed and pointed, and reserve its clinching effect to the very last word or phrase, its success, like its existence, depends upon a skillful laying out of the lead-in. The relationship between the two parts of the joke is deeply symbiotic; a mixture, even a mild blending of each with each can undermine the whole gag and debase its craft.

Consider two jokes. Both are execrable, as ethnic slurs tend to be, but craftsmanship is the concern here. First there is "They had a Polish Beauty Contest in Atlantic City. Everyone lost." The punch line satisfies the usual criteria. It is short and somewhat surprising, and cleanly refers back to the lead-in. Just in its own terms it does not seem the only choice that could be made (e.g., "My brother-in-law won"), but the genuine communicational weakness of the joke is that the lead-in anticipates and thereby deflates the punch line. In the context of opinion in which the joke would be told (and who would tell it otherwise?) the very idea of a Polish Beauty Contest is ludicrous, a little gag by itself. The lead-in would have been better had the joketeller provided more diversionary information: the stereotypical image of the beauty contest, with young women in bathing suits and smiles, banners athwart their bosoms, flags, pageants, music, and a toothy, genial announcer. One would not want to drag the thing out, but at least one could repair some of the damage done by the "Polish Beauty Contest."

Then, by contrast, there is a joke used by Greeks against Turks and so on, or in this version Ukrainians ridiculing Poles. (One recalls that the Ukraine was occupied by Polish feudal lords ca.

1560–1660.) "Why wasn't Jesus born in Poland? Because they couldn't find three wise men and a virgin." The joke form is reversed: the punch line becomes the lead-in. It is a captivating question because of its absurdity. Why wasn't Jesus born *any-where* other than Bethlehem? The listener is not given time to ponder, and if his thoughts are running in any direction it is toward a logical answer such as, "He wasn't Polish."

The answer is the joke's great achievement. It accomplishes the racial insult implied in the lead-in, but with considerable artistry and power. The hypothetical search is ludicrous in itself; one imagines patriarchal figures poring over a map and choosing sites for the Immaculate Conception. What immediately catches the listener's attention is the surface effect, the semantic content of "three wise men" and a "virgin."

There is a deeper layer of meaning, however, in the use of "they" and the specific order of terms. Who are "they"? Churchmen of some kind, perhaps a Polish contingent advocating its home location? But whoever they are, they must be generic figures of the church. Their action exhibits pride, an overreaching assumption of power. Then "they" get things mixed up. If one is to search out a place for the birth of Jesus, one seeks a virgin first. "They" put the three wise men before the essential matter. Depending upon one's feeling about the church, we either have a genial ribbing of patriarchal ineptitude or sharp ridicule of pride, assumption of power, and a loss of the true meaning of the Im-maculate Conception. Whichever, the joke has genuine depth and resonance because its play is with surface words and meanings *and* with underlying structures such as word order and the ambi-guity of "they," verbal equivalents of the deep perceptual con-figurations exploited by Cioli, Hogarth, and Klee.

The basic operation of the joke presents problems for our un-derstanding only when we dwell on just how its underlying struc-tures operate, when they do. Koestler put this operation in Gestaltist terms: the lead-in establishes a network of associations, a "perceptual matrix," which is conceived as a lateral plane of symbols, clusters of meaning, and linking concepts. The punch line cuts across the lead-in, radically reorganizing that matrix by supplying its own configuration and connections between phe-nomena.[3] At that point of bisection (his term is "bisociation") we laugh, or so the joke teller hopes.

Reasonable for the verbal joke; however, if one sees the form as a primary structure which has numerous permutations, analo-gous structurings of response, all amounting to sleight-of-hand, the cognitive explanation of its workings seems inadequate. (A bewildering number of factors enter into response, the stickiest of which to articulate are emotions; more on these later.) Yet there is undoubtedly an element of cognitive, or perceptual, play running through the joke's protean forms and analogues. The pattern of expectation, turn on expectation keeps recurring, as do deception and drawing in of the respondent. Variations on the pattern are numerous.

Just in verbal humor the joke takes a number of mutant forms. The pun has as its "lead-in" the expected, normal meanings of a word, and springs on us a remote, unusual one. The lead-in can be a conventional expression, where both terms and syntactical form are fixed; and the punch line is either an insertion of a new unusual term or play with the syntactical structure. Wilde chooses to leave the structure intact in his transposition, "Work is the curse of the drinking classes." So with the Spoonerism, which retains the structure but displaces expected sounds to come up with nonsense that almost has a Jabberwockyan sense, e.g., "done in one swell foop!" and so on to include any recognizable rhetorical form or organization.[4] What is important to note is that whenever expectations and the perceptions involved in them collide with new or other perceptions, there is the possibility of play taking forms resembling or analogous to the joke structure.

These forms operate beyond sentence and rhetorical organization, within the semiotic language of a medium and in its terms. Thus in theater, novel, and film (short stories, television, etc.) we find episodes frequently structured as enlarged jokes: an elaborate lead-in capped with a relatively compact, sudden "punch line." Furthermore, though a character in the work is usually the fool, as often as not we are, too. Psychological transference still works, only now we see the "joke" enacted or narrated before us.

For instance, Fielding plays with the reader's perception as well as Tom's when, in *Tom Jones,* he has his hero, fallen in love with Sophia, go to express his concern for his now former mistress Molly Seagram.[5] After much wailing about her betrayal and pangs of guilt on Tom's part, the curtain that makes up her "closet" at one end of her attic room falls, revealing Philosopher Square in his nightshirt. We should have known from Molly's sister earlier answering Tom "with a malicious smile" that Molly was in bed and from the odd time of day for sleep. But in the normal course of reading such "plantings" of the lead-in are unremarkable.

Besides, Fielding does everything he can to divert us, including his usual elaborate confidences to us through the narrator with whom we share a superior position ("Imagine, dear reader, the emotions that now . . ."). We have been had, of course, but do not acknowledge it. In any case our whole focus is on Tom—the narrative point of view is his—and his anguished guilt, then on his shock at finding his philosophical mentor in such an unedifying position. Thus point of view, the perspective we adopt in narration, can be itself something of a lead-in, drawing us on in a situation which can easily be turned to a wholly new perspective, the punch line.

There would seem to be less possibility of this kind of play between audience and author in theater, where normally we are privileged to know all that is happening while some characters do not, that is, usually the audience has superior awareness.[6] It is a perdurable device of the stage, and is not inherently comic. Othello is ignorant, and we share superior awareness with Iago, but the outcome is hardly amusing. Still, the discrepancy between our awareness and a character's is high in potential for trickery, for ridicule of a character and what he or she embodies (age, position in life or in the family, and personality quirks), and an almost sure-fire crowd pleaser flattering to our egos.

Nor is the device simple or mechanical. It can operate in the manner of locker room humor—a bucket above the closed door, everyone waiting for the entrance of the class fink—or with considerable delicacy and nuance. Ridicule is not a quantum thing, nor is it necessarily undifferentiated. We express a vast range of feelings through our response, the result of the artist's fine tuning of comic effect. That can be accomplished by generating some sympathy for the comic victim, for instance, or, conversely, by undermining our respect for his or her motives. Or it can be accomplished by making fun of more than one figure, or by having contending sympathies raised in our response. (More on these later, since they are properly a matter of how comedy "means.") So we encounter wider possibilities of play between audience and author, and subtler duplicities than the simple device of discrepancy of awareness suggests.

While we usually occupy a privileged position of awareness, a gag can be sprung directly on us; we can be kept totally in the dark. When that occurs, the result is a sense of surprise and delight, of looniness or madcap zaniness. However, we still tend to fasten laughter on some character, or in any event we do not stop to marvel that we ourselves have been duped. Pace and timing of a show hardly allow for it even if we were so inclined. Nor do we recognize in the ordinary run of gags, where we have superior awareness and there is a victim on stage, that there is always an element of play at our expense. We can know exactly what is coming—e.g., the planting of the letter in the garden for Malvolio to find (*Twelfth Night*, 2.5). Yet we can still be surprised and delighted at the specific revelations: Maria's carefully worded ambiguity, Malvolio's leaping to conclusions, and his strutting self-satisfaction as he decides that the Lady Olivia is conferring her affections on him.

In this range of comic effect, however, the joke has ceased to be a tritely predictable structure. It has been transformed into dynamic play between perspectives capable of generating complex significations. In other words, we have gone beyond skillful handling of a technique to artifice and art. Family resemblance gets clouded, true, and the joke form proper appears to lose its essential shape in, say, the happy ending that is a gag at the expense of its own convention: the finale of *Joseph Andrews*, brought about by fortuitous discovery of a strawberry mark on the hero's torso, or the resolution of *The Importance of Being Earnest*, hinging on Miss Prism's discovery that the fateful handbag is indeed hers (she is glad to have it restored after so many years) and on Jack's discovery that his true name is Ernest. But both endings are "punch lines" in their effect and bounce off our expectations. Interplay between an author's perspective, a character's, and our own (otherwise called point of view) and equivocation between the reliable and unreliable narrator[7] are the joke in more elaborate versions.

On the other hand, I admit that at a certain depth what can be construed as a mutant form of the joke can be, and is usually considered to be, a strategy used by serious artists for somber purposes. As we saw in visual art, surface effect establishes comic intent; thereafter, the artist uses the full resources of the medium, comic or serious, to flesh out what could otherwise be a thin, cartoonlike gag. The artist's full use of the medium taps some deep energies, usually without our knowing it. Only, when that occurs, we are beyond signification by a recognizable structure characteristic of comedy. We are beyond turn on expectation and into deeper consideration of what expectation itself includes.

When a substantial element of or the whole work is a joke at our expense, what the comic artist plays with are not merely anticipated meanings and customary associations. Time, space, cause and effect, and probability—the very framework of our mental world—are fair game. All are part of our almost somnambulant, unconscious, seemingly dormant regions of response.

Consider two cases. In *Winnie-the-Pooh*, A. A. Milne creates a play world of stuffed animals come to life. It is nonetheless a phenomenological world that reverberates off our own.[8] In the Hundred-Acre Wood time is only loosely temporal. Other than a vague suggestion of seasons, there is no calendar; things happen "that morning" or "one day." Space is a large "somewhere" (to a child, at least, a hundred acres is huge) marked by copse, tree, or den but having little sense of distances or coordinates. Episodes just occur, and are not connected by clear cause and effect. Improbabilities and fortuitous happenings abound. And over all presides a benevolent, loving deity, Christopher Robin—not he of the frame story, a normal cranky child, but the one within the main narrative. All in all, Milne does a delightful takeoff on our adult mental world. The Hundred-Acre Wood is phenomenally much closer to the mental world of the child, to whom it appears quite natural. For adults there is the apparently meaningless experience of a fantasy existence which nonetheless registers in our unconsciousness, perhaps one day to move us to perceive our world from a fresh perspective.

Then there is the phenomenological world of Joseph Heller's *Catch-22*. Time moves chronologically, but is broken by glimpses of Snowden dying, always in the present. Narrated time for us, as for Yossarian, drags. Pianosa has a geographic location, but its confined space becomes the center of our existential world, a rather grim Hundred-Acre Wood outside of which we see combat, destruction, and the ruined, surrealistic cityscape of Rome. Rationality and cause and effect are thwarted by the upping of the number of missions men must fly before going home. Probability ceases to operate, as when a young airman's torso is cut off by propeller blades of a plane. The purpose of the military is constantly undermined by petty egos, as military effectiveness is by advancement of a recluse like Major Major Major or the detested Scheisskopf. Sanity is twisted into "you lose no matter what." If there is a deity presiding over all this, he is no Christopher Robin. Yet Heller's phenomenological world is a play world like Milne's. It, too, flips our expectations over. Only the joke is grim: the Janus-faced nature of play again.

All of which is not to suggest that comedy always touches the deepest element of our existence, only that it can. By now it should be apparent that the structurings of comic effect are by no means a paltry grab bag of tricks when bolstered by the semiotic power of the several arts. That is why if we would know what comedy "means," we need to grasp the peculiar operations of its language.

Thus far I have kept to the perceptual aspects of signification;

inevitably these overlap with emotional and judgmental elements of response. Perceptual play is essentially phenomenal. It is a quality of experience that carries in itself the "meaning" that art conveys. Not all comic artists are Paul Klees, though; in fact as a group they tend to be engaged in issues of the world. Often they have flagrantly partisan views. What is more interesting than the messages artists elicit is the quality of vision embodied in them. Most interesting of all is how artists express an abiding fascination with the imponderable inconsistencies of human nature, or as Eugen Fink said of play, with the "tantalizing ambiguities of dialectic."

3

The "Meanings" of Comedy

In the usual sense of the word, there is no meaning to comedy. Meaning is what comedy plays *with*. (This is viewing comedy absolutely and as play, an idea that may never occur to the comic artist; he or she is engaged in the world, driven to express a point of view, not to think about ontology.) Certainly our comic tradition, primarily Menandrine or New Comedy, has been dominated by the necessity to "say something" beyond laughter. As histories of ancient comedy tell us, Menander brought narrative form, recognizable characters, and thematic statement to the frenetic, boisterous clownery of Aristophanes. No more cloud cuckoolands, impossible mistaken identities, unrealistic characters, and sleazy humor for its own sake. Literary and dramatic formalisms exerted their influence, primarily through the cultivated, civilized work of Terence rather than the energetic shows of Plautus.[1]

The net effect was to cleave comedy into two modes: the genteel art form of the mainstream and its "other," meaning farce, slapstick, *buffo*, burlesque. From the perspective of *play*, of course, the "other" is the heart of comedy, its genteel expression a dilute, debased form—hardly the most popular view in literary and dramatic study.[2] Tension between the two modes is often felt, perhaps most deeply in acknowledged works of art. Run-of-the-mill comic entertainment lacks this tension between literary and dramatic form and play, but then, it lacks exploration of underlying attitudes to begin with. The richest comic experience comes from an opening up of our sensibilities to incertitude, to play with rather than producing meanings themselves. Nor is this richness generated by literary-dramatic form primarily. It comes from the operations of comedy just sketched out.

To ask how comedy can have meaning, or at least signification, if it does not "mean" is like asking how a poem can be summarized in clear expository statement and yet remain richer in inference, more compelling and evocative as communication than its abstracted content. Though the "meaning" of comedy is partly explained by perceptual play with our mental habits, it has a contentual element, a bewildering number of intellectual, emotional, and prejudicial factors in our response. It is no easy matter to specify how these work. Although it may occur in the flick of an eye as we catch the whimsical effect in a Klee painting or the nuance of an Oscar Wilde line, our response is most complex, out of the range of awareness, and as deeply buried as the structures of our perception. The conception of surface-deep effect applies here as well, so that the earlier diagram can be enlarged. The element on the left represents the operation of perceptual play between semantic content and frameworks of perception shown earlier. The element is extended now into the context of "meaning" or signification. The source of meaning is a bundle of judgments, beliefs, and values we bring to the experience.[3] These are largely communal in nature, but, humanity being what it is, one can expect individual variation in them. Just how communal *are* they, and how are they to be expressed?

Diagram of Relationship Between Perceptual Play and Content-Meaning of Comedy

Humor is a guide. It is largely culture bound. Chinese Communist jokes do not do well here, just as ours tend to be duds in Beijing. The humor of a Chicago street gang will not work in a retirement home, even one in Chicago. Regional, age, gender, and social differences all enter in. Yet there is a range of humor that works for a broad, variegated audience. The very existence of comic films is testimony. While there are those which have only regional or age appeal, most comic films are made for a wide, national audience. We have every reason to believe that Shakespeare's comedies were equally wide in appeal, given his predominantly London audience. So it is with Molière, Neil Simon, Mel Brooks, and Monty Python.

For another thing, humor either touches upon genuine, live values and issues or it does not work in the first place. That explains why teachers of Shakespearean or any historical comedy have to give "background," the filling in of exactly those values and social patterns, those attitudes and expected behaviors, on which comic effect rests. Or, there is our common experience. No matter how gracious we may try to be, we find ourselves looking a joke teller in the eye and saying, "my cousin is mentally retarded; I don't think that's funny." Or, sometimes we chide ourselves after laughter has subsided, "Why did I laugh at *that?*" meaning, "Do I really subscribe to the implications of that gag?"

Two things, then, can be asserted: comic effect *requires* a grounding in psychologically alive values, and many of these values are shared by a large segment of our culture. Were one to do a detailed study of the matter one would find that Neil Simon's early work, up to and including *The Odd Couple,* presumes a largely suburban, middle-class clientele. That three or four or ten people out of a given night's audience probably did not share the underlying presumptions makes little difference. The shows' long, successful runs attest to Simon's ability to forecast what his audiences were thinking, right down to some very fine points of judgment on marriage, male and female roles, and family.

None of this should be news, yet it has not been utilized much in discussions of comedy. The problem is still how to formulate these observations from daily life into a workable notion of "audience." One can approach the problem by assuming a minimal, tentative set of values (say the Ten Commandments and the Beatitudes) as, so to speak, the official morality of a hypothetical audience. ("Official" means the standards we apply to others; applied to friends or ourselves, the standards are less rigorous.) In practice, the comic work itself will show whether our tentative assumptions have substance. Much more slippery than moral judgments are those having to do with behavior: manners, enactment of roles and positions in life, habits of speech and of dress. What makes Malvolio's yellow stockings ridiculous? What if they were green? That is where knowledge of a time and culture is helpful, along with a fairly broad acquaintance with comedies. Still, no matter how conscientious one may be, presumption of "an audience" can only be an approximation. Fortunately, we have a much more reliable guide than serious values, an historically verified and perdurable factor in comic response.

Common experience in humor and comedy provides this factor. We have all used or heard expressions like, "You can't trust him for a minute, but *funny*? He is hilarious!" or, conversely, "She has a heart of gold, really, but dull? God she's *dull.*" (Gender can be reversed, of course.) The theatrical equivalent is our mixed response to a character. Falstaff is the classic instance. He is a liar, a thief, a lush, and a fat, unkempt, gross parody of knighthood. That does not stop our admiring his wit, cleverness, agility of mind and imagination, and his ability to playact numerous roles.

In other words our response is compounded of both ordinary judgment and a quite different, *comic* assessment.[4] The two kinds of evaluations are inextricably mixed in the comic moment, their interpenetration making up something resembling cooked spaghetti. Purely as a conceptual device, however, the two evaluations can be seen as wholly separate: serious, moral judgment on the one hand, comic judgment on the other.

In and of itself, the ethic of comedy operates by its own determinations. To be witty, clever, imaginative, and successful no matter by what means is to be virtuous. According to this ethic to be dull, stupid, unimaginative, and a failure, no matter how, is to be flawed, a loser. We judge by this ethic; all other things being equal, we judge only by it. What happens with Falstaff—he of *Henry IV, Part 1*—is that admiration for his comic virtues far outweighs repugnance on moral grounds.

The point is that we can presuppose a comic ethic without being arbitrary. It has, in fact, existed since the time of Aristophanes, while moral standards and protocols of behavior have changed from society to society, time to time. It is a part of our psychological makeup, with every sign of its continuing to be. This comic ethic gives some firm grounding to a hypothetical audience one imagines; it gives us a solid point of reference providing a sort of calculus, a way of handling numerous and shifty variables. Most of all, it helps pin down the serious undercurrents of response, the amorphous emotional and judgmental elements from which signification or meaning ultimately derive. The problem is how to conceive of *these* elements, what methodology to use.

There is nothing wrong with becoming, say, a surrogate Elizabethan. Doing so can enrich one's experience. But far more important is conceptualizing the responding mind, the sentience in which comedy occurs. Other considerations aside, that should correspond with what we know of ourselves when we are engaged in comedy individually and collectively. More the latter, however. For the most variable elements in response are our individual values, beliefs, and prejudices. One can only deal with these by seeing them in overview, as a generalized value system—as a methodological necessity, and *not* to reduce the fullness of individual experience. As the games of comedy have changed very little over the centuries, so our judgment by the ethic of comedy has changed not one bit.

After all, how *do* we know that a gag episode occurred in Molière's work in the first place? Because it shows the structure of perceptual play and because it has someone, somewhere making a fool of himself, another character the comic winner. We have no objective evidence that 90 percent of the jokes and episodes we call comic actually raised laughter. What we do have is the perdurability of human psychology and the persistence of a comic ethic (or counterethic, if you will) in any comedy dealing with meaning.

Conceived as a polarity with serious values on one side and comic values on the other, our response appears as a tension between the two since they are incompatible by nature. This tension is at the heart of the comic experience. In practice, however, the comic artist makes all sorts of alignments between the two sets of values. Historically and up to the present the predominant pattern is distribution of comic power on the side of moral good, fudging a bit on the hero or heroine's allowable weaknesses. (Love excuses a great deal; youth is privileged.) Conversely, stupidity and dullness are allocated to morally defective characters, typically figures of authority or wealth who misuse their positions. The pattern makes for good box office. An audience comes away with its prejudices affirmed and its feelings vindicated, all while having had a good time. Only, this is not all that comedy can do; it is in fact the least it can do.

The artist can give comic power to a character who is morally reprehensible—Falstaff again—and thus have us "explore" serious values by way of a mixed response. Or the artist can give us a dominant alignment of comic success with moral virtue, then undermine that "meaning" by a minor character who is evil but hilarious. In short, the range of possibilities is immense, as wide as human concerns the artist wishes to comment on or explore, as varied and nuanced as artists' interpretations of those concerns. (A teleological function to comedy after all? No doubt the artist creates with a purpose, but no final end or *telos* is assumed in my position here.) *And*, it has to be noted, the powerful effects that can be achieved have less to do with literary and dramatic form, the well-made plot, the happy ending, than with the configurations of emotion underlying our experience.

Roughly, then, that is how comedy "means" whatever it may mean. Looking at operations of comedy by way of juxtaposition and the joke, one is considering these operations phenomenologically, in terms of how they strike us and how we respond to them perceptually. That is always an element in how comedy "means," and *the* way in which it signifies in nonrepresentational painting and sculpting. But when the artist chooses a representational mode, irrespective of the medium, then the tricks and games of sleight-of-hand inevitably involve content or meaning. They involve ourselves and the judgments, beliefs, and values we bring to the experience. Slapstick or a pie in the face may have more phenomenal immediacy than content, yet in the fully developed comic work they occur in a dynamic field of audience responsivity to values and issues. It is a question of whose pie, specifically, in whose face? Who is the comic winner, who is the loser, and what aspects of humanity are embodied in each character?

For when an artist creates even a quasi-representational character, there is a contentual entity produced. However shabby by mimetic standards, comic characters *are* in the theatrical or fictional moment men or women; young, aging, or old; educated or unlearned; sound of heart, or devious and overbearing; and so on. Furthermore, they represent a position in the hierarchy and often have an occupation or calling, not to mention political beliefs and class prejudices. Justice Wills in *The Bench* is a figure of authority, a substantial, well-fed, well-off member of the establishment. Malvolio embodies stewardship: the manager, the keeper of order, the humble servant to his betters and tyrant to his inferiors. Stereotyping further assists in conveying what a character embodies.

Such being the case, in theater and its related narrative media there is no surface effect that does not register in the unconscious emotional underlayment of our response. There is no pun, joke, or gag that does not reverberate off our judgment and its largely emotional underpinnings. Hence, in the previous diagram, comic response is shown, by way of an arrow, moving between surface effect and deep response, accumulating from deep registerings

implications, nuances, conflicting sympathies, and the like to become "meaning." That the arrow does not go through surface
games suggests that we are not wholly unaware of what is going
on. We know, or feel, who is losing and who is winning in a
particular gag situation. But during performance or in reading we
do not stop and say to ourselves, "Wait. Just a minute here. How
can you have a hero who is a rogue and a lecher and expect me
to excuse that just because he is charming, witty, and in love?"
Although that is what is happening, if the comic artist has any
skill at all, we are, at best, only dimly aware of these goings on.
Similarly, we are seldom if ever aware that we are indeed making
our deep response known through laughter.

What is meant by that is merely that our overt response,
whether a snicker, a chuckle, or an open guffaw, expresses our
feelings about the comic effect at hand. The general situation is
that we ridicule, or make fun of, characters on stage, screen, or
in a novel. But just as our reactions to jokes has a very wide range,
from open compliance to genial tolerance for sleazy implications,
so our response to the comic moment is highly variable. When
we laugh at a political cartoon showing a politician we dislike
doing something stupid, our response is harsh, vindictive, no
matter how we express it physically. When we laugh at a child
ineptly imitating adult gestures, the response is genial and sympathetic. Or, as the folk saying has it, there is laughing at and
there is laughing with.

Binary formulations belie the incredible range of comic response, however. We can literally laugh and weep at the same
time, an effect Charlie Chaplin's little tramp aroused and that
Woody Allen often strives for, or feel genuinely amused and dis-
gusted at once, as in the bloody "organ transplant" episode from
Monty Python's film *The Meaning of Life* (1983). That is, comic
response involves virtually the whole of our personalities and can
hardly be expressed by scalular gradations. That is even more the
case in the accumulation of feelings moving under response to a
play, film, or novel. In any given moment ridicule can move in
multiple directions, enriched by what has preceded it, affecting
that which follows, which is to say what has already been observed: the meanings of comedy can be complex, finely discriminating, and subtle in nuance.

Exactly how comedy can produce such effects can only be
shown by particular operations on its surface. Surface effects are
not to be sneered at, though we are inclined to think of them as
a repertoire of tricks, and rather shopworn ones at that. For in-

stance, there is the mainstay of stage and film comedy, discrepancy of awareness. The situation of an audience having superior awareness, usually shared by the hero or heroine, and the comic butt being ignorant of the true state of things has been looked at as a form of perceptual play. It is also a powerful, supple instrument for generating meanings.

In *As You Like It*, act 3 scene 5 Shakespeare uses the device, as Corin the shepherd introduces it, to show a "pageant truly played" between true love and the red glow of scorn and proud disdain (3.4.48–50), that is, discrepancy of awareness clarifies a major concern of the play, the proper roles of man and woman within the protocols of courtly love. In the later *Twelfth Night*, he uses the device to clarify an equally important issue, appropriate grief versus the need for life to go on, but with quite different effects than those of the scene in *As You Like It*.

With Corin and Celia, Rosalind observes the pleadings of Silvius, the lovelorn shepherd, for some pity from Phebe, the scornful shepherdess. Silvius's images of execution at her hands get a bit excessive, but on the whole we are sympathetic. Phebe's putdown of them *is* excessive (and twice their length). When Silvius pleads that one day she may know the hurt of love's keen arrows, her reply is blunt: until that time, come not near me, and when that time comes do not pity me, "As till that time I shall not pity thee" (3.5.31–34). It is then that Rosalind, disguised as the young man Ganymede, steps in, unable to contain herself-himself:

> And why, I pray you? Who might be your mother,
> That you insult, exult, and all at once,
> Over the wretched? What though you have no beauty
> . . . .
> Must you be therefore proud and pitiless?
> Why, what means this? Why do you look on me?
> I see no more in you than in the ordinary
> Of nature's sale-work. . . .
>
> (3.5.35–43)

And on the insults go: Phebe has inky brows, bulging eyes, black hair. The topper is Rosalind-Ganymede's catty remark, "For I must tell you friendly in your ear, / Sell when you can, you are not for all markets" (3.5.59–60).

In our response to this unrelieved and witty put-down of Phebe (with some of it directed at Silvius as well), the ridicule is harsh, the harshest in the play. Given the expectations of how a woman should respond to unwanted advances—gently, civilly, with recognition of the power she holds—Phebe deserves every bit of the sneering and cackling an audience gives her. But to make her look more foolish Shakespeare has her become infatuated with the strident, forceful Ganymede. For an Elizabethan audience, in all probability, the idea of a woman falling in love with a woman was absurd. That may not be a strong element in our response to Phebe, but since she does not know Rosalind's true identity she is made to look an idiot, and perverse to boot: she would rather hear Ganymede chide her than Silvius woo.

The power of awareness is all on Rosalind's side, which is why ridicule of Phebe is so strong. For, we note, Rosalind is *aware* that Phebe is falling for her-him: "'Od's my little life, / I think she means to tangle my eyes too" (3.5.43–44). That is crucial, for had Rosalind not been aware she, too, would appear ridiculous. True, there is a bit of ridicule that comes her way. She overdoes, and although intending to straighten things out, she succeeds in generating another love mix-up. But on the whole Rosalind's superior awareness saves her. All in all then, there is harsh ridicule of Phebe mitigated by Rosalind looking slightly foolish and, more strongly, by Silvius's grovelling manner. For if Phebe is clearly at fault, it is in relation to the wooing of Silvius, hardly a model for young men in love. However, the alignment between moral and social values and comic values is a common one, to be found in contemporary film and the television sitcom: the good guys win, the bad guys lose.

In *Twelfth Night* Shakespeare uses the device of discrepancy of awareness with quite different results. Viola is disguised as Cesario, a young courtier in service of Duke Orsino. She-he is sent to deliver the Duke's love overtures to Lady Olivia. Olivia is made to look the fool because she becomes infatuated with the witty, sprightly Cesario. The situation parallels that in *As You Like It* but involves a different dynamic. For one thing, the play suggests that Olivia is wrong in sequestering herself away from life in mourning the death of her brother. But her grief is an excess, something needing correction not excoriation. For another, one must consider the context of her refusing to hear Orsino's profferings of love. (Orsino's love is overblown; anyone so self-indulgent as to want a surfeit of music, the food of love, so his appetite may sicken and die makes us wonder if Olivia may not be right after all.) So Shakespeare modulates the effect of discrepancy of awareness considerably.

In act 1 scene 5 Viola-Cesario enters jauntily; Olivia veils herself so that she cannot be recognized. Thus there is a device within the device: Viola does not know who the lady of the house is. Furthermore, Viola herself is in a ridiculous position. She loves her master, the Duke, yet must deliver his love tidings to Olivia. Viola's resolution is to deliver the Duke's message in an upstart, inept manner, which turns out to charm us and, more importantly, Olivia. (The exact tone of Viola's manner is reflected in Olivia's, "Are you a comedian?" 1.5.74.) So until Olivia reveals her identity about a third of the way through the episode Viola-Cesario looks a little silly and Olivia clearly has the upper hand. It is as if Shakespeare in the earlier scene from *As You Like It* had given Phebe comic advantage.

On the meeting goes, with Viola trying to give her message, and Olivia scorning and mocking it. The mockery itself, witty though it is, becomes heavy, a flippant rejection of anything Orsino has to say. In a more socially elevated position than Phebe, Olivia nonetheless begins to sound as cruelly disdainful. This does not help Viola-Cesario look any less foolish, however, for she-he yearns to see the face that is, after all, her competition.

At Cesario's request (that, too, inept) to see her face Olivia acquiesces, in itself a tip-off that she is becoming interested in this upstart messenger. The balance of ridicule is exquisite. Olivia unveils with a complacent smugness: "Look you, sir, such a one I was this present. / Is't not well done?" (1.5.221–22). But if she earns a sneer for that, Viola-Cesario's response evokes an outright chuckle: "Excellently done, if God did all." The catty reply, like Rosalind's "You are not for all markets," is at the expense of women, but rather mild ribbing, all considered.

From there on out in the episode it is Viola who is comically on top, not so much because of what she says or does as because of the slow revelation that Olivia is infatuated with him-her. Olivia looks progressively more foolish as she inquires into Cesario's parentage and virtually invites his coming again (1.5.265–68); she appears unladylike when she has Malvolio chase after Cesario to return a ring the messenger never left. Still, one notes, the ridicule is dispersed and lightened somewhat by Viola-Cesario's sharing in it. Whereas Rosalind picked up immediately that Phebe was "looking" upon him-her, Viola never does catch on to Olivia's growing interest. There is a drift of counter ridicule at Viola's expense: she hardly notices the sly overtures of Olivia, as any courtier worth the name would.

Compared to Shakespeare's use of the same device in *As You Like It*, the handling of it in *Twelfth Night* act 1 scene 5 is far subtler, its effects carefully tuned. Discrepancy of awarenesses is as conventional a technique as one is likely to find in comedy, yet it is extremely powerful and capable of articulating fine discriminations. In the case of *Twelfth Night* it would appear that Shakespeare cannot afford, at this early point anyway, to have Olivia look the utter fool. (That comes when Viola's brother, Sebastian, turns up.) If she is cruel and scornful, we understand why she is. Again, all is in relation to Orsino, whose depth of love we have reason to question. The specific handling of who is aware of what and exactly when shows Shakespeare establishing precisely how we should feel about Olivia—not a simple, undifferentiated response by any means, but one carefully controlled nonetheless.

The effects in the two scenes detailed above pass in a few moments of playing time; they have little chance of being recognized by an audience. Too much is happening on stage (figures moving, gestures and reactions to them, the sheer phenomenal impact of theater) to allow for it. Yet each word or phrasing or gag registers in our unconscious response. These registerings are rather simple in the case of Rosalind's put-down of Phebe. But the issue of correct or incorrect attitudes in love is central to the whole of *As You Like It*, and theatrically speaking act 3, scene 5 comes at a crucial place in narrative development.

The registerings on underlying emotions of our response in the scene from *Twelfth Night* are far more complex and interactive. According to our serious judgment, Olivia is flawed: grief is to be respected, but life must go on. Yet if she is proud, she is also witty, and no dullard when it comes to putting down the excessive claims of the love-filled Orsino. How her comic virtues weigh, precisely, against our disapproval of her indulgence in grief is no easy matter to decide, but it is clear that Shakespeare evokes a mixed, complex response from us. In that sense there is less condemnation, as in the case of Phebe, than exploration of the factors involved. When the episode ends, our feelings are indeterminate, approving and disapproving, sympathetic and critical, or, in a word, ambivalent.

So it is that surface play can produce deep effect, generate meanings or, as with Viola and Olivia, play with meaning. No matter that by the end of *Twelfth Night* play gets turned to more or less clear thematic statement; at the moment we feel pulled in two directions. We feel the emotional equivalent of dialectic or two incompatible judgments, each having its claim on us. Nor need there be some transcending resolution. Ultimately, play is play, endlessly and pointlessly. In fact, indeterminacy, ambiguity, and irresolution may well be the natural condition of play with meaning toward which all comedy gravitates to one extent or another. The scene in *Twelfth Night* is only one moment in a comedy dominated by meaning and quite in the Menandrine tradition of the well-made play ending happily. Without such moments the play would be the thinner as comic experience, the artist's vision less articulated and responsive to the complexities of existence.

Unresponsiveness is exactly what occurs in run-of-the-mill popular entertainment, what we call farcical or low comedy but which I would rather name "sub-comedy," meaning risible works that have no genuine element of exploration through emotional dialectic. They are not therefore execrable, merely aesthetically unrewarding. They also are forgettable precisely because they have not touched us deeply, had us feel our way through complex considerations. Comic power is given to the morally and socially acceptable characters, while the heavies are comic losers. Our response is undifferentiated. Where it is not, we recall the experience with deep pleasure. For instance, we remember out of a legion of television comedies the arguments of Ralph and Alice in Jackie Gleason's *The Honeymooners* and the clash of attitudes in Norman Lear's *All in the Family*.

More precisely, however, how can the comic artist explore attitudes when, in our mainstream stage comedy at least, the demands of literary and dramatic form must be met? How can one have a happy, fulfilling ending which leaves us in an ambivalent mood? The answer has already been suggested: literary and dramatic conventions are one thing, comedy and play another.

Neil Simon's mid-career comedy is an instance of the artist's struggles with play of meaning. In *Barefoot in the Park* (1964) Simon opposes the free spirit of Corie with the dull dependability of Paul, her husband. For the first two acts the equally free spirit of Velasco the neighbor supports our sympathies for Corie. Corie's wit, charm, and general looniness win us over, at least until she mentions divorce. But when Paul begins to act in the same carefree spirit, wandering around inebriated and barefoot in the park, and when her mother gives her some heavy-handed middle-class advice, Corie relents and sees clearly for the first time that she loves Paul and should try to maintain her marriage.

In the final distribution of things, the tension we had felt earlier, between our admiration for Corie's wit and spirit and our common-sensical regard for the stability of marriage, gets resolved simply and neatly by having Corie "converted," or come to her senses. When Corie gives over thoughts of separation, middle class values are affirmed, and the genuine emotional is-

sues raised in the interplay of contending sympathies are aban-
doned. The ending, like the mother's insipid speech to Corie in
act 3—give up part of yourself, make him feel important—
touched the hearts and thinking of a 1964 middle-class audience,
as did the film made from the play. We might assume that the
pressure to flatten emotional dialectic comes from demands of
form, of the happy ending. Not so.

The Odd Couple, two years later, shows a remarkable deepening
of Simon's own vision as an artist, greater technical command of
the stage, and a genuine exploration of some complicated issues,
the role of man and woman and the nature of marriage. The
play is propositional. If we have two divorced men with different
temperaments and outlooks, what would happen if they become
"married" by sharing the same apartment? Out of the clash of
these temperaments comes some delicious comedy.

Oscar the sportswriter is the typical male of the times: Sloppy,
as careless about the contents of his refrigerator as he is about
meeting alimony payments to his former wife, Blanche, happy,
outgoing, enjoying an evening of poker, or sex when it is available. Felix the newswriter is fastidious to the point of obsession,
morose and self-pitying, guilty about his marriage and how he is
hurting Frances, and vaguely suicidal. His excessive tidiness and
interest in cooking would have been associated with the stereotypical image of women at the time. Whereas Oscar's attitude
about divorce is that it is unfortunate but life must go on, Felix
sees the breakup of marriage as failure. The two points of view
cause friction, until the pair squabble like a married couple, as
when Oscar comes home an hour late without phoning and Felix's
London broil is ruined.

The "marriage" between Oscar and Felix, funny in itself, only
supports the general alignment of our sympathies. Of the two
characters Oscar is the wittier, more perceptive, more buoyantly
cheerful and optimistic. The comic power Simon vests in him is
advocacy for Oscar's acceptance of divorce, just as the comic put-
down of Felix is an undermining of the idea that marriage must
be preserved at all cost. Two-thirds of the way through the action,
however, Simon uses discrepancy of awareness to shift this
alignment.

Oscar has invited the Pigeon sisters from upstairs for drinks.
The birdbrained women try small talk with Felix while Oscar goes
to the kitchen to mix drinks. Felix gradually brings the conversation around to the pain of divorce, shows photographs of Frances
and his children, and finally breaks down in tears. By the time

Oscar returns full of cheer and with drinks to help the dating game proceed, the women are tearfully reflecting on their own lost happiness. The mood is funereal. The gag is at Oscar's expense, but ridicules, as well, the social ritual of dating and the male role Oscar is trying to fulfill. However inadvertently, Felix is comically on top. Oscar is the loser in his attempt to recoup the carefree, sexually predatory life of the single male. And thus the undercurrent of our response switches direction.

The mixed implications of gags continue until the end of the play. Ironically, after there is an "annulment" of the marriage, Felix is taken in by the Pigeon sisters ("That sweet, tortured man"), the very position Oscar would like to be in. Felix turns out on top once more. But we have not lost respect, comically, for Oscar. And when we learn he has been paying his alimony and has sent a goldfish to his son, our serious judgment approves. Felix has become "Oscarized" to an extent, Oscar has become "Felixized" to the point of emptying ashtrays and warning the poker players that this is his house, not a pigsty.

When Oscar asks if he will still join in the Friday night ritual, Felix replies, "Marriages may come and go, but the game must go on." The literal meaning is that life must go on, but the image of the game continuing whatever happens also expresses what has been occurring in the comedy of the play: there is no ending, no flattening of the complex crosscurrents of feeling concerning male and female roles, marriage and divorce, and issues related to them. There is finally only the interplay of meanings, the tantalizing dialectic of play which becomes the "meaning" of the comic experience.[5]

The same dynamic of comedy in respect to content and meaning operates in other media. Comic novels and films show signs of the same tensions between surface form and the subterranean movements of response. What is involved in this tension is more than formal tidiness and aesthetic wholeness. It is a question of how two kinds of meaning—signification through perceptual play alone and implications accruing in the emotional and judgmental underside of our response—work together, if indeed they do. Further, it is a question of how comic "meaning" can be reconciled with literary form.

The comic novel has the same problems of tension between the demands of literary form and those of comedy that show in theater. A well-known example is Twain's handling of comic effect in the last chapters of *The Adventures of Huckleberry Finn*. Literary critics may argue that the ending of the novel has thematic purpose, for instance, to introduce an element of society, its complications, and idiocies symbolized by Tom Sawyer's "literary" pranks from which Huck will soon flee for the frontier. But readers feel, and the fact is, Twain shifts modal gears on us. Up to chapter 33 the comedy of the novel has relied mainly on discrepancy between Huck's perception of things and our own. Interplay of perspectives has generated such rich comic moments as Huck's awed admiration for the dark, romantic "crayons" of Emmeline Grangerford and her terrible "Ode to Stephen Dowling Botts, Dec'd." The introduction of Tom Sawyer in chapter 33 pushes Huck aside and engages us in Tom's "literary" games ridiculing romance writers. This new element collapses the dynamic of readers responding to a first person narrator, and gives us another kind of game, which not incidentally makes Jim look an utter fool. Perhaps the ending can be justified in literary terms; comically, it abandons the emotional alignments Twain had created in the bulk of the novel.

How *might* the dynamic of response be maintained irrespective of narrative ending? One answer is provided by Swift in Book IV of *Gulliver's Travels*—a satire, to be sure, but one with strong comic elements. In Books I–III Gulliver, like Huck, has been both reportorial observer and naive participant, for instance when he urinates on the palace fire and cannot understand why the Lilliputian Queen refuses to enter the structure, or when he admires the "scientific" experiments of the Academy in Book III. In Book IV the same dynamic is intensified by Swift making Gulliver a Man of Reason who refuses to associate himself with the beastly Yahoos, even though when he is attacked by a female one while bathing he should recognize a distant kinship. Instead, upon return to England and that odious Yahoo, his wife, he spends his time with horses.

The relationship between reader and narrator is the same one Swift has maintained in the earlier books. Only, in Book IV Gulliver is less charming, and his gullibility stems much more from pride than naiveté. It is not the first time he has been the target of ridicule (recall his sycophantic offer of gunpowder to the ruler of Brobdingnag) but now ridicule of him is harsh, and we have the humane ship captain Pedro de Mendez as a contrast to the cranky misanthrope. But we also have a slight, lingering affection for Gulliver, and, cantankerous or not, he *is* funny. What is the exact mixture of our disdain and amusement? That is the same as asking, what precisely does Swift mean in his overall satirizing of the Man of Reason? (Scholars argue the point to this day.[6]) To that extent Swift evokes open-ended, indeterminate play with our judgment and emotions. Yet, unlike Twain, Swift maintains the strategy of dramatic irony and provides a suitable ending—the more so because it circles back to the opening letter to "Cousin Sympson," written in the crotchety manner of Gulliver of Book IV. Thus, Swift gives us narrative closure of a kind, but does not flatten our mixed feelings.

All of which is not to suggest that narrative—the meanings generated from surface action, character's views, ideas, etc.—is somehow incompatible with undercurrents of play and comedy. But, as one might expect, the more playful, tolerant of ambiguity, and indeterminate an author's outlook, the less amenable it is to narrative closure. In *Catch-22* Heller presents the grim, sometimes hilarious, and existentially absurd world of war. As noted earlier, it is a phenomenal fictional world in constant play against our own conceptions of existence. As narrative the novel does not have the strong development of cause and effect, the pattern, say, of *Pride and Prejudice;* things tend to just happen, though there is a distant force operating and manifest in the reasoning of *Catch-22.* The hero, or antihero, of this narrative, Yossarian, simply wants to get out, not be where he is, to live. His escapades have the simplicity of the picaresque hero, only they move toward survival and moral sanity rather than toward getting cash and a girl. He does not see a clear way, however, until his unrecognized mentor, Kid Orr, ends up in neutral Sweden. The final narrative action is a move toward freedom and safety, and it follows quite naturally from its narrative genetics as well as from emotions Heller evokes in us.

The alignments of our response generated out of the novel's satire and comedy run a parallel and complementary course. Satiric treatment of higher echelon officers like General Dreedle, or flunkies like Lieutenant Scheisskopf, guarantees that we feel utter contempt for the military establishment. Comic treatment of Yossarian, who could appear to be a mere shirker, is set against this dark background. So contrasted, his flaws and lunacies appear charmingly innocent. And he ranks high in comic values, managing to squirm his way out of duty and into hospitals, and taking bold, imaginative action such as appearing nude in formation. The sporadic visions of Snowden dying explain Yossarian's motives and bolster our sympathy for him.

Meanwhile, there are those who drift about in befuddled confusion, Doc Daneeka and Chaplain Tapman, for instance. They are controlled by the same arbitrary, crazy power against which Yossarian struggles. In Doc Daneeka's case the power lavishes wealth on his wife, supposedly his widow; in the Chaplain's case the power selects him as the criminal who perpetrated the Washington Irving letters. Positive or negative, the play element of comedy—play in its full Janus-faced nature—becomes a message in itself: We are in a zany, cruel, hilarious world.

Yossarian's final determination to gain freedom is thus supported by the subterranean implications of satiric and comic response and by the surface developments of the narrative (as the implications of the ending of *Huckleberry Finn* are not). Freedom has been the insistent theme of the novel, Yossarian's goal and humanity's as well, and it is a metaphor for all that values life, all in us that seeks to be happy and fulfilled. In its negative, ironic way the book's satiric element moves in the same direction. In their more complex, positive way its comic elements do also. Freedom—escape, life, happiness—is an apt metaphor for the manifold implications of comic episodes throughout the novel.

Furthermore, both narrative and comedy and satire are bound together by the fictional world Heller embodies in the novel, a terrifying, insane, absurd existence against which life struggles to be free.[7] We know that world through narrative detail ranging from computer mistakes with Major Major Major or Doc Daneeka's "death" to the bizarre, surrealistic cityscape of Rome or the cutting off of a young airman's torso by accident. But we feel it more deeply, phenomenally through the lunacy of play, the very experience of our reading described earlier in connection with *Winnie-the-Pooh*.

The ending of *Catch-22* is both meaning by direct narrative statement and "meaning" by its structuring as a joke. Kid Orr is never taken seriously by us or Yossarian, and he drops out of the action and our consciousness for a long while. Yet it is the puffy cheeked, impish, and sly Kid Orr who proves to be the master of escape when we learn he has made it to Sweden. The joke is on Yossarian, and on us of course. Perhaps because it is a joke on us, critics in general have been unhappy with the ending; some few, however, regard it as suitably inconclusive, or "opening outward."[8] From the perspective of play the ending's formal weaknesses, such as a sense of deus ex machina, seem minor compared to its encapsulating and summarizing the comic and satiric elements of the novel as a whole. That is, the subterranean registerings in us as readers surface, or reach a conclusion, in the final illumination of a way out that comes to Yossarian. It is a joyous, happy moment of reading, and though there may be a faint "click" of being put upon at the time, it is no more than we have experienced with many an improbable happy ending.

Reflection on *Catch-22* reminds one that there are essentially two ways in which comedy "means," by play between comic and serious judgment and with perception. Discussion thus far has emphasized how surface gags, situations, turns on expectation, and the like register in deep response and thereby generate meanings, leaving the impression that this is the only way comedy conveys a message. It surely is *the* major way in traditional comic theater, and an important way in any piece that is representational. Yet a good many works convey most of their "meaning" through the phenomenological, experiential impact of flippings of our perception, and there are those, like *Catch-22*, that do so in part. Both forms of sleight-of-hand tend to gravitate toward the open-endedness and indeterminacy of play itself. The tendency is countered, usually, by the demands of form and by artists' comic interpretations of life. For while play may have no *telos*, comedians have purposes, positions to defend, transgressions and stupidities to ridicule. Their outlooks are expressed in a bewildering array of statements manifest in a wide spectrum of forms and types of comedy.

4
Modes of Comedy: "Meaning"

Anyone proposing a clear scheme of things in comedy is likely to be seen as a quirky taxonomist, a kind of Felix Ungar compulsively emptying ashtrays and cleaning up after the careless of the world. Nonetheless, typologies have their use. In addition to providing a common basis of reference, a typology insists that we be clear about secondary attributes and those inherent in the art itself.

While there are a number of bases for typing—genus and species, historical derivation, the media artists use, or some final end or purpose—my choice, obviously, is play. Whatever one may choose as a basis for discriminating between types, it cannot be what we now have, a loose assortment of designations resting on rickety underpinnings, if any. There are names for comedy based on historical development (Old, Middle, New, or Menandrine Comedy) or on styles and fashions of a period (Restoration Comedy of Manners, Eighteenth-century Sentimental Comedy). There are designations based on content (Love Comedy, Black Comedy, meaning that of black people as distinct from black or dark comedy), on content and overall style (Moralistic, Romantic, Realistic, Sentimental, Domestic Comedies, and Comedy of Manners again), and on implied comparison with other kinds of comedy (dark, problem, black, satiric, absurd). There are designations by technique (Comedy of Errors, of Intrigue), by whether or not comedies were written down (*commedia erudite* was; *commedia dell' arte* was not), and by "level" of effect (low, high, vulgar, farcical or slapstick, *buffo*, sophisticated). Designation can be by formula (Menandrine Comedy as a pattern, the television situation comedy or sitcom). Or distinctions between kinds can rest on overall impression of "tone" (e.g., "comic-serious," "mordantly witty," "ribald," or "mordantly ribald"). Then there are designations by generalized style of particular artists (Shakespearian, Jonsonian, Molièresque, perhaps Monty Pythonian), even though the work of each changed and grew throughout their careers.

Not only are our names for comedy products of different bases, they have arisen haphazardly through periods of commentary reflecting the particular set of assumptions of this or that kind of criticism. Nor are many of them defensible as entities. What comedy is *not* a Comedy of Manners to some extent? Which is not to some extent a Comedy of Errors? How truly "realistic" are plays like *Volpone* or *The Alchemist*, how free from coincidence and improbability, supposedly part of what distinguishes them from "romantic" comedy? What the history of our naming confirms is that comedy encompasses a staggering variety of modes, types, forms, genres, subgenres, and vogues, not to mention styles and types within a communicational medium. There is no reason they should be reduced to a schema. All one asks is a bit of sorting out, a way to speak of comedy, quite within itself, with a shared, accepted terminology resting on a firm conceptual basis.

Toward that end I offer a sketch of a typology derived from observations on the operations of comedy and the "meanings" they generate. A full typology would be immense in scope, and never could include the infinite number of possible cases. I only suggest what one would look like. Here "mode" refers to an aggregate, large or small, of works with features sufficiently shared to make it distinguishable from other aggregates. Comedy is a mode. So is satire. The two are amorphous aggregates of works within a larger group, the arts of the risible. Humor is another aggregate within that group. The only terms needed here are mode and submode, the latter merely a subdivision of mode and not a type or genre. (I avoid "genre" because generic designations bring with them associations of a body of study and criticism that would only litter discussion of the art of comedy.)

The mode of comedy, a vast playing field, is less a discrete entity than a spectrum of possible kinds and forms, identified here as submodes. Not even demarcations that apparently distinguish comedy as comic, such as a risible response, opposition to the serious, and a playful nature, can establish its boundaries. For instance, satire evokes laughter, too, and the play element in comedy has parallels in other kinds of aesthetic expression: Mozart's working of variations on a theme, the play of light and texture in impressionist painting, or of symbolic shapes in space in Miró's work. Still, there is a thing called comedy, and it appears less amorphous when seen as its own art. That implies to be comedy works must have a substantial element of skill or artistry providing aesthetic value and, in general, have a certain customary size and substance. Often rich in artistry, humor is nonetheless taken to be a contiguous, overlapping mode. (There is also the matter of intention; art is a happy byproduct of an essentially social act and not *why* humor occurs.) The series of jokes making up the cabaret performer's "bit" can form a little work in itself, like a short story, but bears the same relation to a comic work that a finely carved jade pendant bears to a piece of sculpture.

On the other hand, because a piece stands so high, has so many chapters or acts, or hangs on the wall of a museum is no determinant of aesthetic achievement. The important thing to recognize is that there is a perceptual and semantic center to comedy. In a very general way a comedy is a consciously devised work that evokes a risible response and elicits significations transcending literal, surface "meaning," thus offering aesthetic experience to some degree or another. To what degree depends upon realization of its dual operation as play with perception and with meaning.

Seen as play in relation to "meaning" comedy appears as clearly recognizable types. But there is also perceptual play's signification embodied in the work itself. A full typology would have this double axis, the first based on significations or meanings arising from our serious and comic values, the second based on perceptual play. The two axes are interactive in works having semantic content (in general, representational art, drama, or literature). But to deal with both at once would require analysis of the kind done on Klee's *Revolution of the Viaducts,* for instance, with each cartoon strip or gag sequence in a stage comedy or novel, an unnecessary confusion at this point. So for now concentration will be on the wide spectrum of significations and meanings created by the artist through manipulation of the judgments, values, and emotions we bring to the comic experience. Further, because of its familiarity I will use Menandrine or New Comedy as exemplary of what occurs in other kinds of comedy.

What was said earlier about the verbal joke and surface and deep response applies: what we feel as "meaning" is compounded of moral values and social protocols on the one hand, and on the other the values of a purely comic ethic. (For convenience, hereafter I will use the term "moral-social values" to include such things as the Ten Commandments, but, as well, expectations of proper behavior, appropriate dress and manners, in other words, accepted social decorum.) From a broad perspective, the shades of "meaning" really come down to the *relationship* between serious and comic values, the two polarities of judgment. One kind of value can dominate either in a comic moment or throughout the work, and usually morality does. But the two kinds of values can also be opposed to produce emotional dialectic, again in a comic moment or through the whole work. The possible configurations of response are endless.

There are two kinds of response, generally: a single, undifferentiated, and determinational ("my mother-in-law is a witch"), and multiple, differentiated, and explorational response ("my mother-in-law is devious but lovable"). What we apprehend as something of an emotional and judgmental blob is the product of the artist's manipulations of surface effects and, more importantly, of what transpires in our deep response. There is where we find accumulated implications, switchings back, qualifications, and, on occasion, clear meaning registered. The shorthand expression for this registering is the relationship between serious and comic values. Or, to see it another way, these registerings are the net result of the artist's allocation of ridicule, its precise strength and quality in a given moment of laughter and collectively throughout the work. So to say that this or that comic turn on stage elicits a mild, genial response usually means that the figure being made fun of meets with our approval, seriously, comically, or both. Conversely, harsh ridicule is a sign of disapproval, comically or seriously but usually the latter. And this harsh ridicule may be mitigated by some extenuating circumstance, as it is in our day-to-day response to life. In either case crosscurrents of feeling can contend. We can be left in genuine ambivalence.

The earlier diagram of interaction between surface and deep response can be expanded to show the overall effect of the numerous registerings of gags, jokes, turns on expectation. The figure summarizes, on the left, the operations of registering meaning as if they were a single result. That is seldom the case in actuality. (Or we would have a dull comedy indeed.) But the cumulative effect of comic moment followed by comic moment—every pun, joke, gag situation, and their nuances of implication—does end up being the afterglow of "meaning" we carry away from the experience. It is what we "know," that is, feel intuitively to be the message. The range of messages is indicated on the right, and in a highly schematic way. It would be impossible to indicate all gradations along this spectrum, and fruitless if it could be done. But three clusters of meaning stand out, comedy which affirms, explores, and attacks. One could, I suppose, select ten or twelve groupings of works,[1] but three will have to do; even those will require considerable explanation. Furthermore, what comedy does not affirm or attack something, or at one moment or another

PLAY WITH
PERCEPTION & MEANING

OVERALL MEANING
(EXPERIENCE-AS-"KNOWING")

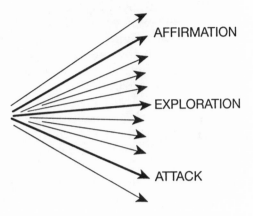

AFFIRMATION

EXPLORATION

ATTACK

Surface Effects: Gags, Jokes, etc.

Registerings in Deep Response
(Largely Unconscious)

Comedy as Overall Meaning

explore contentious matters? That is, though the clusters on the spectrum are submodes, they themselves have considerable gradation—more or less intensity, greater or lesser depth, etc.

At the center of the spectrum of comic meaning is exploration, characterized by a high degree of emotional dialectic. The more genuinely and deeply comedy plays, the richer the experience it offers. One could even say that any ludic work which does *not* have a significant element of play is not a comedy—something else in the arts of the risible, but not comedy. According to this position there are two classes of ludic works which fall outside the spectrum of comedy, and important ones too: satire and what I earlier called subcomedy.

The latter is what we usually refer to as popular entertainment—all of the eminently forgettable plays, films, and so on whose surface effects carry us toward a happy, vacuous conclusion. It is a legitimate ludic mode, however, and is characterized by the lack of emotional dialectic, a thin, undifferentiated response, and pandering to our prejudices (qualities, in fact, it shares with satire). All it shares with comedy is a community of techniques, dramatic and literary form, and risible response. What it lacks is that searching through our feelings that is the sign of comedy-as-play doing its work, and, not incidentally, of the artist seeing into and feeling his or her way into the matter at hand. Subcomedy has certain formal, surface characteristics. It strongly inclines toward stereotypical, one-sided characterizations, shopworn formulae of comic action, and clear, binary meanings. None of these are execrable in themselves; the *farceur* uses them regularly, but then farce is about its real business of perceptual play and makes little pretense at doing what comedy does. Subcomedy presents itself as comedy, that is, it deals with meanings and our underlying judgments and emotions. It is just that it does not do much with them—the basis for the earlier distinction between *Barefoot in the Park* and *The Odd Couple*.

At least Simon's *Barefoot* raises issues to explore them in some depth, and at least there are the figures of the mother and Velasco to give something of a countermessage to the thudding advocacy of serious values at the end. A good many television situation comedies do not offer even that. The same is true of most comic films, and probably for the same reasons: artistic control is pressured by production costs and the need to make a profit. While subcomedy is escapist entertainment, and valuable as relaxation, esthetically considered, of course, it is another and lesser mode than comedy because it lacks the interest of play with meaning and tends to traffic in stereotypical characters and situations that elicit an undifferentiated response.

Much the same is true of satire, though it, too, overlaps with comedy by virtue of sharing certain techniques. Satire is not play with meaning. Quite the opposite: the satirist has a clear message, usually one fully acceptable to an audience. That is so because the audience of satire is preselected. While satirists claim to better mankind by showing us our vices and follies, it is a tongue-in-cheek argument. Who pays good money to see his or her esteemed values harshly ridiculed? (Alas, as with sermons those most in need of them are seldom there to hear.) The idea of anyone going to a theatrical or filmic satire and rising in a burst of illumination to say, "There I am!—what an unprincipled, vicious swine I've been!" is highly unlikely, especially for unprincipled swines. If one is generous and open-minded, application of satire's message to one's self may come later; for most of us it comes begrudgingly, if at all. Furthermore, the overall "speech act" of satire is not that of comedy. If one can generalize and say we participate in comedy in the spirit of play and carnival or holiday, then we would have to say that we engage in satire in the spirit of communal exorcism and bloodletting.

The qualities of satire's presentation contribute to the mode's overall tone of negation and censure. The characteristics of satiric presentation are heavy reliance on irony; focus on a target or targets, usually of topical interest; use of characters who are stereotypical, flat, and without redeeming qualities; and the eliciting of sneering or harsh laughter. In general, the net result of these is response that is largely negative and, more importantly, undifferentiated. The prevailing position of an audience in irony is a superior one. We are in collusion with the satirist and sit in judgment on characters' follies and crimes. Though satire may engage in perceptual play, and we may be surprised at sudden turns, there is little or no play with the judgmental and emotional underside of our response. Satiric characterization assists in this privileged exemption from genuine play. Who can "identify with" or relate themselves to one-sided figures, often inconsistent in their psychology, with few if any engaging qualities, and about as fictionally "real" as cartoonists' drawings of Moammar Khadaffi, Saddam Hussein, or some other political enemy? In short, we find ourselves responding much as we do in subcomedy, with a closed mind.[2]

That is looking at satire as an aggregate or mode distinguishable from comedy by its lack of deep play. But very few satires are without comic elements—as I earlier noted about *Gulliver's Travels*—just as few comedies are wholly free of satiric effects. What is confusing is that the two modes share the same repertoire of techniques to engage us in similar forms of surface games. And at any moment either satire or comedy can become farcical: they can rely upon perceptual play to convey their significations.

With this sketch of satire and subcomedy the spectrum of comedy appears as a wide field of possible meanings, overlapped at

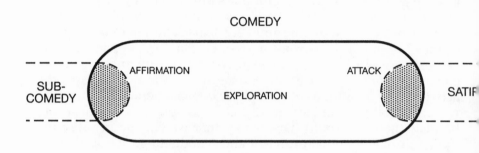

Spectrum of Comedy Based on Play with Meaning

either end by two modes. The diagram shows meanings generated out of play with perception and underlying values. The same three prominent clusters of meaning appear as in the previous diagram: affirmation and attack, with exploration at the center. It seems reasonable enough that the contiguous modes of subcomedy and satire appear where they are. Subcomedy is a mode which wholeheartedly confirms audience values. Satire is akin to attack, and though it, too, confirms audience prejudice, its main business is to assault. Essentially, what distinguishes comedy from both is its commitment to play with meaning, to exploration of values, judgments, and emotions. Hence exploration as a kind of message is at the center of the diagram as it is at the heart of comedy. In this typology other kinds of comedy range along the spectrum, more or less this, more or less that, but tending toward affirmation on the one hand, and attack on the other.

Perhaps the finest example of affirmative comedy is Shakespeare's *As You Like It*. The earlier discussion of the Phebe-Silvius episode for its operation as discrepancy of awareness implied what is the case overall: Shakespeare affirms the desirability of a code of social relations involving the proper attitudes of men and women in love, or the Elizabethan vestige of courtly love. (The doctrine of courtly love is epitomized in Cardinal Bembo's great peroration in Book IV of Castiglione's *The Courtier*.) Phebe's problem is that she lacks the grace and humanity to turn off an unwanted suitor gently. Silvius's is that he lacks the proper self-worth of the gentlemen and grovels; furthermore, he does not know when to take no for an answer. As Corin the shepherd says, they are a "pageant truly played," an *exemplum* of how not to woo.

Rosalind, on the other hand, embodies the grace and humanity that Phebe lacks, and just as ridicule of Phebe is harsh, so ridicule of Rosalind is mild, when there is any at all. Rosalind is the comic winner with only a few exceptions. Her superior wit, cleverness, buoyancy, and charm are an endorsement of her courtly virtues. Only she has a problem. The man she loves, Orlando, is a male Cinderella, noble by birth but denied the proper upbringing of a gentleman by a selfish elder brother. Orlando's boorish ways, such as his refusing to speak to Rosalind when she congratulates him on his defeat of Charles the wrestler, have to be corrected. The opportunity comes when Rosalind is banished from the court of the usurping Duke Frederick and, with the duke's daughter Celia, flees to the Forest of Arden. There Rosalind takes the guise of a young man, Ganymede, while Celia becomes a shepherdess, Aliena. Thither comes Orlando.

While Orlando has little wit (Shakespeare keeps insisting he does, however), his upbringing excuses him somewhat, and we pity him for his misfortunes. He appears downright dullheaded as he plays out a game with the young man Ganymede, an imitation love game calculated to cure Orlando of his "quotidian" or passion for Rosalind. That he does not know Ganymede is Rosalind puts him in a ridiculous position. Meanwhile, Rosalind-Ganymede sets about training herself a husband, and except for some chiding by Celia—"you have simply misused our sex in your love-prate" (4.1.191–92)[3]—she remains in comic control. The frame story of a dukedom taken from Duke Senior, who has sequestered himself in the forest, serves only to generate action, such as bringing Orlando's brother, Oliver, to Arden where he falls in love with Celia. The upshot is that the play ends in multiple marriages, blessed by no less than the god Hymen, and the realm is returned to Duke Senior, Rosalind's father. The ending of *As You Like It* has a peculiar quality of put-on, however.

Marriages fall in line, a literal deus ex machina (or from the shrubbery) appears on stage; the nefarious Duke Frederick, who has come to wipe out his opponent, is converted upon meeting an old religious man and gives up the world and his dukedom for a life of contemplation. All this happens in a brief time on stage. Probability is thrown to the winds. Yet the last scene is a wrapping up of action, however perfunctorily, in a happy, appropriate ending. Good is rewarded, evil expunged. The wet blanket, morose Jaques, absents himself after giving his blessings: all this happiness is too much for him. It is a delightful spoof of the happy ending that is, at the same time, a happy ending in true Menandrine style.

While the main action affirms the values of courtly love by allocation of comic power, there is a countercurrent without which *As You Like It* would be flat, not to say unctuous, subcomedy. This counterelement centers on the character of Touchstone the clown. An appendage to the main action, Touchstone nonetheless provides a running counterpoint to the high-flown ideals of courtly love. He is comically on top, wittier, even, than Rosalind. Unfortunately, his wit gravitates toward bawdry and sleaze. For instance, there is his lampoon of Orlando's execrable love poetry, redolent with animal and rutting imagery in his galloping verse that ends with, "He that sweetest rose will find, / Must find love's prick, and Rosalind" (3.2.109–10). However, since everyone else seems to be engaged in it, Touchstone, too, would be wooing. He chooses the dull country wench Audrey.

The scene in which he woos Audrey is the nexus of Shakespeare's counterstatement on his own advocacy of courtly love. Observed by Jaques, Touchstone tries to persuade Audrey with arguments far above her head but which provide ample amusement to us, the audience. He wishes Audrey were poetical, but Audrey does not know what that means ("Is it honest in deed and word? Is it a true thing?" 3.3.14–15). No, Touchstone continues, for poets are feigning, and he wishes the gods had made her poetical for if she were he would have hope that she feigns when she says she is honest. On the argument goes, with Audrey thanking the gods that she is not a slut but foul. "Well, praised be the gods for thy foulness; sluttishness may come hereafter," says Touchstone (3.3.34–35). Sir Oliver Martext, a scatterbrained itinerant preacher, enters. Touchstone has sent for him so that he and Audrey can be married. At that point Jaques steps forth to give the bride away and to advise Touchstone that he should be married in church with a solid clergyman who knows how to minister vows. Touchstone's aside is revealing:

> I am not in the mind but that I were better to be married of him than of another, for he is not like to marry me well; and not being well married, it will be a good excuse for me hereafter to leave my wife.
>
> (3.3.81–85)

The "marriage," then, is the equivalent of our one night stand. Or, as Jaques later puts it in his final blessings, "thy loving voyage / Is but for two months victualled" (5.4.190–91). What is crucial is the final treatment of Touchstone. By rights he should be ridiculed, his lust exposed and his superior wit bested, if not demolished. No such thing happens. Other than the remark by Jaques, Touchstone comes off comically unscathed. In effect, Shakespeare has it both ways: a solid endorsement of courtly love, and a condoning, if not advocacy of lust.[4]

This counterstatement is primarily what makes *As You Like It* such a clear case of affirmative comedy. Without it we might have subcomedy of a high order, of the order of Lodge's *Rosalynde.* Touchstone is Shakespeare's major comic addition to his source material. There are other elements in *As You Like It* that contribute to the mixed emotions we have about the purity and sanctity of love, however. There is the ending and its implications. The wrapping up of things is just exaggerated enough to be self mockery, yet it is not an outright disavowal of its own triumph of love and good. In other words, it is play between a serious outcome and a comic one, neither yet both at once. This final ambivalence perfectly fits *As You Like It* itself.[5]

If *As You Like It* is a fine example of affirmative comedy, it is also an unusual one, both in the general run of comic theater, and, indeed, among Shakespeare's own comedies an exceptionally rich, playful, fully crafted work. In most comedies interplay between attitudes and values is given over by the last act to assure a happy, morally appropriate outcome. Sometimes it is done by withholding information from us—the police officer at the end of *Tartuffe* who turns out to be the king's representative and seizes Tartuffe rather than the victimized Orgon, the deed of trust by which Mirabell saves the estate of Mrs. Fainall and Lady Wishfort at the end of *The Way of the World,* and so on. The more usual dodge is manipulating characters' attitudes to swing them toward an appropriate conclusion, Corie's change of heart at the end of *Barefoot in the Park,* for instance. But the difficulties of ending comedy are formidable because they arise from a deep, generic incompatibility between play for its own sake and the constraints of dramatic and literary form. It is rare that the artist finds a way to let play and exploration just be.

Ben Jonson was to produce such a rarity in *The Alchemist,* a fine example of comedy of exploration. His handling of emotional dialectic satisfies both the demands of a happy, morally acceptable ending and the registerings accumulated in our deep response, the demands of play. His heroes—Face, Doll, and Subtle—are petty, vicious thieves, but they are also witty, brilliant con artists. Their inventiveness, like their ability to assume virtually any role, knows no bounds. While Subtle is always the alchemist, he plays the fast-talking hustler at one moment, the devout religious recluse the next. Doll can be one of her own multiple personalities of the prostitute, or the sister of a lord gone mad from reading a Protestant tract writer, or the Queen of Fairy as needed. And they enjoy the game as a "venter-tripartite" doing battle against the dullards of the world. Still, as Jonson reminds us in our first sight of them, they are cutthroats who will rob anyone they can find. They do not have far to look, for word of the "miraculous stone," "the elixir," has spread. The house they inhabit, whose owner Lovewit is out of town to avoid the plague, becomes a magnet for a fair cross section of society, only part of whom we see. Those we do see are carefully graded by Jonson; some are greedy, some not. He uses the ploy of "no sin to gull a guller." It is a powerful instrument.

Our estimate of the alchemists, though high comically, is closely tied to the nature of their victims. Drugger merely wants a propitious setting for his new tobacco shop. Kastril, the country bumpkin, wants only to learn how to be a "roaring boy" and swagger around taverns, snarl oaths, and outface all opponents as the gallants of London do. The wealthy Dame Pliant merely exists, vaguely in want of a husband. (It is hard to know; she is one of Jonson's most silent, vacuous stage characters.) When the alchemists gull innocents like these they appear what they are, predatory. However, they appear in a somewhat brighter light when they con Dapper the law clerk, who wants to use the power of the miraculous stone to win in all gambling and betting. And when they dupe Tribulation Wholesome, the power hungry

church administrator, and Sir Epicure Mammon, the randy hedo-
nist, they almost perform a needed public service.[6]

Tribulation Wholesome, the Puritan churchman, uses the wid-
ows' and orphans' funds of his congregation to invest in the elixir.
For what purposes? Not for self-aggrandizement, heaven knows,
but for the cause. As Subtle correctly assesses it, the cause is after
power:

> Have I not discoursed so unto you of our stone?
> And of the good that it shall bring your cause?
> Showed you (beside the main of hiring forces
> Abroad, drawing the Hollanders, your friends,
> From the Indies, to serve you, with all their fleet)
> That even the medicinal use shall make you a faction,
> And party in the realm?[7]

We are in the England of 1611, when the forces of Puritanism
were receiving help from Holland (a growing maritime rival) and
were gaining the strength that would erupt in the civil war of
1642. Even if this were not the case, Tribulation is himself a devious, casuistical hypocrite of the kind not unknown among our
own evangelists.

The situation with Sir Epicure Mammon is less clear to us because our own times are far more tolerant of sexual and monetary
lust than were Jonson's. Sir Epicure appears to us a charming
rogue of gargantuan appetites. But consider him from the perspective of 1611 and ask what is always a fair question in comedy:
What would the world be like if its greatest power *were* controlled
by Epicure Mammon? He will have his oval room filled with por-
nographic pictures and subtly cut mirrors to multiply the images
"as I walk / Naked between my *succubae*" (2.2.47–48). He will be
misted in perfume, fall into baths, and emerge to roll with his
succubae in gossamer and roses. Well and good, but he goes on
to project that when he finds a wealthy citizen with a "sublim'd
pure wife," he will give the fellow a thousand pounds to be his
cuckold; only a pure wife will do (2.2.55f). No, he decides, he
will have fathers and mothers as his bawds; they do it best. And
on the visions of power and corruption go; he will dispense the
blessings of the "stone" for a fee, like a public utility. Even in
our jaded times the idea of vesting all medicinal, restorative, and
aphrodisiac power in the hands of *Crotch Shots* or a similar enterprise is excessively liberal. To Jonson's audience the notion was
monstrous.

Thus we move toward the final act with thoroughly mixed feelings about Jonson's alchemists. Emotional dialectic has pressured us to feel our way through some complex considerations—no less than greed and the nature of man. If anything, by the time Lovewit returns in act 5, only a comic ethic is in force: Who is the winner, who the loser? When Lovewit shows up, we expect the return of moral sanity, the working out of justice. What do we get? As neighbors press around him to report the crowds, the comings and goings ("Another Pimlico!"), Lovewit takes a technical interest, wondering what Jeremy-Face could have done to attract so many. He runs through a catalog ranging from bawdy pictures of the Friar and the Nun to peep shows of the knight's courser covering the parson's mare. While calling in the sheriff would seem the right approach, instead Lovewit outfaces all claimants searching for their lost goods, keeps the loot in the basement for himself, and takes Dame Plaint and her considerable estate to wife. He lets off Jeremy-Face; Doll and Subtle escape over the back fence. In short, the game goes on, as the poker game goes on in Simon's *The Odd Couple.* There is only continuation and intensification of play.[8]

In this thoroughly explorative comedy, there is a happy ending to be sure, complete with marriage, perfunctory though it is, and with dispensation of a kind of comically poetic justice. Dramatic and literary formalism are served, or given lip service. Jonson swings his efforts toward concluding the ambivalent feelings he has raised in us. There can be no conclusion to these other than their continuation and intensification. Jonson effects an ending that has all of the surface elements convention requires yet remains true to the moral ambiguities deeply embedded in our response, the undercurrents of feeling in which the "meaning" of comedy lies. All this may help explain why comedies which are genuinely explorative are rare.

If exploration through emotional dialectic is rare in the spectrum of comedy, it would seem the submode of attack is even more scarce. That is not the case, however. The possible reason is that comedy of attack merges easily with satire, on the whole a simpler mode than comedy, and, given the right audience, one that guarantees an acceptable result. Just as affirmative comedy teeters toward subcomedy and pandering to audience tastes, so comedy of attack gravitates toward satire and its panderings. Comedy of attack may have many of the characteristics of satire, such as stereotypical, one-sided characters, heavy use of irony, etc., but it relies mainly on the play of comedy to achieve its aim.

And all the more effective it is, too, for engaging us in the snares of emotional dialectic rather than depending upon our prejudices alone.

Machiavelli's *La Mandragola* (*The Mandrake*, 1520) exemplifies the submode of comedy of attack. It has its satirical figures, notably the corrupt priest Friar Timoteo and the unnamed, birdbrained Florentine lady who grieves over her dead husband but who thrills at the terrible prospect of being "impaled" by the Turks (3.2. pp. 208–9).[9] That is, Machiavelli rakes over the church, or at least a church administrator, and takes a dim view of women. These are not his main concerns, however. What he is after are a number of cherished values of his early sixteenth-century Florentine audience: the sanctity of marriage, the exalted position accorded women, the concept of the courtly gentleman, and, most of all, the ideal of romantic love.[10] Rather than excoriate these and related values by satire, Machiavelli chooses to ensnare us in the dialectic of comedy. For this purpose he takes the supposedly magic powers of the mandrake root and the conventions of Menandrine comedy, or, as it would have been known then, *commedia erudita*. One ingenious variation he makes on the work of his predecessors is to have a heroine who is virtuous. Young Lucrezia is married to old Nicia, an idiotic *senex* straight from Plautus. But unlike the ladies of Roman comedy in similar circumstances, Lucrezia staunchly upholds her marriage vows. Word of her beauty has reached a Florentine in Paris, young Callimaco, and he must return to see this paragon. So he does.

The usual plot is set up: young love will find a way to be fulfilled. Its justification is inherent in the situation of a young, beautiful wife and an aged, foolish husband. Nature demands rectification. On the other hand (so the Menandrine pattern goes), it is best if the young lover is sincere, caught up in a passion over which he has no control. It is well, too, if machinations, disguises, and plots are left to a witty slave, or in this case, to Ligurio, a down-at-the-heels gentleman. Callimaco certainly is caught up in passion for Lucrezia, so much so that he appears more a lovelorn adolescent than a young gentleman of breeding and station. In the opening of act 4 he soliloquizes that his legs shake, his stomach turns, his heart pounds itself loose in his chest, his voice is lost, his head spins. In act 5 scene 4 he determines that he will have Lucrezia or hang himself, throw himself in the Arno, or stab himself on her doorstep. Obviously he is in no shape for intriguing.[11]

Lucrezia, meanwhile, bears her marriage as a dutiful burden.

Nicia and she do not have children (her fault, of course). They *must* have a child, he feels, and so does Lucrezia's mother Sostrata. So Lucrezia is set upon from all sides, including, eventually, that of her father confessor, Friar Timoteo. Ligurio's solution to all this is to have Callimaco disguise himself as a famous physician who has cured many a case of infertility by applying a potion made of mandrake root. Nicia, himself a *dottore*, is completely swayed by the reputation of the "doctor," by medical gibberish, and by schoolboy Latin (2.2). However, the magic potion has a death benefit, so to speak: whoever sleeps with a woman who has taken it will surely die thereafter (2.6). By agreeing to have the potion given to Lucrezia Nicia acquiesces to homicide.

Our feelings in all this are clearly tipped toward Callimaco, partly on account of his passion, but mainly because Nicia is such an egregious fool, and a morally reprehensible one at that. Wit and cleverness are all on the side of Callimaco's cause, or more specifically in Liguiro, the initiator of the plot and the manager of its operations. Once Nicia has agreed to administering the potion, there is the hurdle of Lucrezia's adherence to her marriage vows. Hence Ligurio enrolls the aid of Friar Timoteo. The Friar's arguments in 3.11 are masterful. Doesn't Lucrezia want to help create another soul for the Lord? Sometimes, it happens, people do not die from the potion. Is it not better, then, to eschew an uncertain outcome and take a certain, positive one? As for the act itself, it is the will that sins, not the body, and her intent is pure. What with pressure from her mother as well ("There are at least fifty women in this town who would thank Heaven for this opportunity" 3.11.), the arguments of her father confessor finally win Lucrezia over. All that remains is to set up the occasion and to snare in a man off the streets—a wandering lute player, as it turns out, who is Callimaco in disguise.

In effect, Machiavelli has pushed his audience into accepting an extramarital affair, which they presumably would not condone in their saner moments, by making it the lesser of two evils and by granting it comic sanction. It is difficult to side with a marriage and a husband when the union is against nature to begin with and the husband agrees to homicide. Added to that are Nicia's gross stupidity and pride, not to mention his treating his wife as chattel, a breeder. Ridicule of the church, seemingly a satiric byproduct, works in favor of young love's consummation, too, by undermining the sanctity of marriage vows and by suggesting that, in the corrupt world Lucrezia inhabits, what is another sin, more or less? So, as the surface effects of disguise, plot, and machinations run along, there is a strong accumulation in our response moving us toward joyful acceptance of the night when Lucrezia receives the potion. Furthermore, the scene, 5.2, is hilarious in itself. Nicia checks over the merchandise snared off the street and feels under the covers to make sure the potion is being applied.

The outcome of all this is a *ménage-à-trois,* or *-quatre* if one includes Ligurio, which keeps Lucrezia and Callimaco happy, and with a child to please Nicia and Sostrata. One could hardly ask for more. Beneath the hilarity, the surface gags and rapidly paced action, of course, is a profound attack on Florentine values. What the audience finally accepts is Machiavelli's own somewhat cynical, existential amoralism.[12] *La Mandragola* relies, as comedy of attack must, on our habit of psychological transference: we do not acknowledge our being made fools, hence the true meaning of the comic experience lies below what we think we are laughing about.

Still, as suggested in the last diagram, comedy of attack easily overlaps with satire. *La Mandragola* has a number of satiric elements, such as flat, one-sided characters (Nicia) and heavy use of irony. One could argue that a number of the play's effects are satiric: the more than needed emphasis on Friar Timoteo's corruption, the slaps at learning and physicians, the sneering at the venality of women. The dynamics of the play are comic, however. In any event the reference here is to submodes, not to clearly defined, crisp types or genres. Moreover, any typology, even so floppy a one as this, will not account for all mixtures of sub-comedy and comedy, comedy and satire, that artists create. It just so happens that *La Mandragola* fits the pattern. Given their different mixtures of comedy and satire, so do a great many other plays ranging from Molière's *Les Precieuses ridicules* to Joe Orton's *Loot,* and, the most compelling of all, Oscar Wilde's *The Importance of Being Earnest.*

What is interesting about *Importance* as a comedy of attack is its apparent innocence, nonsense, and insubstantial fluff. That Wilde is attacking the values of his audience (roughly upper middle to lower upper-class Victorians) is suggested in the title: What more admirable quality in the thinking of the time than earnestness? The range of targets is considerably wider than that, however, and includes class structure, education, religion, the concept of proper behavior for a man and a woman, romantic love, and marriage, to cite the most obvious ones.[13] Wilde's overall approach is to treat these serious matters flippantly, as if they were, or because they were, nonsense. The very playful, airy quality of *Importance* is a statement.

Yet Wilde does use satiric technique. With some exceptions the characters are thin, like cartoons, and have little to which we can attach our emotions or concern. *The* satiric characterization is Lady Bracknell: imperious, aloof, psychologically inconsistent, and never at a loss for comment or censure. Who can like her? Jack wonders if in a hundred years or so Gwendolyn will be like her mother. In fact, Gwendolyn is right now, and so are Algernon, Miss Prism, and, in a more charming way, Canon Chasuble— satiric characters in whom we can take little personal interest. We may admire Algernon's wit and freedom but these begin to pall halfway through, and we find it difficult to feel enthusiastic about his love for Cecily. Miss Prism also leaves us cold. Ever the stern moralist and educator (she hopes that death has taught the scapegrace, fun-loving Ernest a lesson), the only human interest she offers is her sly attempt to snare Canon Chasuble in marriage. Chasuble himself is charmingly befuddled, but other than that he is a pompous fool who seems to have no pastoral concerns at all save administering baptism.

The net effect of satiric characterization is to remove us from the engagement comedy offers. Heavy reliance on irony has the same result. Both Gwendolyn and Cecily *must* marry a man named Ernest. The name gives vibrations, and inspires complete confidence. Lady Bracknell cannot accept Jack as a suitor for the hand of Gwendolyn. He is wealthy enough, has no firm political position, and has an occupation, smoking. But he can hardly expect Lady Bracknell to bestow her daughter on one born, or at any rate bred, in a handbag at Victoria Station, to have Gwendolyn form an alliance with a parcel. On Wilde goes, treating arguments and issues as characters see them with a straight face. The inherent looniness of their views is immediately obvious to us, and, as in most satire, we sit removed from them, laughing and passing judgment. Collectively, both our judgments and the running quips, turns, and one-liners show a pattern of attack on Wilde's various targets.

Yet *Importance* is also comedy both in its action and, to a lesser extent, in two key characterizations. Wilde gives Jack and Cecily just enough personality to elicit our emotional involvement with them. Jack is not nearly as witty as Algernon, but then neither is he as studiously flippant. In contrast to Algernon the Dandy, who has no involvement in the world except seeking pleasure, Jack at least has the responsibilities of keeping a country estate and car-ing for his ward, Cecily. He comes up to London for a good time but also to protect Cecily from premature contact with the world; hence he has invented a mythical brother, Ernest. However wrongheaded his motives, at least he has a sense of principle, which is more than Algernon can say for his foraging about the countryside for women, or Bunburying. Jack also appears to be a tolerant squire, observing that the only people who make anything off his estate are poachers. Cecily, too, has qualities we understand and can become attached to. She has, Jack tells us, a capital appetite; she takes long walks, hates her German lessons, and fantasizes about romantic love, duly noting down her imaginings in her diary. She is a recognizable young woman, and a witty, clever one, too.

What is important about our tepid involvement with Jack and Cecily is that it propels interest in events, makes us want to see if Jack can defeat Lady Bracknell at last, and engages us in something like the emotional undercurrents of comedy. For in addition to being other things, *Importance* is a comedy of romantic love. Wilde frames important episodes as comedy. The tea scene, for instance, is a conventional wit combat, as old as comedy itself and producing winner and loser, thereby generating approval and disapproval of the attitudes of the characters involved—here, Gwendolyn's London snobbery losing out to Cecily's country girl simplicity.

Likewise, the scene in which Jack appears in mourning for his dead brother Ernest is traditional discrepancy of awareness. Jack knows he is faking, but Miss Prism and Canon Chasuble do not, so that they look completely foolish. But Jack does not know that "Ernest" is alive and well, in the person of Algernon, within the house; he looks charmingly idiotic in his somber mourning clothes, mouthing expected phrases. Still, Wilde does not miss a chance to bend his gags toward satire: ridicule of Miss Prism's starched morality, of Chasuble's hollow condolences, of the empty social ritual of grief itself. The dynamic of the scene remains comic, however, and registers on our deep response.

The thing that fuses comedy and satire in *Importance* is Wilde's play with the very dramatic form he uses, the typical well-made romantic comedy of the time. The names are theatrical, e.g., Gwendolyn Fairfax and Cecily Cardew, not Mary Jones and Elizabeth Smith. There are two sets of lovers, or three if we count Miss Prism and Canon Chasuble, who face a "blocking element." For the young lovers it is Lady Bracknell, for Prism and Chasuble the canon's belief in celibacy. The blocking element must be circumvented or overcome, and in theater of the time this was often accomplished by a key property: the will found under a loose floorboard, the letter divulging true identity, or the like. Wilde gives us the handbag. Improbabilities abound but one way or another connect to bring about a final revelation and happy conclusion, e.g., Miss Prism's mistakenly leaving the manuscript of her three-volume novel in the perambulator and the baby in the cloak room. The marvelous spoof of the contrived happy ending builds to the final suspense: What *is* Jack's true given name? As the handy set of army records reveal, he was christened Ernest. So, Lady Bracknell defeated, Gwendolyn's requirement met, the ending moves to its final pun on the play's title.

The spoof is more than a put-on of the happy ending, though: the whole of *Importance* plays off its own form. One could say that the maneuver is essentially satire. True, parody is a satiric form, perhaps the ultimate aesthetic expression of irony, in the same way we would call *Gulliver's Travels* a spoof of the travel narrative or Swift's "Modest Proposal" a lampoon of the proposal or *Joseph Andrews* a take-off of Richardson's *Pamela*. All of these have the form parodied as a target, for instance in Swift's lengthy second paragraph of Book II of *Gulliver's Travels,* a salty hodgepodge of spritsails, lifts, foretop sails, mizzens, foresheets, weather braces, and lee braces.

Wilde's approach is far more tangential and playful. He is utterly straightfaced, as the parodist should be. In performance it is only as we near the ending that we may realize a parody is going on, and even then full awareness is not likely. That is because he has provided enough emotional involvement to have us respond almost as we would to any romantic comedy. Almost. With satiric characterizations and irony distancing us *Importance* still works as a stage comedy: heavy-handed though its devices are, they ensnare our interest. The net effect is both "real" comedy and constant play off of its conventions, play which finally erupts in the manifest improbabilities of the last moments, including the wholly unprepared for embrace of Miss Prism and Canon Chasuble ("Laetitia!" / "Frederick, at last!"). For most audiences it is only then that the gag played on them comes to light, if it does.

No wonder commentators on *Importance* run out of adjectives for its overall effect—"farcical," "satiric comedy," "sophisticated satirical farce," and so on.[14] The work is an amalgam of comedy and satire. It is a parody, or at least parodic. Most of all it is play. Wilde plays with our expectations in the manner of all comedy, but with greater intensity. There are few comedies, in any medium, which offer as many gags per square inch, so to speak, as *Importance*. Very little is wasted on narrative development or on the serious elements that take up a third to a half of a work in the Menandrine mold. Very few opportunities for a one-liner are passed over, even when it does not fit character or moment. Like the *farceur* Wilde pushes play to its limits.

We have no name for Wilde's achievement. In respect to meaning or content, *Importance* is easily typed as comedy of attack, teetering more toward comedy than satire by virtue of its playfulness. But there is its strong element of the flippant, erratic, and loony, which brings us to that other axis for typing comedy, play with perception, with our phenomenal world and all the habits of mind embedded in it.

5

Modes of Comedy: Perceptual Play

The point of examining Paul Klee's *Revolution of the Viaducts* earlier was to isolate the important factor of perceptual play in comic art that is nonrepresentational. Representational art, and much of drama, the novel, and film, is weighted with semantic content. To the ordinary viewer or reader it has "meaning." How can it not, since characters and things presented look real? Quite aside from the problem of what is "real," there is the matter of art embodying its message in its own phenomenal existence. How it does this leads to the other axis of the comic experience, perceptual play.

No comic work is without play with perception. But not every comic work has this play as its fundamental condition of being. Those that do are often considered anomalies outside the realm of aesthetic concern. Slapstick—farcical effect in general—is considered low, or as in Shakespeare's youthful *Comedy of Errors* exuberant apprentice work that will lead to mature comedies which "say" something. For example, the description of farce in the 1974 *Encyclopedia Brittanica* is "a dramatic genre having no pretensions beyond provoking laughter . . . it is good-natured, pointless horseplay and is aesthetically and intellectually inferior to comedy" (*Micropedia*.IV.53). That somewhat overstates the case but captures a general literary bias and underestimation of what farce can be, attitudes that are still with us.

What the encyclopediast does not grasp is that farce works first and last phenomenally. Apparently that was the case with Elder Olson when he called Wilde's *Importance* theatrical *badinage*. However, if one frees one's mind from the notion that comedy must have content—in other words must satisfy literary and dramatic formalism—the *badinage* (persiflage, flippancy, impertinence, whatever) of *Importance* is a substantial part of its phenomenal "message." While Wilde's work has many comic and satiric elements, perhaps the generic term that best applies to it is farce.

As used here "farce" is a designation for those works that take play as their primary condition of being. How primary is primary, though? Virtually every comic work has an element of play, a certain amount of pointless clowning with words or actions. The *farceur* takes the play element latent in all comedy and intensifies it, revels in its energy and wackiness. So far from being a meager, impoverished activity, farce—perceptual play largely for its own sake, unconcerned about meaning—may well be the ultimate mode of expression to which arts of the risible tend.

Farce is less a distinct group of works than a matter of degree. And while it is useful to refer to it as if it were a discrete but overlapping mode of comedy, it is distinguished from other modes, say subcomedy and satire, mainly by the extent to which it is committed to perceptual play. Its content is often embarrassingly thin; it relies heavily on stereotypes; it is as careless of subtleties as it is of probability. No matter, the *farceur* would say, the dynamics of the art lie elsewhere. Reckless, extravagant, erratic, bordering on lunacy, farce is the chanciest of art forms, teetering on its edge, risking loss, even, of its own fictional underpinnings. It is the comic mode that most approaches a state of pure play.

On the other hand, in order to communicate, farce must have some order and coherence, or the appearance of them. For the *farceur*, narrative form is a scaffolding on which to hang action, as frail as steel piping and angle irons supporting a pyrotechnic display. Psychological probability, causality, and the like are games to be played *with*, as are conventions, formulae, and expected configurations of experience, including the ones the *farceur* uses. Though the play of farce has a number of substantive messages (the little man has a chance, love conquers all, and so on) these are almost trivial compared to the impact of play on our consciousness, and even more on our unconscious mind. It is as if substance, narrative point, and what the experience is "about" are not just illusions but diversions. The expectation that all jerks, turns, and pointless and excessive joltings will somehow come together is the grand, enduring lead-in of the joke the *farceur* plays on us. And, evidently, we have never quite caught on. While the mad, impulsive embrace of Miss Prism and Canon Chasuble at the end of *Importance* hints at the play on form in which we are snared, full awareness comes with Jack's finally realizing "the vital Importance of Being Earnest."[1]

Representation in farce, then, provides enough semblance of the "real" to give the impression of actuality, when its true function is to be part of sleight-of-hand. Once we are into our habits of response, we are setups. That is so even with only partially mimetic representation, as in the cartoon strip. The cartoonist presents a symbolic, confined world that bears little resemblance to the one we know. No matter, the strip itself evokes conventions of viewing, and the very act of looking at it engages our habits of perception. Furthermore, there is often a halo of awareness we bring to the experience, knowledge of the symbolic "world" of the strip and the characters populating it.[2]

In the case of Berke Breathed's *Bloom County*, we have acquaintance with the character Steve, whose more-liberal-than-thou attitude often bumps against common sense. The strip evokes our usual habits: reading and viewing left to right, focusing frame by frame, emphasizing facial expressions and words. Little is done, after the first frame, to change perspective or distance of viewer in relation to image. Overall, we are in the same position as with a television situation comedy: in the room, fictionally part of the family.

Details add to the semantic texture (Steve's Vegetarian Chef apron, a badge of liberalism, his shaking his wooden spoon at his mother, etc.), but the strip moves in the accustomed pattern through five panels of lead-in to the "punch panel." The only significant element of play—contentual as well as visual—is the father, who makes up a little countermovement. Heavy in caricature of the television addicted, elderly man, he augments the words of the mother while providing a delightful spoof of fathers. But playfully distracting as he may be visually—his wiggling elbow, the bending down of his head—the father is firmly tied to overall content. In short, the strip is good visual comedy, or social satire, but meager in play.

By contrast there is Breathed's statement on gun control. (See page 98.) The situation is that Milo, the hero of the strip, is conducting a presidential campaign for the Meadow Party. The eternal naif and loser, Opus the penguin is assisting and passes on to Milo a contribution by the National Rifle Association to influence the party platform. The NRA wants to block gun control. The figure in the last panel is Bill the Cat, an execrable, filthy, loony character who is emotionally expendable for most readers of the cartoon strip. (That is, the last panel has no comment to make on cats.) Suspension of the request on behalf of the NRA spans the seven panels; its completion makes up the punch line in Opus's final statement. Thus Breathed's pro–gun control message is finally made clear by words.

The treatment of visual elements of the strip adds immensely, however, enhancing the play, or trick, of witholding information

Berke Breathed, *Bloom County*, (c) 1989, Washington Post Writers Group. Reprinted with permission.

Berke Breathed, *Bloom County*, (c) 1989, Washington Post Writers Group. Reprinted with permission.

until the last panel. The very surprise of "BLAM!" in the second panel is play: unexpected and delightfully absurd, considering that Opus is supposed to be persuading Milo to take a position opposing gun control. The next panels juxtapose Opus's reassuring words—"I've got it . . . under control!"—with images of violent, self-loading fire from the revolver. In panels four, five, and six, Opus is hardly master of the situation. His vision is blocked by his arms, he shakes, his mouth is open in shock, his figure off balance from recoil. His assurances and the "blam's" of the gun are equal in visual weight until the next to last panel. There the sound of gunfire visually dominates, especially since it is on the right of the panel rather than on the left side. (Left to right reading assures the last element seen receives emphasis, as the terminal position in a sentence does.) The tilting of the fifth frame to spill it over onto others adds to the general impression of lack of control, of a fortuitous, inexplicable happening. Details reinforce the confusion. In the tilted panel Opus's eyes are wide with surprise; in the next to last panel they are squeezed shut; in the punch panel hair stands on his head to symbolize his frazzled state.

Viewing left to right, by the time we arrive at Bill the cat, a hole neatly cut through his midriff, the major statement of the strip has been made. But Bill's figure and the innards splattered behind it play off the words of Opus to the left, especially "every American's right to feel safe." "Feel safe" packs its own irony generated by the panels preceding. Without them it would be a straightforward statement expressing the position of the National Rifle Association. But the words' calmness, following such visual violence, works in another way: it establishes that Opus is merely the messenger doing his job and is not implicated.

All in all the vastly richer visual play of this strip, compared to that of the first one, not only gives a stronger phenomenal impact but conveys its own message, violence. Had words never been used, visual play would have carried its embodied "meaning." Not that play *is* the main communicational outcome; Breathed curbs its impulses toward the overall statement he wants to make. Perhaps only Bill the cat and his innards suggest excess of play for its own sake. Often in his other work Breathed lets his impulses loose to become a genuine *farceur* among cartoonists; in this second strip he merely inclines in that direction.

Though not so readily apparent, farcical play operates much the same way, and in varying degrees, in the comic film and novel. Mainstream film comedies tend to stay within the bounds of conventional games, seldom risking the excesses of farce, possible alienation of audiences, and reduction of profits. A typical case is Gene Saks's 1968 film version of Simon's *The Odd Couple*, earlier cited for its power as a comedy of exploration. In respect to content and to Simon's handling of underlying issues and values, *The Odd Couple* is indeed rich. As a film and considered in terms of perceptual play, it is drab.

Other than two episodes added to the playscript (an opening suicide attempt by Felix, at which he fails, and a useless search by members of the poker group in Murray's police car), the camera pretty much records action as it had occurred on stage. Camera angles and cuts are used wisely, if conservatively. For instance, in a scene mentioned earlier, Oscar goes off to prepare drinks, leaving Felix to entertain the Pigeon sisters. As Felix gradually transforms the dating game into somber reflection, the camera has Felix centered, ready to burst into tears, but includes, as well, the face of one of the Pigeon sisters looking blankly confused. The juxtaposition makes mild fun of the woman and helps divert us from thinking of Oscar, helps to maintain the "lead-in" that will soon be flipped over by Oscar's returning with drinks in good spirits. It is responsible filming, but as use of the medium for comic effect, it is meager in perceptual play.

By contrast there are the films of the Monty Python group. In the spirit of Music Hall skits and the *Goon Show* of radio, Pythonian comedy is bumptious, fast paced, given to slapstick, or, in a word, farcical.[3] The group's films have been somewhat restrained, all things considered, but still show within the usual games of comedy an irrepressible urge to play. In *Monty Python and the Holy Grail* (1975), there are nicely conceived gag sequences leading up to a visual "punch line." King Arthur and his knights confront a castle held by detestable Frenchmen. Seige equipment is needed. After much banging of hammers and thunking of timbers, the frame shows us shrubbery, leaves trembling, boughs shaking to a mighty rumble that makes the ground quiver. The seige machine appears, a huge wooden rabbit on wheels. The timing is effective, the lead-in superbly diverting. In addition to flipping over expectation, the rabbit delightfully parodies the Trojan Horse.

Still, a good many episodes are both loosely tied to narrative development and excessive in their play. When an Englishman meets dark, Germanic knights blocking his way (all the Germans say is "Nicht"), we have a rousing sword fight. Plucky as he is, the English knight fights on after losing various parts of his body, including his legs, ending a mere stump on the ground but gamely belligerent and swinging his sword. The episode serves scant narrative or thematic purpose. By literary or filmic standards it goes on far too long; its spurting blood is gratuitous. As play—dark and bloody play, admittedly—the scene makes perfect sense: It carries the conventions of chivalric bravery to their absurd extremes.

Again, in *The Meaning of Life* (1983) the opening sequence is a satiric attack on the church. We are shown a working-class neighborhood, its run-down houses teeming with scruffy children. A line of nuns in black habit sing a song against birth control while doing high kicks with all the verve of a Broadway musical. The message is abundantly clear through juxtaposition of the chorus and children. Yet for a moment the camera moves low to the ground; we glance up to see that the nuns are wearing black gartered, net stockings suggestive of the streetwalker. A comment on hidden desires, on the hollowness of holy vows, or both, the brief view has little to do with the satiric point being made. Like later episodes in the film—a fat man gorging himself with food and vomiting all over a posh restaurant, a grotesquely bloody organ transplant—the jibe at nuns is genuinely farcical in spirit.

More extreme yet in farcical play is Mel Brooks's *Blazing Saddles* (1974). It is a patently obvious attack on stereotypes, especially racial ones, by way of parody of the Western film. There are the usual figures: the greedy land tycoon Hedley Lamar; a corrupt, idiotic governor; frightened townspeople of Rock Ridge who need a lawman to protect them; a has-been gunfighter named the Waco Kid; and assorted cowboys and Indians. The townspeople hire a sheriff, sight unseen, who turns out to be a black man. He is dressed in stylish, fitted clothes and rides a palomino horse, the kind used in parades preceding floats in the annual Rose Bowl Pageant. Fortunately, the Sheriff is supported by the quick as lightning guns of the Waco Kid. The narrative line is simplicity itself: Hedley Lamar raises a small army of gunslingers to attack the town, but by a clever ruse the Sheriff and the Waco Kid save Rock Ridge, only to be pursued by Lamar's men. Eventually the heroes escape.

What happens in the meantime, however, approaches lunacy. Some actions are thematically relevant, others only tenuously connected to the film's main message, undermining stereotypes. When an Indian chief (Brooks) speaks in a Brooklyn Jewish accent or Klu Klux Klansmen turn around to show on their white robes a smiling yellow face saying "Have a Nice Day," the gags make a kind of thematic sense. But a good many incidents are pointless in these terms, e.g., cowboys punching an old lady, the bad guys slapping leather as they pursue the Sheriff and Waco Kid, only to be stopped in the middle of the desert by a toll gate that requires them to deposit a quarter.

The pursuit spills over onto a modern day film studio, where men in tophats and tuxedos are rehearsing a Busby Berkeley dance routine, and, it is suggested, are homosexual to boot. Pies are thrown in the ensuing melee, but the heroes escape on horseback to enter a movie theater showing *Blazing Saddles*. They climb up to the screen, enter into their own film's ending, and ride off happily in a limousine. Time, space, and probability are thrown out. The very framework of narrative and theme is demolished, and with it our belief in the fictional "world" of the film. In its own loony way the ending is most appropriate. Increasingly over the course of the movie, play had become the filmic experience, theme a mere pretext for sudden jolts and turns generating hints, suggestions of meaning leading nowhere. How better to bring this experience to an end than by intensification, a playing with the medium of film itself?[4]

An extreme case, nonetheless *Blazing Saddles* is in the tradition of the *farceur*'s commitment to zany, pointless effect, to risking the very implied contract with audience on which his work rests. This commitment is less obvious in, say, Wilde's play with his work's form at the end of *Importance*, or Feydeau's stretching of probability to its limits in the chance meetings at the Coq d'Or bordello toward the end of *A Flea in Her Ear*, or even the accidental happenings and mistaken identities of *A Midsummer's Night's Dream*. But the risky play of farce erupts throughout our comic tradition, from Aristophanes to the films of the Marx Brothers, and is not, of course, limited to stage and cinema.

With the novel the *farceur* works with an altogether less congenial medium. Unsupported by the holiday spirit of play or film and by the laughter of others, the isolated reader can be easily put off, made to feel ill at ease with slapstick effects. Most readers are quite comfortable with the games of comedy, and more particularly with the superior awareness granted by the author in the conventional comic novel. In Kingsley Amis's *Lucky Jim* (1953), we sympathize with the good-hearted hero, enjoy his bumbling, and in general do not observe the games being played on us. We enter into our usual condition of semiconsciousness, expecting only to be amused. Amis does all he can to maintain our mindlessness.

For instance, at the end of chapter 5 Jim has had too much to drink and, room tilting, mantelpiece fluttering, tries every conceivable position to get to sleep. He finally succeeds. Chapter 6 opens the next morning with Jim struggling to gain full consciousness. He discovers a hole in the sheet, a larger scorched hole in the blankets, and a brown channel in the rug, ending in ashen paper—all this in the guest room of the house of Welch, his boss. That Jim smoked was known by the reader, and cigarettes were mentioned at the end of chapter 5. But Amis obscures the information, so that with the convention of the chapter break (end of episode; new subject matter) we are not thinking of smoking as we follow Jim's struggles to awaken, his head thudding, his mouth tasting awful.

The sleight-of-hand has been played on us, as usual, but we do not acknowledge that, and in any event we piece together the implications of burned bedding and rug before Jim does. He is the fool once again, and we are in the comfortable position of sharing the author's superior awareness. The craft lies not only in burying key information and diverting us with irrelevant details, but in using conventions of form—here the break between chapters—to deceive us. Given the game being played, it is crucial that Amis keep us unaware of what is really transpiring. Wisely, he does not bring attention to his use of form evoking a predictable response. And so it is with the conventional comic novel. By and large the author maintains a smooth surface, letting events unfold as if fate or some cruel deity played jokes on characters, letting language operate as a translucent recorder of fictional "reality." Not so with the author inclined to be the *farceur*.

In *Riotous Assembly* (1971), overall Tom Sharpe uses realistic fiction to create games similar to those of Amis. However, Sharpe has a strong satirical bent and a propensity for play with and beyond the bounds of the conventional comic novel.[5] His general satiric target is apartheid, and more particularly the authoritarian mentality of the South African police—Afrikaaners all, as are the doctors, judges, and prison warders who represent other aspects of white domination. His secondary target, treated much more comically, is British colonialism, or more exactly idealized concepts of empire nostalgically valued among some English. There are other matters that come in for ridicule (women, sexuality, and the church) but with these Sharpe's tone is light and jovial by comparison.

The action of the novel is propositional: What would happen if an elderly, socially prominent English lady were to kill her Zulu cook and lover in a *crime passionel,* and if the investigating police commander deeply admired British culture, or cultivation, though he himself was an Afrikaaner? Kommandant Van Heerden is shocked to learn of the longstanding relationship between Miss Hazelstone and the now deceased Fivepence, a love the more lasting because they shared a fetish for rubber (they met in a tire retread shop). Naturally it would not help peace or tranquility if the crime were known; the cause of white supremacy could be damaged beyond repair in the provincial town of Piemburg. The difficulty is that Miss Hazelstone wants to give herself up. Her father having been a judge, she has a deep, compulsive love of justice. But Van Heerden can scarcely allow such a scandal to occur. Thus begins a battle of wills that generates most of the actions, and idiocies, to follow.

Sharpe's strategy as a satirist is to exclude blacks from the novel—the scattered remains of Fivepence, blown apart by an elephant gun, a boy on a bicycle, prisoners, but no fully drawn characters—so as to concentrate on whites. We see the naive Kommandant Van Heerden trying to dissuade batty Miss Hazelstone from confessing, the bumbling Intelligence Officer Verkramp misreading information and concocting files, and the barely human Konstabel Els abusing his power to rape and kill blacks.

As is typical of satire, the main vehicle is irony. The police see their actions as rational and in support of law and order; we see them as absurd. So with Miss Hazelstone, although she is more a comic than satiric characterization. There is a kind of loony rationale to her actions, and with the reader she perceives clearly that apartheid is wrong. Yet she has an imperious, aggressive, unself-conscious manner that embodies the very spirit of the British upper class. And it is difficult for us (for males, anyway) to accept her solution to Fivepence's tendency to ejaculate prematurely: a shot of Novocain in his penis. Still, the considerable we see of white society confirms Miss Hazelstone's judgment that the inmates of a mental institution are as sane as South Africa itself (p. 149).[6]

Few aspects of white South African life escape attack through ridicule. Sharpe's typical mode is to let lunacy speak for itself. His ironies can be outrageous, or merely wicked, for instance when the prison chapel has colored glass windows showing not spiritually moving figures and scenes from Scripture, but forms of execution ranging from a pincushion St. Sebastian to an electric chair haloed in blue sparks (pp. 167–68).

In addition, Sharpe uses devices of comedy extensively. He is fond of double-entendre, as when Konstabel Els is about to be attacked by his nemesis, Toby the Dobermann. We see Toby prowling behind a barricade upstairs in Miss Hazelstone's Jacaranda House; the point of view shifts to Els downstairs. The Konstabel has the feeling "something is in the air." A moment later Toby lands on him, initiating a fight to the death (pp. 103–5). The most frequently used and powerful device is discrepancy of awareness. Miss Hazelstone and Kommandant Van Heerden talk from different frames of reference, while the reader observes. Or Van Heerden foolishly gives the gun happy Els permission to fire if need be to keep people out of Jacaranda House. Unknown to Els, Verkramp is leading a column of men to assist. From a block-house at the front gates Els opens fire on his fellow policemen. In the house some distance away the Kommandant hears gunfire and believes something may be wrong.

It is the extent to which Sharpe carries out such scenes that shows his impulse toward farcical play. It would be joke enough to have Verkramp, ordered to be inobtrusive so as to avoid upsetting citizens, loudly rumble through the little town of Vlockfontein with his six armored cars hung with signs announcing outbreaks of rabies and bubonic plague (chap. 5). But Sharpe adds untrained police dogs, one biting a boy who made faces at it, another chasing a cat. As the latter runs down alleys and over fences, the dogs of the town get excited. By the time the police column leaves on the way to Jacaranda House shots are heard as citizens slaughter their dogs for fear they are rabid. Further, some dogs, trying to prove they are useful, kill rats. The appearance of dead rats is taken as a sign of the plague. Roads are blocked with people fleeing the town.

True, the episode is a lead-in for Sharpe's fine understatement, that the objective of quiet movement of men and matériel was not being met; but it is delightfully excessive, a spinning off into play and the improbabilities of slapstick. So, too, when the column reaches the gates of Jacaranda House (chaps. 5–6). Konstabel Els opens fire, kills some twenty policemen, thoroughly perforates an armored car, and drives Verkramp into a deep ditch with sharp iron spikes set in its concrete bottom. One or two bodies would have made the satiric point: the police are bumbling fools, Els a thickheaded animal. But Sharpe cannot resist and spins the episode out into a virtual battle, complete with skirmishes, retreats, advances, and the attackers' confusion over the mysterious "bush" or shrubbery that has so much fire power. Again, narrative and thematic statement yield to the play of farce.

It is not that Sharpe is irresponsible in craftsmanship as a novelist. The major satiric attack is accomplished and secondary targets included. Details are not irrelevant to the overall themes of *Riotous Assembly*. The very existence of the blockhouse at the gates (built to accommodate naval cannon), the fence, and the deadly ditch surrounding it bespeak the enlightened rule of General Hazelstone, Miss Hazelstone's grandfather, and the symbol of the British Empire. It is just that the action becomes self-generating, propelled by its own absurdity.

That is even more the case in the celebration instigated by Miss Hazelstone when she is a patient in Fort Rapier Mental Hospital (chap. 18). Playing off the Boer War heritage of Dr. Herzog, she persuades him to stage a pageant celebrating notable moments in the history of South Africa. Schizophrenic Zulus play their part, spears tipped with rubber replicas left by a film company. Welsh guards and county regiments are manned by compulsives, with the Scots regiment made up of women patients led by a chronic depressive.

All goes well until the Zulus get caught up in the action and place knitting needles on their spears; the whites respond in kind, while Miss Hazelstone loads field cannon with chlorate and sugar. Kommandant Van Heerden tries to bring order, but the battle begins in earnest and he barely escapes with his life. To the *1812 Overture* Zulus attack, raping Scots, and a detachment of frogmen appear and join in the fray. Cannon go off, blood is all over the parade ground, and the Kommandant, freeing himself from the embraces of a private of the Black Watch, finds only a large hole in the ground where Miss Hazelstone had been. The staged illusion of history becomes slapstick on a grand scale, yet remains fictional "reality." Again the point is made: South Africa is insane. But the overall effect is as if the episode had been written by the Marx Brothers or Monty Python. The farcical impulse in Sharpe brings the action to the verge of destroying its own credibility as fiction.

How far, one wonders, can the novelist as *farceur* go before, like the ending of *Blazing Saddles*, the work itself comes to pieces? Tom Robbins provides something of an answer in *Even Cowgirls Get the Blues* (1976),[7] a novel that examines women and sexual stereotypes more through the play of comedy than the harsh ridicule of satire. Compared to that of *Lucky Jim* or most of *Riotous Assembly*, the play is deep, beginning with the very concept of a heroine. Sissy Hankshaw is as propositional as Sharpe's opening situation of a policeman confronting the murder of a Zulu cook by a white woman who wants to give herself up. What happens, Robbins asks, if the heroine is a strikingly beautiful young woman who has abnormally large, huge thumbs? Our concepts of beauty and woman are put to the test.

For, thumbs aside, Sissy is remarkably engaging as a character. She is independent in action and thought, a free, happy spirit existing outside society yet undeterred by its rejection of her. After an uneventful working-class upbringing, she ventures out, as a model for the Countess, a homosexual manufacturer of vaginal powder (Yoni Yum/Dew), and devotes her life to hitchhiking. She encounters a group of women who run a guest ranch, The Rubber Rose, and a philosophic recluse named The Chink. In their various ways the women are playful characterizations, but at least they are explicable by normal psychology. The Chink is enigmatic, tantalizingly beyond understanding, and as serious as he is amusingly eccentric.

Sissy and the Chink dominate a fictional society crowded with stereotypes that provide light satirical commentary: Miss Adrian the finicky manager of The Rubber Rose, a cranky old lady in a town nearby, federal agents, and, inevitably, a fee conscious psychiatrist. And there are odd, comic characters such as Julian, the American Indian artist, who has sold out to be fashionable, or Bonanza Jellybean, who lives out her childhood fantasy of being a cowgirl. But in Sissy and The Chink Robbins goes beyond stereotype and the quirky "humor" character. The irreconcilabilities of Sissy—beauty/deformity, sexual explorer/yearner for emotional stability, outsider/insider—become somewhat resolved in her pregnancy at the novel's end. True to the spirit of play and openness, The Chink's contradictions never do.[8]

Robbins plays as well with fictional mode, beginning in the vein of realism, or as much realism as his ironic style allows, moving into simplistic alternated with discursive, meditational, "philosophic" episodes with little narrative happening. After a teasing introduction which tells vaguely what will befall Sissy, Robbins switches back to her early years. The style is playful, but lapses into fairly straight narration, for instance, in "South Richmond was a neighborhood of mouse holes, lace curtains, Sears catalogues, measles epidemics, baloney sandwiches—and men who knew more about the carburetor than they knew about the clitoris" (p. 19). Partly because, and often in spite of Robbins's flippant running commentary, Sissy's trials and pains of childhood come through clearly. Dialogue capturing the working class mentality helps. So does local color, the telling details of a milieu: typical foods, brand names, *The Saturday Evening Post, Playboy,* and the Bible.

As things proceed, however, the novel takes on the quality of cartoon animation. One-dimensional characters contribute to this effect. The Countess wears a monocle, taps it with a cigarette holder, and says repeatedly "shit O goodness"; Dr. Goldman speaks in Freudian psychoanalytic and therapeutic clichés. But action itself becomes equally flat, released from the motive and probability the novelist usually weaves into events. Effects have causes of the flimsiest kind and rather than revealing complex motivations as they occur, they simply take the form of X happens, leading to Y.

Three quarters of the way through (Part V), whooping cranes appear as a major element in the plot. We had seen them before at The Rubber Rose; now Robbins enlarges their role, which leads to a confrontation between the environmentally conscious, beauty loving cowgirls of the ranch and the Keystone Cop, brainless agents of government (chaps. 107, 112, 117). In the standoff Bonanza Jellybean is killed, which leads later to serious treatment of Sissy's grief, and the whooping cranes take off, saved. The cranes come as something of a surprise, but we are in a world, like that of the animated cartoon, where anything can happen. Occurrence validates existence. Events clip along rapidly, leaving little time for nuance, or for embodiments of motivation in action that characterize a "real" fictional experience.

Equally distant from "real" experience are the sections concerning The Chink. Actually Japanese, Chink had escaped from a wartime internment camp, lived with a band of Indians who worshipped The Clockworks, and migrated to the Dakotas to live in a cave high up in a butte overlooking The Rubber Rose ranch. There he eats yams, meditates, and rejects would-be disciples come to absorb his wisdom. As occasion offers he has sex with girls from the ranch, including Sissy, whom he impregnates.

No guru he. Yet Robbins treats him as one, hinting throughout that the crusty old man has philosophical and spiritual insight by having him speak in short, pithy statements, say nothing at all, or snicker "Ha ha, ho ho, and hee hee." Though he is removed from our tainted world, Chink goes down fighting when he sees Jellybean shot by lawmen and government agents. Recovered, he returns to The Clockworks Tribe to await cataclysmic events sure to come and wipe out much of the human race. Meanwhile, he assures Sissy, there will be pockets of people free from consumption as a goal of life, and humanity may be regenerated.

Contact with The Chink and the assistant of Dr. Goldman leads Sissy into lengthy philosophical speculations. While Chink refuses to be her spiritual mentor, she learns from him—about life, the necessity of magic and poetry, even about love—and decides to have her enormous thumbs removed to enter the world of normalcy. The plot shows a loose pattern of cause and effect and of novelistic development. Narrative functions, however, seem incidental to Robbins's intent. When Chink is not uttering profound, dogmatic statements disavowed by a "Ho ho, ha ha, hee hee," Robbins is. Like Chink, Robbins's reflections on philosophy and life are serious and comically ironic, both polemic and slapstick, or, in a word, playful. As author he attempts to have it both ways: a giving up of the world of consumption, politics, and action in favor of a life centered in magic and poetry; and a rejection, through ridicule, of the possibility of a feasible alternative to our hopelessly tainted existence. For the reader, however, an alternative is suggested: play.

To the extent that there is any point or "message," it lies in experiencing the novel itself. Playfulness becomes its insubstantial substance. We may bring accustomed habits of reading to *Even Cowgirls*, but for Robbins the structure of fictional response is fair game. So with the conventional novel; our expectations are lead-ins. The difference is that Robbins is not duplicitous. Early on he establishes his authorial presence, a voice chatting to us on the side about the novel we are reading and he is writing.

> If he has confused you, the author apologizes. He swears to keep events in proper historical sequence from now on. He does not, however, . . . embrace the notion that literature should mirror reality. . . . A book no more contains reality than a clock contains time. (p. 124)

A book consists of sentences. And, since Robbins is not under contract to any of the muses "who supply the reputable writers," he has access to a considerable variety of sentences, for instance:

> This sentence is made of lead. . . . This sentence is made of yak wool. This sentence is made of sunlight and plums. This sentence is made of ice. . . . *Like many italic sentences, this one has Mafia connections.* . . . This sentence may be pregnant, it missed its period. This sentence suffered a split infinitive—and survived. . . . This sentence is proud to be part of the team here at *Even Cowgirls Get the Blues.* This sentence is rather confounded by the whole damn thing. (pp. 124–25)

So are we for a moment, and either delighted or put off by this wrenching of our position as readers. But precisely speaking, there *is* a team of voices and *Even Cowgirls* is a place, a "here" where author and reader engage in pointless play.

This passage is not unusual, nor does Robbins bracket it as an authorial aside. Play with style and novelistic conventions is the norm. Narrative gets accomplished, sometimes proceeding in entire stretches with "realistic" evocation of sensation as if a quite sane, normal author were writing. More often, Robbins cannot resist a pun or restrain language from playing itself out. Chapter 40 opens, "Bang! Bang bang bang! Bang squared and bang cubed. Bang conjugated and Bank koked. They arrived at the ranch to the sound of gunfire. 'O merciful Jesus!' cried Miss Adrian" (p. 138).

Pure sensation (Bang!), straightforward narrative (arrived at the ranch), and dialogue maintain fictional "reality." It would seem that play with "bang" and the double play of "koked" would prevent our usual semiconscious immersion in narrative. Yet we shift easily from one mental state to another, and by now we are used to Robbins's flippancies. We may also recognize that the novel, qua realistic fiction, must be continually reestablished for play to occur in the first place.

Robbins's style keeps *Even Cowgirls Get the Blues* thoroughly disruptive and disjointed, seemingly working against itself. He takes the further risk of undoing author and reader collusion by including himself as a character, Dr. Robbins. He is the anti-Freudian assistant to Dr. Goldman and Sissy's analyst, or a participant in mutual therapy. Appropriately, the novel ends with Dr. Robbins, identified as "your author," struggling in the darkness up to the cave formerly inhabited by Chink, now the home of a pregnant Sissy and her mate, Delores del Ruby. He has "all the material for this book," but how will he fit into Sissy's destiny? He does not know, and we can only guess. However, echoing The Chink he, now the authorial "I," believes "in everything; nothing is sacred / I believe in nothing; everything is sacred. Ha ha ho ho and hee hee" (p. 415).

As the ending of *Blazing Saddles* had done, that of *Even Cowgirls* demolishes the basis of its own fictional existence, requiring us to accept a new order of experience, play. Still, if Robbins is a *farceur* in this respect, he has messages to convey through conventional means. In the passages dealing with "girl love" (e.g., pp. 172–79), he talks to the characters, discourses to the reader on various aspects of sexuality, and plays with language, but still devotes considerable detail to setting, physical sensation, and emotions quite in the manner of the romance writer. Nor does he much interrupt a political message when satiric irony will carry the point, as in describing the reactions of the president, the FBI, and government officials to a "lost" flock of whooping cranes (pp. 333–37). On the other hand, he is sharply aware of his own predilections and ridicules them as well. Like his aesthetic forebears, Rabelais and Sterne,[9] Robbins is consistently, deeply committed to play.

Though usually to a much lesser degree than in *Even Cowgirls* or *Blazing Saddles*, all comedy juggles linguistic and other habits of response. Perceptual play is not a quantum, or quantifiable. When it is sufficiently intense to become the work's essential mode of being, according to the meaning given the term here, the work is a farce. Another distinguishing characteristic of farce is that it plays with a medium's own fictional and semiotic conventions to the point of risking their collapse. Most of all, farce pushes reader, audience, or viewer to a drastic realignment with the work, pushes us to join in play or reject it altogether. Though they may have farcical elements (mistaken identities, chance encounters, etc.), few comedies carry play this far. Whatever its degree and intensity in specific works, perceptual play is a major axis in the operation of comedy. With this axis superimposed, the previous diagram of modes of comedy according to "meaning" appears different.

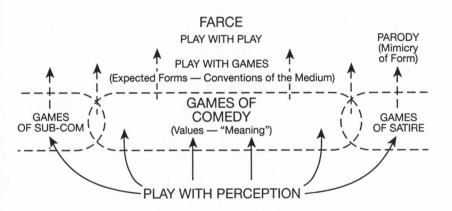

Axis of Perceptual Play Overlaid on Modes of Comedy According to "Meaning"

In the interests of visual clarity only major kinds of play are identified. The vertical arrows—intermittent, without pattern—are meant to suggest that how much perceptual play a specific work or genre has is highly variable. And while it may seem odd that subcomedy or satire are included in this axis, recall that *Blazing Saddles* is low level satire, viewed in terms of its meaning or content, and, seen another way, high farce, rich in its phenomenological assault on our habits of mind. Or, again, Wilde's *Importance* is seen by Elder Olson as mere theatrical *badinage*, having little or no content and not meeting Aristotelian requirements, whereas from the perspective of farce, it is highly accomplished perceptual play.

All in all, this schematic representation implies not only a new typology of kinds of comedy, based on two axes rather than one, but a radical shift in our customary valuation of the "other" in our tradition: Aristophanic Old Comedy, *buffo*, slapstick, and vulgar or "low" comedy. For ontologically considered perceptual play is as legitimate a mode of existence as that based on content. One could even say it has a prior claim as a feature of all ludic modes, while content and meaning are not indigenous to the art. (The works of Klee, Miró, Calder, and many postmodernists in painting, literature, and the performing arts are simply ungraspable as content or meaning.) To confer this legitimacy, of course, one must recognize the authenticity of play itself as a mode of being.

Even granting that play is an irreducible, primary element of existence, a further question arises. How can play as comedy blend so easily with the serious? Play and seriousness appear to be deeply, inherently incompatible with one another. But as Robbins's *Even Cowgirls Get the Blues* has shown, and *Waiting for Godot* and a good many other works testify, coexistence of comic with serious statement is neither impossible nor unusual.

A shorthand suggestion as to why the comic can turn deadly serious, or the reverse, has already presented itself. Play is not exclusively cheerful, buoyant, and genially loony. It has its dark side. The image of Janus comes to mind again: neither of the god's faces can exist free of the other. Every kick in the pants is an assault upon order, a cruel debasement of humanity, especially if it is *your* pants. No doubt every genocide has seemed slightly humorous to those perpetrating it. It seldom occurs to us as we laugh that the object of our ridicule is thereby dehumanized, made an object in a game of power and subjugation in which we are assured winners. We are spared such thoughts, or are until the mixture of comedy with the serious forces us to recognize how deeply the two are entwined.

6

Comic/Serious, Serious/Comic

Few persons or situations are absolutely, inherently comic in nature, just as there are few that cannot be seen as ridiculous to someone, somewhere. All depends upon point of view and the context in which they are placed. It takes no comic to see the ridiculous. It takes the artist, however, to perceive absurdity and embody its comic/serious duality in a work.

Often this double effect is achieved by yoking inappropriate form with subject matter, or the reverse. For instance, in *Death of a Toad*, Richard Wilbur evokes an experience which is at once somber and lightly playful:

> A toad the power mower caught,
> Chewed and clipped of a leg, with a hobbling hop has got
> To the garden verge, and sanctuaried him
> Under the cineraria leaves, in the shade
> Of the ashen heartshaped leaves, in a dim,
> Low, and a final glade.
>
> The rare original heartblood goes,
> Spends on the earthen hide, in the folds and wizening, flows
> In the gutters of the banked and staring eyes. He lies
> As still as if he would return to stone,
> And soundlessly attending, dies
> Toward some deep monotone,
>
> Toward misted and ebullient seas,
> And cooling shores, toward lost Amphibia's emperies.
> Day dwindles, drowning, and at length is gone
> In the wide and antique eyes, which still appear
> To watch, across the castrate lawn,
> The haggard daylight steer.[1]

The subject, at first a lamentable but insignificant happening, grows into a genuine, poignant demise. Not that the poet is involved; the power mower did it. The toad is the focus of attention. From an unimportant creature he becomes a distinct individual. His death inclines him toward a sort of Jungean collective unconscious of toads, "Amphibia's emperies." And as the day, or life, dwindles in his antique eyes, the poet's own day is "haggard," and its daylight "steers" across a "castrate lawn." Or, one could say, the poem has awakened us to our own man centered universe to see in a longer perspective, to sense ourselves relative newcomers among ancient races of beings that were here before continents were fully formed.

Whatever one's interpretation of the essential statement of the poem, its seriousness is undermined by light ridicule. "Chewed and clipped of a leg, with a hobbling hop" evokes a grim but awkward, slightly absurd movement. The opening is in the reverse word order of ceremonious address. Then there is Wilbur's choice of Latinate words where English ones would do—verge instead of edge, sanctuaried, cineraria, ebullient, castrate—or antiquated terms such as spends and wizening, and the Elizabethan emperies. Most of all there is the controlled, repeated stanzaic form recalling the Pindaric ode, typically reserved for celebration of grand deeds.

The discrepancy between elaborate, dignified ode form and lowly subject generates interplay between the serious and the comic. (Further, there is the old mocking expression, "Ode to a Toad," which Wilbur takes literally.) The toad is both dispensable in our anthropomorphic scheme of things and yet elevated to a position of dignity. Its blood is rare. Rather than expiring under an aster or azalea the toad dies under the ashen, heartshaped leaves of the cineraria, with its classical resonances. The toad is not an insignificant piece dropped out of the chain of being. It goes back to a sort of froggy nirvana, causing us to wonder: Do toads have a heaven too? What does Amphibia look like, Elizabeth I, Queen Victoria, our own First Lady? There is no end to the sparks thrown off by juxtaposing comedy with the serious.

Juxtaposition is not apparent, however, on first reading. The two blend into tongue in cheek solemnity. Interplay between the comic and serious works well because both are essentially two sides of the same thing, play. In this case the interaction is between content and form, not very far from the parodist's favorite device, mismatching subject matter with a recognizable, conventional vehicle. Things get rather more complicated when the artist suddenly flips a serious situation into comic perspective, and back again. Just as every comic moment can turn grim, every somber situation can become the lead-in for a sudden turn—all the more hilarious because of its dark context. Ultimately the comic and the serious not only play off one another, they mutually reinforce and intensify each other.

Such is the case in Comedy of the Absurd, where slapstick is often used in a dark context to express the purposelessness of existence. The works in this genre of playwrights like Beckett, Arrabal, Ionesco, and Frisch are more farcical than comic. Like farce they assault our habits of mind. But whereas farce is play largely for its own sake, in Comedy of the Absurd it is bent toward a reiterative message: man is helpless in the face of a contradictory, alienating universe.

In *Waiting for Godot* Beckett's old music hall gags and routines, such as the hat exchange in act 2, are painfully hilarious. Vladimir and Estragon's attempts to generate significance out of their bleak existence lead to marvelous non sequiturs, as when they discuss hanging themselves, or, just as often, to comic deflation. For instance, Vladimir wants Estragon to say he's happy to be back with him.

> *Vladimir:* Say you are, even if it's not true.
> *Estragon:* What am I to say?
> *Vladimir:* Say, I am happy.
> *Estragon:* I am happy.
> *Vladimir:* So am I.
> *Estragon:* So am I.
> *Vladimir:* We are happy.
> *Estragon:* We are happy. *(Silence.)* What do we do now, now that we are happy?[2]

The juxtaposition of "happy" and their grim, drab setting (a stage bare except for a dying tree) is reinforced by Estragon's flat delivery of his lines. Repetition dulls, too. And the skewed logic of Estragon's last question (as if happiness had to be used in some way) is only one instance in a running gag: the two tramps seek meaning and purpose in an existence which has none.

Therein lies the joke on the audience as well. With what has since become a convention in itself, Beckett plays with audience expectations, especially customary response to "realistic" theater. Space is a "somewhere"; time passes but does not; cause and effect are inoperable; and action ends where it had begun, with waiting. Meaning, like Godot, is tantalizingly out of reach. The complex game Beckett plays—embodying "message" in the experiencing of the work itself—is a basic tenet of postmodernism.

Not surprisingly, the comic and the serious often become inseparable. Is that not the case, however, with more conventional treat-
ments, with, say, traditional theater?

In *The Playboy of the Western World*, for instance, Synge lets the
whole play become a grand lead-in for the comic flip at the end.
Not that the events leading up to his denouement are without
humor. The hero, Christy Mahon, is a country bumpkin who
believes he has killed his Da with a potato shovel, an action the
villagers of Mayo take to be a manly deed of heroic proportions.
The people of Mayo are themselves humorous, an admixture of
stereotypes and colorful local characters. There is Michael James,
the master of the public house, who is overly fond of poteen;
Shawn Keogh, a cowardly, sniveling young farmer; and Sarah,
Susan, and Honor, giggling girls of the village who flock around
the exciting figure of Christy. More seriously conceived, but humorous in her way, is the Widow Quin, ever on the lookout for a
man. Perhaps the only straightforward character is Pegeen Mike,
daughter of Michael James, de facto mistress of the pub, and
eventually Christy's intended.

Humorous a lot as they are, the villagers have a shadowy side.
Hunger for excitement leads them to aggrandize Christy. They
encourage him to tell the tale of his dark and bloody deed. Un-
used to such attention, and falling in love with Pegeen Mike,
Christy obliges them, becoming in his own mind the hero they
crave. Since for much of the action all goes well, we tend to over-
look the villagers' motives. Increasingly we gain respect for
Christy as he blooms into manhood. He wins at jumping, leaping, and racing donkeys in village festivities. His language reveals
the soul of a folk poet, as when he tells Pegeen,

> It's little you'll think if my love's a poacher's or an earl's itself when
> you'll feel my two hands stretched around you, and I squeezing kisses
> on your puckered lips, till I'd feel a kind of pity for the Lord God is
> all ages sitting lonesome in his golden chair.[3]

And Pegeen, whose intelligence has earned our respect, confers
her love on him. As the end of the play approaches, with Christy
and Pegeen happily engaged, we feel buoyantly content, at least
until Christy's father shows up, bandaged around his head but
alive after all.

Suddenly all is changed. The Mayoites, and especially Pegeen,
feel cheated. Poor Christy is shown to be the innocent he always
was, but the loss of Pegeen's love and his pride force him to

violently attack his father offstage to show that he indeed can kill.
There is a long silence. Christy returns alone. His reasoning is no
crazier than the villagers', his emotions no more paradoxical than
Pegeen's. Though she had pledged herself to him and only a
short while before had received her father's blessing, it is she who
places a rope around Christy from behind so that he can be hung
or dragged off to the police. She now realizes that there is a huge
gap between a gallous story and a dirty deed and does not want
herself and the villagers implicated in this heinous crime. When
Christy tries to squirm free she burns him with the coals of a sod.

Like that of the villagers, her viciousness shocks us. On reflection we might see that there always has been a streak of violence
in the Mayoites, a mixture of adulation of heroism and law-
lessness. At the moment we only recognize that they are betrayed
by their own dark impulses, not by Christy. Repulsive as their
ugliness is (all the more because we had been charmed by their
humor and eccentricity), it is intensified by Christy's naive efforts
to redeem himself in their eyes. All of his genuine value as a
man seems tragically sacrificed to petty, murderous intent. Or so
Synge lets his lead-in progress until he plays his joke on Christy,
the Mayoites, and us.

Old Mahon comes in on all fours, unnoticed by all, including
Pegeen, who is burning Christy's leg with the coal. It is a powerful
theatrical moment. After we had seen Mahon chased by his son,
potato shovel flailing, heard the blows and groans offstage, and
waited through the silence and Christy's return, we had been
convinced that the already wounded old man was dead. The Irish
head is thicker than we thought, however, and painful apprehension is flipped to exquisite comic effect. The whole mood changes.
Christy declares himself head of the family, pushes Mahon before
him, and thanks all for turning him into a likely gaffer who will
romp through life from now on. Pegeen is left to her just desserts.
The detestable Shawn Keogh sidles up to her and receives a box
in the ear; she wails she has surely lost the only playboy of the
western world. The grand joke of the ending sets everything
aright and concludes the play in a deeply satisfying resolution.

The depth of satisfaction comes less from a suitable ending
to action than from the conclusion's being generated out of and
resolving inconsistencies that had existed all along. Had the villagers been more "realistic" and seriously portrayed, they might
have satisfied outraged Dublin spectators who attempted to
drown out actors during the play's initial run. But much would

have been lost. Fortunately, Synge gives us clownish figures whose charm obscures their petty, violent natures.

Small details early on hint at the dark side of the village folk. The Widow Quin, says Pegeen, had done in her man with a pick whose rust poisoned him, and suckled a black ram at her own breast. Even Pegeen, apparently levelheaded and businesslike, has a streak of violent romanticism. To Shawn's claim that these times are as good as any she recalls folk heroes of Mayo:

> Where now will you meet the like of Daneen Sullivan knocked the eye from a peeler, or Marcus Quin, God rest him, got six months for maiming ewes, and he a great warrant to tell stories of holy Ireland till he'd have the old women shedding down tears about their feet. (act 1, p. 59)

Hitting a policeman hard enough to knock his eye out, "maiming" ewes, and telling great stories are odd heroic traits. When Christy first tells of killing his Da, Pegeen responds, "Is it killed your father?" and a little later, "And you shot him dead?" (act 1, p. 73). Then, with the same detached curiosity, she wonders if he hung him as Jimmy Farrell hung his dog "screeching and wriggling three hours at the butt of a string" (act 1, p. 73). Her thoughts turn readily to blood and violence, and she is so attracted to excitement that she urges Michael James to hire this young murderer to protect her that night from harvest boys, tinkers, and soldiers of the militia while he is away.

These and other inconsistencies, not the least of which is making a hero of a man who killed his father because "he was getting old and crusty" (act 1, p. 73), are felt rather strongly at the beginning of the play. However, sheer accumulation of action tends to distance them. We never quite forget the underlying violence, but Synge transforms Pegeen from the blunt, domineering mistress of the pub to the more likable young woman in love. And Christy's development from shy, frightened, closemouthed fugitive to active, self-confident hero fastens our attention on him and his efforts to win her.

The first appearance of Mahon near the end of act 2 introduces a threat to this development, and we are relieved when the Widow Quin sends the old man off on a wild goose chase. Yet Mahon also removes an impediment to our admiration for Christy; we know now that he is not a killer. In addition Mahon destroys the whole false basis of hero worship, leaving the way clear for genuine admiration for Christy's accomplishments. At the beginning of act 3, however, Mahon returns, threatening to undo Christy's success. While Philly and Jimmy excitedly report Christy's athletic feats on the strand below, the Widow Quin convinces Mahon he has gone insane and should leave.

Thus Christy is saved once again, entering in jockey's silks to the adulation of all. That is, Synge uses the device of the near escape of melodrama to heighten our involvement. It works. More importantly for the ending, it displaces our attention, shifting it away from the potential violence of the villagers. With Mahon out of the way and Christy's triumphant entry, all on stage is happiness and good feeling. This is followed by a lyrical love scene between Christy and Pegeen, a comic turning away of Shawn, and the blessings of Michael James on the marrige to come. Then there is the *third* appearance of Mahon, and, Christy's happiness apparently demolished, Synge completes his lead-in by having Christy "kill" him off stage. We have been snared into sympathy by love blocked, innocence defeated, and happiness thwarted— old formulae, but effective ones.

Synge's deceit is skillful, and he is no more duplicitous than playwrights ever have been. Rather, the final turn on our expectations—Mahon's fourth and last appearance when Christy is about to be hauled away for his murder—merely expresses in a moment the comic/serious view of existence Synge had had all along.[4] This double-edged perception is evident elsewhere in his work, for instance in *The Well of the Saints*, drawn from a fifteenth-century French farce. Or the comically serious, seriously comic could be particularly noticeable in the Irish sensibility. Yeats saw Synge's "grotesque plays with their lyrical beauty, their violent laughter," *Playboy* most of all, as "holding so much of the mind of Ireland."[5] If so, this cast of mind is reflected in the wake. Michael James sees no contradiction when he says that as Kate Cassidy's bones were sunk in her narrow grave there were "five men, aye and six men, stretched out retching speechless on the holy stones" (act 3, p. 151).

But, in fact, in a rather more complex way the quite English Shakespeare shows the same quality of mind, and not just in "problem comedies" such as *Much Ado About Nothing*. Like Synge, Shakespeare uses theater's capacities for perceptual play, fusing the comic and serious not so much by thematic connections as by manipulating audience awareness, or, in other words, by theatrical scam. I am thinking of the ending of *Henry IV, Part 1* and the supposed death of Falstaff in battle, one of Shakespeare's most audacious gags. Theatrically it is kin to Synge's lulling us into false expectations, but the comic element of *Part 1* is more overtly hilarious than the charming idiocies of the villagers of Mayo, and the serious matter of the chronicle involves dynasties and a nation. Yet the same principle holds: the vision of the playwright is embodied in a script and is fully known to us only through our experiencing the play in performance. Then what is one to make of Falstaff's faking death, rising, and claiming the body of Hotspur as his own victory? What is this grotesque clownery *doing* at the high point of battle, the culminate moment of the serious issues of the chronicle play? The implication is that not only was Shakespeare's conception of the reign of Henry IV ambivalent, as scholars repeatedly remind us,[6] so was his conception of man.

This, of course, is viewing *Part 1* from the perspective of comedy and play rather than that of history, political theory, and the like which have dominated critical commentary. Perhaps because of the prevailing emphasis on the serious elements of *1 Henry IV* there is to this day a problem with the work's "unity," candidly summarized by Robert Ornstein when he wrote that it is easier to appreciate Falstaff than to "explain how the comic scenes join with the 'serious action' of the play to make up a larger artistic whole. When we see a fine performance of *Part 1*, we have no doubt of the unity of its plot and its conception; when we try to analyze this unity, it proves ineffable."[7]

The problem of unity has been addressed in various ways, e.g., by seeing *Part 1* as "metadrama" and by rejecting the idea of the mimesis and form on which "unity" rests. James L. Calderwood sets up an opposition between mimesis and artifice, the first being of the order of historical fiction, the second of the order of liberated artifice embodied in Falstaff, while Prince Hal exists in both kinds of dramatic experience.[8] Calderwood was to influence Edward Pechter, who finds the ending of *1 Henry IV* irresolute, the play both pleasurable and a thwarting of our anticipations.[9] Elizabeth Freund attacks mimesis and form another way: the chronicle play shows "strategies of inconclusiveness" as its dramatic structure, and is essentially rhetorical in nature, hence inconclusive and open-ended.[10] While the explanation fits critics' recognition of Shakespeare's ambivalence regarding the reign of Henry IV, it does not respond to Ornstein's observation that we *feel* the unity of the play in performance.

One difficulty is "unity" and the notion of the "organic text" that underlies it. Let us rephrase the question, then: How do the two strands of action—serious dynastic struggle and clowning around at Gad's Hill and the Boar's Head—fit one another theatrically? That they connect thematically has been shown in article, book, and preface, most recently by David Bevington.[11] What Ornstein implies is that there is a phenomenal, experiental compatibility, a deep "fit" that is difficult to explain. No wonder. The play's comic elements are not easily articulated, and quite on its own its treatment of history is clouded with issues.

These issues stem from Henry's gaining power outside the rules of succession; his rise was a break in the royal Plantaganet line. Shakespeare had examined the situation in his own *Richard II*, and his audience knew the debate well: Can a crown be legitimate if it is taken by force? Was England ready for a Machiavellian justification of rule by power alone? (With Queen Elizabeth aging and no clear succession in sight, the question was pertinent in 1597–98.) For although Richard II was a weak, frivolous king, he did name an heir-designate. The designation was ignored. Bolingbroke, later Henry IV, was brought back from exile to lead the forces of the nobles, chiefly of Northumberland, or the House of Percy. So he did, to victory. Only, what was to be done with the emprisoned Richard? That was resolved by overly eager courtiers (or so it is presented in *Richard II*), and apparently Henry's hands were left untainted.

They could not be, of course. Henry's reign was one long struggle for legitimacy. As *1 Henry IV* opens he plans to atone, or to make a public show of piety, by a crusade to the Holy Land. That plan is interrupted by renewed battles with the Scots and with the Welsh under Glendower. Meanwhile, his earlier supporters, the Percys, now feel slighted. Harry Percy ("Hotspur") has captured many noble Scots, worth considerable ransom, and refuses to give them up to Henry. The dispute grows into rebellion. Led by Hotspur the forces of Northumberland are joined with those of Glendower to the west, Douglas the Scot to the north, and others, and just as importantly by Mortimer, the heir-designate proclaimed by Richard.

The major action of *1 Henry IV* concerns the rebels' growth in power and the King's response to it, leading up to his victory at the Battle of Shrewsbury. A key factor in that outcome is the emergence of his scapegrace son, Hal, from the taverns of Eastcheap to become the true Prince of Wales (and, later, the great Henry V). The same age, Hotspur and Hal represent two views of honor: Hotspur the chivalric code of medieval times, Hal a more pragmatic, political, "modern" outlook. Well and good, except that with Hal Shakespeare includes a strand of comedy dominated by the fat, broken-down knight Falstaff. The later scenes in which he appears—from the one outside Coventry with his ragged troop of conscripts to his presence in battle and soliloquies on the hollowness of honor—make perfect thematic sense. It is the comic element of the first two acts that does not seem to fit the overall pattern of the chronicle play, and who can admit that Shakespeare's finest comic scenes may be superfluous?

Yet in one sense they are. They insist upon legitimacy of an order of experience that runs counter to the whole tenor of the chronicle play. It is usually said that the clowning of the Gadshill robbery (2.2) and the first Boar's Head Tavern scene (2.4) contribute to the theme of the Prodigal Son returned, the education of the prince, and the fulfillment of Hal's "I know you all, and will awhile uphold / The unyoked humour of your idleness" (1.2. 183f).[12] Yet the first two acts are dominated by the liveliness and excitement of play as comedy. Shakespeare gives his early comic scenes a phenomenological heft disproportionate to their function. Part of it comes from sheer scale. The famous Boar's Head Tavern scene is twice as long as the important earlier one in the council (1.3) where rebellion is plotted. Had the line ratios been reversed, however, and more weight given politics, the first Boar's Head Tavern scene might still rank among Shakespeare's most dynamic, compelling moments of theater.

Why is that? The relationship between the serious and comic enters again: they not only play off, they reinforce and intensify each other. Falstaff's escapades as would-be thief and wounded defender of manhood would be the less hilarious were there no grim affairs of state to serve as backdrop. Conversely, the pointless clowning of the first Boar's head scene serves as a frivolous preface to the somber meeting between Hal and his father (3.2), in which Hal pledges to reform and 1 Henry IV turns—slowly, with transition—to the "real" world of dynastic struggle. But while it is there, the loony play of Gadshill and Boar's Head is a counterexperience (not a counterstatement) that asserts the ontological authenticity of play itself. And that, apparently, is why the issue of comedy's place in 1 Henry IV remains up in the air.

The two major comic scenes of acts 1 and 2 are one extended gag, chiefly at Falstaff's expense. Initiated by Poins, the jest will be to stage a robbery, steal the loot from Falstaff to return to its owners, and then listen to the incomparable lies the fat knight will tell when all gather at the Boar's Head. The scenes display the popular image of Prince Hal as "madcap," a tavern roisterer, but otherwise they do little for the overall development of the chronicle. Seen another way, however, they present a world that is nonserious, nonobligatory, and flippant, existing only in the present without regard to some end beyond exercise of its own creative energy. What counts in this world is who wins the games being played, not whether the games themselves are significant in some other order of experience.

In the Gadshill robbery (2.2) Falstaff is the major loser. Huffing and brawling about, cursing whomever took his horse, he is one of the loudest sneakthieves on record. Yet the old knight's corpulence and general ineptitude signal only one kind of game. There is wit combat between Hal and Falstaff, and in that, at least, Falstaff is the winner. When the Prince objects to helping Falstaff onto his horse, the knight replies,

> Hang thyself in thine own heir-apparent garters! If I be ta'en, I'll peach for this. An I have not ballads made on you all and sung to filthy tunes, let a cup of sack be my poison: when a jest is so forward, and afoot too! I hate it. (2.2.41–44)

Given the nature of the contest, to see who can best the other in rich, pungent insult, Falstaff is the better player. Yet he is also the main target of ridicule, genial though it is.

That he is made fool of when Hal and Poins steal his loot only means that he has lost a skirmish in the larger battle of wits between Hal and himself. For the moment it is important that he loses. That is an essential condition for the great action to follow. Furthermore, before the Boar's Head Shakespeare inserts a scene in which Hotspur reads a letter from a lord who declines to engage in rebellion. That over, the rest of the scene is given to a charming domestic interlude in which Lady Percy and Hotspur tease one another, playing man and wife games that end in confirmation of their love. This interlude, too, is an essential element in the play at the Boar's Head. Shakespeare gives considerable care to preparing us for one of the great comic moments of theater.

The greatness of the first tavern scene, 2.4, comes from its intensity as play. Nowhere else in Shakespeare are so many kinds of play and games, so many flips on expectation, or so much foolery compacted into some twenty minutes of performance. And few of Shakespeare's scenes are so carefully crafted. Act 2 scene 4 is made up of the "prologue" of Hal and Poins awaiting Falstaff's return, the consummation of the jest of the robbery, the "play extempore" in which Hal and Falstaff practice for the upcoming meeting between Prince and King, and a final gag at the fat knight's expense as the "real" world intrudes on merriment. Each element involves different kinds of play, games within games; undercurrents of ridicule move in multiple directions, often colliding; gags fragment, implications spin off.

The scene opens with Hal in high spirits as he awaits Falstaff. Two preceding episodes generate the dynamics of this "prologue," Falstaff's fleeing at Gadshill, and Hotspur and Lady Percy joking with one another. The first puts Hal in a superior position comically; he holds all the cards and will pounce on the fat knight when he arrives. The second is important because it helps establish the level of play. The Prince displays his cleverness by baiting the wine drawer, Francis, and by mimicking the Percys. The humor is coarse. Having Francis scurry between a customer, Poins, in the next room and the Prince is sure-fire slapstick, and shows Hal's meager wit to advantage. Not so with Hal's parody of the Percys: "He that kills me some six or seven dozen of Scots at a breakfast, washes his hands, and says to his wife, 'Fie upon this quiet life, I want work,' and her reply, 'O my sweet Harry,' says she, 'how many hast thou killed today?'" (2.4.100–4). It degrades the charming man and wife episode we have just seen, and makes Hal look juvenile.

"Prologue" done, Hal's schoolboy wit established, the main point of 2.4 begins with Falstaff's entrance. The knight is in a foul mood. A plague of all cowards, Falstaff blusters, unable to bring himself, quite, to call the Prince one. When he does, and includes Poins, the latter threatens to stab him. Falstaff retreats, as usual, into bravado. Then follow the "incomparable lies" Poins had anticipated: Falstaff gives a rousing account of what happened to the booty. A hundred villains came to rob them, no a dozen, or sixteen, fifty at least, but Falstaff peppered two, no four, and these become nine, then eleven. Finally three knaves in Kendal green came at him, and—but Hal interrupts: how could you see them in Kendal green when it was pitch black?

Falstaff eludes the trap by, "What, upon compulsion? 'Zounds, an I were at the strappado, or all the racks in the world, I would not tell you upon compulsion" (2.4.229–31). But the noose tightens. Hal says he can no longer brook these lies and launches into one of his catalogues of insults. Falstaff is a sanguine coward, a bed-presser, a huge hill of flesh, to which he responds, hoping to divert the Prince, "'Sblood you starveling, you eel-skin, you dried neat's tongue, you bull's pizzle, you stockfish!" (2.4.237–38). Although it works for us as an almost poetic conjuring up of unsavory images, the diversion does not succeed with Hal.

In spite of Falstaff's nimble wit and fund of metaphor, he is a comic loser. His flaw is that he does not know what happened at the robbery. Hal tells a true account, ending with, "What trick, what device, what starting-hole, canst thou now find out to hide thee from this open and apparent shame?" (2.4.254–56). Poins seconds it with, "What trick hast thou now?" Falstaff appears to have been trapped, fatally. Without pause he counters,

> By the Lord, I knew ye as well as he that made ye. Why, hear you, my masters, was it for me to kill the heir apparent? Should I turn upon the true prince? Why, thou knowest I am as valiant as Hercules, but beware instinct. The lion will not touch the true prince. Instinct is a great matter. I was now a coward on instinct. (2.4.258–63)

Hal is defeated, utterly. (He does not take the loss with good grace and mentions running, cowardice, and instinct some six times later in the scene.) Without our being aware of it, we have gone down as well. Did we not know the truth? Were we not waiting with anticipatory glee for Falstaff to be ridiculed unmercifully? Yet we are delighted with the knight's sheer power of invention, revel in the victory of the underdog, and admire the irrefutable, "I knew you all along." We approve, too, when Falstaff generously refuses to gloat and, instead, suggests a "play extempore."

While it may seem excessive to point out each twist and flip of comic play as Falstaff evades certain failure, it is worth the effort to catch the full flavor of the first Boar's Head scene. The turn on a turn, the play with play itself compacted into Flastaff's few lines, is theatrically and comically powerful. As well it should be: We have been waiting for this moment since Poins's announcement of the elaborate jest in 1.2. Still, what does it have to do with anything? Thematically speaking, very little. If comedy to this point were cut, the history of 1 Henry IV would have survived as strongly. One brief scene of Hal at the tavern would have established that he is the madcap prince later to reform. Similarly, the play extempore that follows exceeds the requirements of its contribution to the chronicle.[13] True, it bounces off serious matters. Just after Falstaff's argument on instinct, Shakespeare interjects news of rebellion, and we are reminded that Hal must soon meet his royal father. As ever, seriousness intensifies the comic moment, and the reverse. But overall there is indulgence in play largely for its own sake.

The mock meeting between play "prince" and play "king" is in two parts: Falstaff playing Henry and Hal playing himself, and then a reversal of roles, with Hal playing his father, Falstaff the prince. Both parts have an undercurrent of deadly serious issues. How is Hal to explain his profligacies to his sire? Has Falstaff been "an abominable misleader of youth," or is he to be a scapegoat for Hal's own recklessness? And, most seriously from the standpoint of play, what is to become of the old knight if his patron in foolery reforms? Is there no place in the scheme of things for jest and merriment? Practical solutions are all but determined: Hal cannot continue his tavern brawling. Beneath his wit and flippancy thuds the heart of the true Prince, as Falstaff well knows. These considerations give poignancy to the old knight's efforts to amuse, and by their presence make the flips and turns of comedy all the more playful.

Seen just as play, the impromptu "practice session" operates by its own dynamic: Who is winning, who losing in the wit contest between Hal and Falstaff? The Hostess gives the main criterion, "O Jesu, this is excellent sport, i'faith!" (2.4.376), and Falstaff reminds us of the game when he says to Hal, now assuming the part of King, "Nay, I'll tickle ye for a young prince, i'faith" (2.4.427–28). And indeed he does. As excellent sport Falstaff's performance is superb, ranging from parody to non sequitur, one-liners to gag sequences, puns to dislocations of style.

Falstaff opens with a delightful spoof in King Cambyses's vein, "For God's sake, lords, convey my tristful queen, / For tears do stop the floodgates of her eyes" (2.4.3.80–81). (Flow is stopped by floodgates, not the reverse and massive, soggy planks are not the most flattering metaphors for eyelids). He continues as the King,

Harry, I do not only marvel where thou spendest thy time, but also how thou art accompanied; for though the camomile, the more it is trodden on, the faster it grows, yet youth, the more it is wasted, the sooner it wears. That thou art my son I have partly thy mother's word, partly my own opinion, but chiefly a villainous trick of thine eye and a foolish hanging of thy nether lip that doth warrant me. (2.4.384–92)

The most striking play is use of Lylian euphuistic style, which sets up an expected parallel and contrast between trodden camomile and youth, quickly flattened in the obvious "the more it is wasted, the sooner it wears." Then there is bloated, formal phrasing, admirably conveying the mind of a self-important, empty-headed monarch. Lastly, there is the joke about Hal's legitimacy.

The play generated out of that one gag alone is remarkable. By using the structure of the periodic sentence—predication interrupted by a string of secondary grammatical elements—Falstaff again displays the convoluted thinking of the King, while leaving the two insulting phrases, "partly thy mother's word, partly my own opinion," dangling in a syntactical vacuum until the sentence's closure. The play on meaning is delightful, e.g., "thy mother's word," "a villanous trick of thine eye and a foolish hanging of thy nether lip." Implications fly at two targets, Prince Hal's being a bastard and the King's being a cuckold (three, if we include the Queen), even as they insult both son and father by selecting their distinguishing features, villainous, shifty eyes and the hanging lower lip of the village idiot.

Verbal play is enhanced by theatrical context. Since all of this is a mock dramatization, Hal must observe the unspoken rules of the game or risk being a spoilsport; he must receive ridicule and be silent, or come back with a rejoinder that will best Falstaff's gags. He can not top Falstaff, and the knight goes on with his double game of mockery and insult while adding the king's praise of a certain "virtuous man" seen in his son's company, a "goodly portly man, i'faith, and a corpulent; of a cheerful look, a pleasing eye and a most noble carriage" (2.4.407–08).

It is too much for Hal, and he switches roles to become the "king." As a parodist Hal is apt enough, but the result is scarcely better than his earlier sneering at Hotspur and Lady Percy. The best he manages is to heap epithets on Falstaff—"that bolting-hutch of beastliness, that swollen parcel of dropsies, that huge bombard of sack, that stuffed cloak-bag of guts," and so on (2.4.431–42). Although Falstaff sidesteps with "Whom means your grace?" he knows Hal's making fun, as with Francis earlier, is not play at all, but, rather, a power game he must win. Hence Flastaff gives his famous defense of merriment and his appeal not to banish sweet, kind, true, and valiant Jack Falstaff: "Banish plump Jack, and banish all the world" (2.4.461–62). To which Hal responds flatly, "I do, I will."

Metaphorically the world Hal will banish *is* that of innocent play, nonsense, joy, and merrymaking for their own sakes. Shakespeare will do the same. After 2.4 come two lengthy scenes concerning the rebels' plans to divide the kingdom and Hal's meeting with King Henry. We see Falstaff again at the Boar's Head. There will be play between the old knight and Bardolf, and more delightfully with the Hostess, but all in all there is a falling off of comic effect. Falstaff's opening words of 3.3 convey the dampened mood: "Bardolph, am I not fallen away vilely since this last action? Do I not bate? Do I not dwindle?" Falstaff is given a "charge of foot," and the scene ends in a flurry of messages and meeting times, in urgent preparations for battle.

From this point on the comic element of 1 *Henry IV* is appropriately subordinated to theme and events of the chronicle, and changed in its nature. What had been delightful horseplay at Gadshill and the Boar's Head now has a dark edge. Falstaff is funny enough in 4.2 when we see him outside Coventry. He leads his pitiful troop, bare leavings of beggars and prisoners bought cheaply so he can pocket most of the crown's impressment monies. Falstaff as war profiteer does not surprise us, but when Hal says he never did see such pitiful rascals, the knight counters, "Good enough to toss; food for powder . . . mortal men, mortal men" (4.2.62–64). The cold unconcern jolts us, and it emerges again in Falstaff's last words, "To the latter end of a fray and the beginning of a feast / Fits a dull fighter and a keen guest." Usually taken to be a jovial reply, the lines can be read another way. The latter end of a fray is the beginning of a feast for scavengers, the poor and the petty thieves who stripped corpses of valuables. No duller fighter than Falstaff, no keener guest.

Grotesque as the image is, it fits what we next see of the old knight. He appears as an appendage to nobility gathered at the king's camp near Shrewsbury (5.1), an oddly discordant figure in ill-fitting battle gear and a shield far too small to protect his bulk. He says little, yet the scene ends with his great soliloquy on honor. Utter pragmatist, or existentialist, he sees Honour as a word, air, a heraldic symbol on a burial pall. It is to be a countertheme running through the battle scenes, and not just when Falstaff sees the body of Sir Walter Blunt—"There's honour for you" (5.3.32). "Honour" is the focus in the culminating hand-to-hand combat between Hotspur and Hal in 5.4.

Meanwhile, what ever happened to the bumptious, pointless play of acts 1 and 2? For an audience the glow of play and comedy has receded from consciousness, yet emotionally it *has* been felt. There are echoes of the Boar's Head in slapstick such as Hal's asking for Falstaff's sword, only to find in the holster a bottle of sack (5.3.48–54). But this seems woefully out of place in the deadly serious context, as does the knight's cheering when the prince fights Hotspur: "Well said, Hal! To it, Hal! Nay, you shall find no boy's play here, I can tell you" (5.4.74–75). This delightful enthusiasm from the sidelines sets us up for the sudden action to follow: the renowned Douglas enters and exchanges blows with Falstaff. The old knight falls. Rightly staged, the "death" of Falstaff is a gripping, poignant moment for an audience. All that joy and wit, gone! But we are not allowed to sort out our feelings. At the next instant Hal deals a fatal blow to Hotspur.

Reading *1 Henry IV* we know Falstaff is only faking, but theatrical effect assures that in performance we assume he is dead. As usual, the gag is on us as well as Hal. It is heightened by Hal's tender obsequies, first over the body of Hotspur, and second over the lifeless mound of Falstaff. Befittingly, the prince's feelings are balanced off with moral perspective: "O, I should have a heavy miss of thee / If I were much in love with vanity" (5.4.104–5). Yet his mild joking expresses touching remembrance of their past friendship. Hal even goes so far as to see Falstaff is embowelled— a mark of respect. We are deeply moved.

With Hal's exit comes one of Shakespeare's most audacious jokes on his audience. Falstaff rises with "Embowelled!" and the house comes down. The very spirit of the Boar's Head is resurrected. He gives his twisted reasons for "counterfeiting" and utters his famous "the better part of valour is discretion" (somewhat haltingly in performance; the audience's laughter is still subsiding) then reflects that if he was playacting, could not the fearful Hotspur be too? Up to that moment, that precise point, our response is a rich mixture of joy and vindication. The happiness of seeing the old knight palpably before us is reinforced by part of us having felt, all along, that there is a hollowness to war, a futility and destructiveness. All very well for Hotspur to proclaim, "Doomsday is near; die all, die merrily" (4.1.136) or Hal to say casually, "Why, thou owest God a death" (5.1.126); most of us would side with Falstaff's "Give me life," especially since the fat knight stands by Hotspur's corpse.

This bubbling up of joyful affirmation, of life and play, lasts only minutes, however. Shakespeare wrenches it, and us, by having Falstaff make sure that Harry Percy is not counterfeiting: "Yea, and I'll swear I killed him. . . . Nothing confutes me but eyes, and nobody sees me. Therefore, sirrah [*stabbing him*], with a new wound in your thigh, you come along with me. [*Takes up Hotspur on his back*]" (5.4.123–26). Words are offensive enough; the actual stabbing and taking up of the body to dangle upside down off Falstaff's shoulders are grotesque. For we have not forgotten Hotspur's brave death, his final moving lines, and Hal's recognition of his great spirit. His body is now so much meat for scavenging.

Shakespeare returns us to "happy" comedy by having Falstaff throw the body down before the amazed Hal and Prince John: there; "if your father will do me any honour, so; if not, let him kill the next Percy himself" (5.4.137–38). "Honour" in Falstaff's vocabulary is payment; he looks to be a duke or earl. Then follows the knight's account of how he and Hotspur fought a long hour by Shrewsbury clock (rather difficult to see from the battlefield), accompanied by much bluster and threat to any who will deny the truth. Theatrically his words echo the "incomparable lies" of the Boar's Head. Hal acquiesces, will even gild his old friend's ploy with the "happiest terms I have." Whether it is from relief at seeing the knight alive or because he has better things to do as a retreat is sounded, we do not know, nor do we care. Falstaff's wit and cleverness have carried the day, and in comedy that is what counts. Or have they, quite? Not in the same way Falstaff wheedled his way out of traps and gave his virtuoso performance in the "play extempore" of 2.4. In the Boar's Head politics and rebellion were reported from the "outside," whereas the moving death of Hotspur remains with us, as his body does on stage. Shakespeare's theatrical scam, his magnificent gag of the "death" of Falstaff, has brought the Boar's Head to life again, leaving us feeling both joyous and sad, numbed with the complexity of our own response.

So, Shakespeare provides no easy way out. (The final scene of *1 Henry IV* is a mopping up operation, a ceremonial "epilogue.") What he gives us is a yoking of two strands of experience that first seemed wholly incompatible, comedy and history. To cite Ornstein again, theatrically we *feel* the deep unity and resolution of the ending, but cannot explain it. That is because critics have tended to view the chronicle play from the standpoint of the serious, and, in general, have slighted its phenomenological nature as theater.[14] Seen from the perspective of comedy, and emphasizing the effect of action on stage, the "unity" of *1 Henry IV* seems less problematic.

One might even say, from the vantage point of audience response, there is little mystery in how Falstaff's grotesque but hilarious scavenging the corpse of Hotspur caps off the major action. The fight to the death between Hal and Hotspur *is* the actional and thematic high point of the chronicle, and its most intense theatrical moment as well. All is drawn into the single combat: the theme of honor, the matter of the education and reform of the prince, questions of the right basis of rule, and so on. Drawn in too is the diminished Falstaff of acts 4 and 5, a voice from the sidelines reminding us of the larger human context in which this dynastic struggle is to be placed. So when Shakespeare takes the thematically dense, exciting fight between the two young men and turns it into the lead-in of a joke, no matter how theatrically elegant that joke is, one can conclude that his outlook is divided. He celebrates the joy of play but does not ignore its other, darker side. Nor do we. While we applaud Falstaff's wit, how can we not feel, too, the pitilessness of war, and with it, something of the meaninglessness and chaos of existence?

Does that mean Shakespeare was an existentialist? If one emphasizes the grotesque absurdity of the joke played on us, perhaps so. (No more grotesque than Falstaff himself, however; with his kin Iago he is a theatrical descendant of the Vice, or Devil.[15]) But this chaotic side of existence would have been known as Chance, an aspect of Fortuna. Furthermore, Falstaff's hilarious, dark resurrection occurs in an ambience of victory, an overall mood of affirmation and rousing patriotism. Although we are not political theorists, we feel the defeat of the rebels as a victory for a "modern" order brought out of the chaos of contending feudal lords, out of the petty strife exemplified in squabbles and ego contests of the early scene in council, 1.3. The triumph of Hal and the Lancastrian cause at Shrewsbury endorses the virtù of the Machiavellian prince: power belongs to him who seizes it, for the good of the state, of course.[16] Taking place as it does in this buoyant emotional context, Falstaff's triumph celebrates a similar movement, out of the chaos of battle and threat of death and toward life, through the creative power of play of the imagination.

Falstaff is an opportunist, as are Hal and his father, but outshining that is his supremely nimble wit. What does one do, "waking" beside the corpse of the fearsome Percy if one is an utter coward? The reasonable thing would be to run. But Falstaff's thought, flipping through puns on "counterfeit," toying with possibilities as the creative mind must, lights upon another counterfeit, the audacious lie. Having played, his mind turns to strategy. No one sees him; who can confute him? It is another version of the game Hal was playing in his "I know you all" speech of 1.2., only it has greater reach and imagination, the spontaneity of the creative act. (If this makes Falstaff, metaphorically at least, a Nietzschean Overman transcending the meaningless play of existence by the power of the creative intellect, why not? He seems to have been called everything else.) And Shakespeare has Falstaff win. As Shakespeare endorses the energy and determination of the prince, so he endorses the power and trickery of the creative mind at play. If one wants to reduce the ending of *1 Henry IV* to thematic closure, that may be the solution.

However, much of the "message" of the ending, as of all theater, is in the phenomenological impact of what occurs on stage, and one might well be skeptical of attempts to reduce that experience to thematic statement. Whether or not it was so received, my purpose in dwelling on the first Boar's Head tavern scene at such length and in such detail was to capture, insofar as possible, something of the excitement of an intensely comic moment. For without a full sense, or sensation, of the flippancies, turns, and play within games that happen there, phenomenally speaking the problem of "unity" in *1 Henry IV* may be unresolvable.

The problem is essentially one of audience response, of emotional undercurrents, or in this case the glow of enjoyment, the rumble of laughter at Falstaff's lies, evasions, and parodies—a full-bodied experience that seems to dissipate gradually as serious matters come to command our attention in the latter part of *1 Henry IV*. But the glow of comic excitement does not go away; it remains with us even as we watch Falstaff in his new role as war profiteer, commentator on "Honour," and scavenger. Seen this way, the "unity" of *1 Henry IV* comes mainly from Shakespeare's bringing that intensely comic moment back into the action before us—with the mixed results suggested above, but embodied once again in the resurrected Falstaff of the Boar's Head. That, far more than the numerous thematic connections between comedy and history noted by commentators, contributes to the effect Ornstein observed: during a good performance we have no doubt of the drama's unity of plot and conception.

One returns, then, to the statement made much earlier that play is what comedy *is* and what it *does:* play in its double sided, unstable nature as a principle of existence and as the essential sleight-of-hand of comic expression. I am not suggesting artists literally think of play in its philosophic, existential sense, or "see" it, or have it in mind at all. The concept is one way *we* can grasp the phenomenon of comedy as well as its place as an element in serious drama, art, and literature. The joining of serious and comic elements in a work seems to be a problem only insofar as we think of them as irreconcilable modes of being, compartmentalized, so to speak, by our own habits of mind. To judge from *1 Henry IV*, Shakespeare's mind was less fettered in this regard, as was Synge's when he conceived *Playboy*, or, certainly, Beckett's when he created *Waiting for Godot*.

Similarly, though we tend to associate certain games, strategies, and duplicities with comedy by reason of frequency of use, as was pointed out earlier, few if any configurations of effect are inherently comic. When the artist so chooses, he or she can use a technique usually eliciting an uncomic response as a means of diverting attention, or refocusing interest, or, in other words, as sleight-of-hand. The effect may be local: a joke, a scene making up a gag sequence, a sudden turn in a minor action. But when jokes are as extensive as those played by Shakespeare and Synge, they involve our whole experience of the play up to the point of the turn or punch line, including some quite serious matters. Further, their jokes occur in the grim contexts of death on the battlefield, the villagers' latent viciousness and lust for excitement directed toward Christy. How grimly comic or comically grim the resulting "message" is depends upon the playwright's double sided perception and emotional ambivalence. The shades of these are infinite, as are our own mixed responses, but whatever they may entail, they are not determined by certain techniques or devices, only by how they are used.

All that being so, configurations of effect—seriously comic, comically serious—still convey part of the overall "message" of our experience. In other words, perceptual play still signifies, and powerfully. This is most obvious in Beckett's assault on his audience in *Waiting for Godot*. Unnerving though it is, the "meaning" of the work is primarily in its play with our habitual attitudes toward ourselves and the stage. Like the *farceur*, Beckett overturns our phenomenal world, and more specifically our expectations that theater will entertain us. In a less obvious way Shakespeare and Synge are doing a similar thing; it is a question only of how much perceptual play is involved. Whether by choice or convention, Shakespeare and Synge utilize our expected responses as lead-ins. The overall point to be made is that play with our perception may be selective or inclusive, but in any case conveys a phenomenal "message," just as any other configuration in theater does. This, too, runs counter to our accustomed attitude, that juxtaposition, joke structures, and the like (if we are aware of them at all) have no particular significance. They do, and our awareness of them is a virtual necessity if one wants to "read" comedy in all of its varieties of expression.

7

Humor/Comedy, Television

From *Waiting for Godot* to *I Love Lucy* and *Monty Python* is a distance, I must confess, but it is time to get back to the mainstream of comedy and, in any event, the same concepts apply to lowlier art forms as to high drama. Preceding discussions emphasized theater, and within it Menandrine New Comedy. Neither has been treated adequately, nor has the novel. (Where are Aristophanes, Plautus, Cervantes, Molière, Goldoni, Fielding, Marivaux, and so on, but then where are radio, cabaret performance, and film animation?) The aim is to establish basic operations of comedy, not to give an encyclopedic account. The most that can be done is to address a few significant problems. For instance, how far should we reach into the fuzzy territory between comedy and humor? What constitutes a "work"? And, can the concepts presented here be expanded to modes of aesthetic expression other than "legitimate" theater, literature, and the visual arts? Television provides some interesting answers.

Humor was touched upon earlier. It was pointed out that jokes can be little works of art; the stand-up comic's routine or "bit" is analogous to the short story. But folk humor—oral transmission and polishing of a joke—is a communal activity lacking both aesthetic intent and the individual outlook of the artist. From the standpoint of reception, anonymity makes no more difference than it does with Chinese jade or classical amphorae. Intention is another thing; aesthetically speaking, it is usually considered a necessary precondition of art.[1] In any event, my determining a "work" to be of a certain size and scope was arbitrary, a matter of custom and methodological convenience.[2] So was my separation of humor from comedy. It is time to look at both determinations more closely.

Humor and comedy overlap, and nowhere more interestingly than in television. "Meaning" generated out of interaction between serious and comic values applies, though with results that show the overall pattern of subcomedy. Seldom are audience val-

ues questioned or attacked. (Ratings are the life blood of the enterprise.) There are, however, shades and shades of acquiescence
to audience opinion, and moments of true exploration. Perceptual
play and use of the medium are more intriguing because they
involve concepts of artistry versus artifact. So far as comedy is
concerned television has two major genres, by way of the radio
serial the situation comedy, or sitcom, and the variety show
grown out of British music hall, American burlesque, and radio's
comedy hours. The single feature, made for television film is minor by comparison and is essentially a version of cinema.

The situation comedy is an offshoot of Menandrine comedy
adapted to, and partly determined by, conditions of electronic
communication.[3] It is humor with elements of narrative and dramatic form. (How strong these elements are varies from sitcom
to sitcom, season to season, and show to show within a season.)
The genre is unusual for a number of reasons. It is not bound in
time as the film is. It rests on a situation that is, producers hope,
infinitely extendable. Characters may grow somewhat over a season, or minutely over the span of a thematic unit, a loose cycle
of evenings' entertainment bound by narrative turn or shift in
subject matter.

The sitcom's thematic unit is hard to fix. Like cartoon strips,
e.g., *B.C.* or *Bloom County*, the situation comedy generates amorphous groupings of shows held together by a character's falling
in love, getting married, or changing jobs. In the static world of
the sitcom *something* is a happening, and it can be the focus of
shows to come. (It may even produce a spinoff from secondary
characters, as *All in the Family* spawned *Maude* and *The Jeffersons*
or as *The Mary Tyler Moore Show* launched *Rhoda*.) And, since this
thematic cluster evolves more by chance than by artistic design
(a minor character creates audience interest, new subject matter
catches the public's fancy) it cannot be considered a "work" com-
parable to the short story or novella.[4]

The difficulty is with our tendency to think of the work as a
bound, discrete entity. The very nature of the situation comedy
prevents that. Rather than reject it out of hand, though, one can
try to see the genre in its own terms. Like the well-made play of
Sardou, the sitcom has rigorous requirements to meet. Assuming
the situation originally conceived will provide dramatic inter-
change between characters, it must be open-ended. It should have
enough amplitude to accommodate an occasional new character
and enough flexibility to integrate into its vague "story line" subject matter of unforeseen importance. Ever evolving yet the

same—*Fawlty Towers* again, no one growing older, an occasional new guest arriving—the sitcom maintains the same configuration of relationships among its characters, viewing subject matter from slightly different comic perspectives. Hence, though single episodes or a connected three or four shows appear to be the "tagmemic units" of the situation comedy, practically it has only one unit: its initial conception, its situation, and the premises incorporated into it.

However, this oddly static yet changing form *can* produce moments of great comic or humorous intensity. Single episodes can be artfully conceived, and if they never can have the complexity of, say, the first Boar's Head Tavern scene of *1 Henry IV*, that is because the genre precludes formal development, the careful preparation Shakespeare gives in the Gadshill robbery and the teasing between Hotspur and Lady Percy. Instead, the situation comedy hits upon a new subtheme and takes off on a group of episodes resembling a formal entity. In *All in the Family* (ca. 1971) Archie Bunker's neighbors sell their home. It is bought by a black family, whose son, Lionel, had been a secondary character for some time, a thorn in Archie's conservative, working-class mind. Thus begin episodes bound together by the theme of racial prejudice. Only, the boundary to this thematically unified group is not determined by narrative contours. The group is terminated by a new thematic cluster; Lionel and his family are relegated to minor roles. Meanwhile, there have been powerful and hilarious interchanges between Archie and his new neighbors.

So while any comparison one makes between the situation comedy and drama is unflattering to the genre, that may be because one is applying the wrong criteria. Overall, television comedy is more akin to cabaret performance than to the literary, visual, or filmic arts. Slightly delayed it may be, and technologically removed, but audience response is a shaping force in the sitcom. The genre is less a "form" than a socioaesthetic phenomenon. It is balanced between concerns of high production costs and artistic endeavor, but is ultimately dependent upon the vicissitudes of its audience's interests. Last week we learned that character X has developed a psychosis, or character Y has fallen in love, but that does not mean these "plot" elements are to be continued. Audience response, or sponsors' and networks' conception of it, determines. Where writer and director ignore public reaction in order to exercise their creative prerogative to lead and explore, they risk the program itself. For instance, by having the happily married Rhoda and Joe separate, and then divorce, writer and director caused ratings to plummet, the show to die (*Rhoda*, 1976).

The amorphous, open-ended, ever evolving, and formless quality of the situation comedy creates problems for aesthetic evaluation, no doubt, but quite in its own terms and considered a mixture of humor and comedy the genre can do interesting things with subject matter. (It does less interesting things with the medium, but more on that later.) Though one has to characterize the sitcom overall as subcomedy—usually reflecting, rarely attacking audience values—there are degrees of bending to the socioeconomic forces acting upon it. In the one-liners that season their episodes, and in the underlying currents of serious and comic values, writers and directors manage to explore some rather fine discriminations in current attitudes.

Though humor in the sitcom seems adventitious—a turn on meaning, a sneering reply, a gross exaggeration, a malopropism, all involving some topical subject—it tends to take on a pattern. Over the span of a season one-liners become a running skirmish poking fun at stereotypes and attitudes the series as a whole ridicules (the boss, the nosy mother-in-law, the snob, and so on). The danger is in allowing immediate humorous effect to overwhelm consistency of story line and of characters' motivations. That is, the situation comedy is not the variety show, and when statements serve primarily as lead-ins or punch lines rather than springing from character the net effect is to blur narrative and thematic content.

Usually, however, television comedy emphasizes narrative and dramatic situation and allocates wit, cleverness, and the like to a character whose views it advocates, or distributes comic advantage equally in order to explore an issue momentarily—much as in the Menandrine mode. Moral and social values most often determine who comes out on top. A frequent figure is the lovable fool whose idiocies we accept because he or she has good intentions. Lucille Ball's persona in the *I Love Lucy* series is a well-known example. Whether it is producing an eight-foot long loaf of bread that "rises" straight out of the oven to pin her against the sink ("Pioneer Women," 1952) or having a fight with a *paisana* in a grape vat and losing her part in a film ("Lucy's Italian Movie," 1956), Lucy's failures allowed men to laugh at her in confirmation of their prejudices and women to recognize in her the struggles of Everywoman with the complexities of day-to-day life. Whatever the losing situation, Lucy had a heart of gold, as did her husband, Ricky. They *did* have their squabbles and differences, however.

Some of the most interesting episodes of *I Love Lucy* explore fine points of conduct within the sane, middle-class outlook upheld in the series overall.[5] Male domination of the family is questioned but seldom undermined. In "The Black Wig" (1954) Ricky forbids Lucy to get a newfangled Italian haircut, that is, he oversteps his bounds as a husband. She borrows a wig from her hairdresser and, assured she looks a different person, tests Ricky's fidelity by flirting with him, thus overstepping *her* bounds as a wife. That she goes beyond allowable man and wife games is shown in her failure. Ricky is tipped off, plays the flirtation up, and leaves Lucy (and her co-conspirator, Ethel) rejected. A waiter tells the disguised Lucy and Ethel that Ricky and Fred have left the restaurant with a blonde and a redhead, so that the women are wretched *and* the butts of their own trick. Serious point made, the episode ends with Ricky and Fred revealing they had had the waiter lie. The happy ending erases any doubt about male superiority, but at least the episode explored the complexities of unspoken rules of conduct between man and wife.

Similarly, male and female roles are examined in "Job Switching" (1952), and with equally revealing results. Having bounced a check, Lucy is chided by Ricky: she would be more cautious about spending if *she* had to earn the family income. (Once again, Ricky comes down too hard, violating the unspoken protocols of marriage.) With Ethel's support Lucy proposes switching jobs for a week. She and Ethel will earn money outside, Ricky and Fred will take care of the house and cooking. Male egos confronted, Ricky and Fred agree to what they see as the easier task. Lucy and Ethel contact the Acme Employment Agency to enter the world of work. Thus Lucy's and Ricky's tampering with the "natural" order of things is put to the test.

Predictably, the plan fails. Ricky ruins rice and chicken, making a complete mess of the kitchen, while Fred bakes a seven layer cake collapsed to the thickness of a piece of toast. Lucy and Ethel take jobs in a candy factory, leading to the famous scene where they are positioned by a conveyor belt to wrap chocolates coming past. As the chocolates appear at greater speed Lucy has to put some in her mouth, then in her hat, finally in her bosom. To make matters worse, she and Ethel are watched over by a gruff supervisor. Disaster. When the women return home, exhausted, they find a note cautioning them not to go into the kitchen; it will be cleaned up. Ricky and Fred arrive, contrite, and from behind their backs pull out presents, two five pound boxes of chocolates. The women fall onto the couch, groaning.

As with most subcomedy, prevailing audience attitudes about male and female roles are upheld. Folly is equally distributed among men and women; both brag about how easy job switching will be. Yet our sympathies tend to side with Lucy and Ethel, simply because they face the more difficult, almost impossible task: a conveyor belt moving relentlessly, the overhanging threat of the gruff supervisor, the sense, overall, of woman or man against the machine. Furthermore, the men's making a mess of cooking is an old gag routine, though none the less effective for that, while the candy factory episode is freshly conceived, visually powerful, and exquisite in slapstick effect. (Each gag is topped by the next, so that the episode builds to a dense climax before blackout.) Our sympathies are more with Lucy in her failure than with Ricky in his. In other words, within the general demands of subcomedy there are moment of rich play and discrimination of attitudes—here, the wife's carelessness with money, the husband's treating her like a child.

Play with underlying values is more obvious in a sitcom like *All in the Family* (1971–78; based on the British *Till Death Do Us Part*). To this day the series is an exception to the general run of television comedies partly because of its powerful conception by Norman Lear, who not incidentally had considerable artistic control, and partly because of ambivalencies of public opinion in a time of profound social upheaval. The show was concerned with issues, tapping into just those things most argued about in workplaces, bars, and living rooms across the nation: equal rights for blacks, yes, but let's not go overboard; equal rights for women, too, but it will take time; a polack's a polack, a homosexual is a fairy, liberals are air-heads, or, conversely, blue collar workers are thickheaded rednecks, and so on.[6]

Dialectical in nature—Archie losing most of the time to his meathead son-in-law Mike or his "little girl" Gloria, but coming back, often, with folk wisdom that punctured their liberal attitudes—*All in the Family* could be read in a number of ways. Conservatives found their suspicions being at least aired if not vindicated; liberals found their convictions winning out. Most viewers in the vast audience, probably, found that the show was honest, raised issues, confronted both sides. For them the figure of Edith, Archie's "dingbat" wife, presented a stabilizing element: simple-minded she was, but a-political, and above all loving. In the tradition of the wise fool she embodied a primal common sense, a genuine concern, a way out of conflicting attitudes seeming to have no resolution. But that is another reason why *All in the*

Family is most unusual as a situation comedy: it is the fortuitous outcome of television's interaction with its audience in a time of turmoil.

As it happened—the years of the unpopular and divisive Vietnam War, of seismic social upheaval—the show reflected the national mood, one of deep ambivalence. Its doing so gave Norman Lear a great deal of control over his endeavors as an artist (ratings do not lie) and enabled the situation comedy to achieve one of its high moments of potential: rich, full comic inquiry in tune with the feelings of its audience, sufficient flexibility to incorporate timely events in its humor, and sometimes beautifully shaped episodes. Furthermore, the sitcom, like other at least quasi-literary or quasi-dramatic forms, is not received in a vacuum. Intertextuality applies to viewing television as well as to reading the novel. Like *The Honeymooners* before it (and *The Simpsons* afterwards), *All in the Family* brought its down-to-earth, hard-edged dialogue into a context of shows dominated by suburban, double garage, stereotyped families having little to do with actualities of American life. The show was a breath of fresh air.

Though these comments may seem to roam from concerns of comic practice and response, they acknowledge a major problem: the situation comedy is not a "work" in the usual sense, it is a socioaesthetic phenomenon, as inseparable from audience participation as the stand-up comedian's performance. Creativity in the genre requires mediation between aesthetic impulses and practical demands, a kind of high wire act in which writers and directors can easily fall to mindless entertainment. One could say that television comedy proves the Marxist thesis, that creative production is the result of socioeconomic forces, that it embodies an "ideology" whether the creator knows it or not.[7] Be that as it may, here it is enough to recognize the conditions in which this new form appears and to wonder how anything like an artifact can come out of such stifling circumstances. *All in the Family* transcends these and is not truly representative of the situation comedy.

The *M*A*S*H* series is a better example of the genre operating at a high level of performance within television's constraints.[8] *M*A*S*H*, too, was tied to and reflected the overall mood of the country, which was no less complex than that underlying *All in the Family*. Why, one wonders, was a situation comedy on the Korean War of the 1950s popular during the 1970s and 1980s, when social conditions had changed a great deal, when Vietnam had thrown doubt on militarism and the rights and wrongs of war? It would take a sociologist or psychologist to answer the question, but it appears that compared to the confusing cross sympathies of the Vietnamese conflict the Korean experience was the last "real" war, which is to say, one in which there was clear right and wrong. War itself had changed its nature, and, evidently, the nation was ready for a nostalgic look back at simpler issues. Removed in time, the Korean War was ready to be mythologized.

To understand this mythologizing, or at least the peculiar attraction of the $M*A*S*H$ series, one can go back to its source, the novel by Richard Hooker. Published in 1968, Hooker's $M*A*S*H$ was an immediate success, spawning a movie of the same title (1970, Robert Altman), and eventually the television series. But the novel has two fundamental messages that were not carried on: doctors are lordly, women are subservient, on the whole rather deficient except as they serve their lords. For instance, neither in film nor television is mention made of The Epileptic Whore;[9] the thrill, according to Hooker, is mounting a spasmodic body whose jerkings may exceed the customer's own. In fact, by the standards of broad public feeling in the mid-1970s, Hooker's deification of surgeons and reduction of woman to orgiastic thrill or competent nurse would not have been acceptable, so rapidly had the mood of the country changed in a half decade.

That is where the effect of audience in popular entertainment comes in. The film $M*A*S*H$ purged Hooker's novel to some extent. The television series further sanitized the film version to meet the demands of popular sentiment while retaining the essential situation and characters. Two key issues of the late 1970s were war and the status of women. The Vietnam conflict had undermined public faith in government and the military, including the industrial complex that benefited from fighting. Television had helped the undermining. For the first time Americans *saw* combat daily, and also saw protests, demonstrations, riots involving people much like themselves. The Women's Rights movement was equally visible, articulated by capable spokespersons; it was a social change that seemed to have reached an inevitable point requiring action. And these were two major issues that $M*A*S*H$ confronted, within the conventions of comedy and the sitcom as a genre, of course.

The staples of comedy were there. For instance authoritarian figures were riduculed harshly, and so were patriotic flag wavers like Major Frank Burns, or his female counterpart, Major Margaret "Hot-Lips" Houlihan. But then the situation itself, a field hospital, the 4077th, was an antiwar statement. Whatever the contents of particular episodes, all that was seen of war was its destructive effect. The "story" of elaborate jokes or turns on expectation occurred against a narrative fabric of humanitarian concern, usually taking the form of sirens announcing the arrival of helicopters with wounded, medical personnel running and ducking under rotating blades, and the hurried attention given soldiers, ending in bloody work in the operating room. Attitudes about the military and war may differ, but everyone of the 4077th was involved in healing.

Content to let this antiwar message work by repetition, the writers of the series concentrated on attitudes concerning a good many side issues (marriage, shirking duty, class snobbery, children, even love of animals) but most of all concerning patriotism and the relationship between men and women. Quiet, unassuming patriotism is never ridiculed; it is recognized that there is a job to be done. It is *how* the job is to be done, and from what motives, that are important. The heroes, Hawkeye Pierce and Trapper John MacIntyre, are physicians and officers, but doctors first of all. In fact, their attitudes are more aligned with the sensible enlisted men than with the likes of Frank Burns and Margaret Houlihan. One commanding officer of the series, Colonel Potter, is old Army, and a generous, kindly man who shares the heroes' impatience with military protocol. (That is, criticism of the Army per se is mild.) Another, Colonel Henry Blake, is equally humane, but rather inept. Most of the work of the unit is carried out by a corporal, Radar. In short, the writers complement their antiwar message with an antiorganization bias, a sure crowd pleaser for the millions of viewers who had seen military service.

Regarding women, they are both capable nurses and sexually desirable. But there is some ambivalence in their treatment. As nurses they are respected for their abilities, and seldom is their womanhood allowed to interfere with important work. But the men's sexual hunger is constantly present, some liaisons are formed, and extramarital sex occurs—ironically between the straight Major Burns and the all-army Margaret Houlihan, commanding officer of the nurse corps. There is a double message: as nurses women are to be respected, and as human beings their appetites are recognized, for the most part without condemnation. The stressful situation of war allows some latitude, but just how much? (The viewing public as a whole probably had no single answer either.) No nurse in the unit is shown to be promiscuous or tawdry; certain expected feminine behavior is observed, e.g., modesty, attempts to look attractive, avoidance of harsh language. But there is a respect and freedom given women in the fictional world of the sitcom that reflects a changing, and uncertain, public attitude. Some of this uncertainty is reflected in the actions of Margaret Houlihan in her impassioned affair with Major Burns.

One of the most interesting comic elements of *M*A*S*H*, the running love affair between Frank and Margaret, works in a number of directions. It opens the question of infidelity in marriage. One would think, with the two majors cast as starchly patriotic disciplinarians, that Frank's cheating on his wife would add to our scorn for him and Margaret. Certainly they are often comic losers. One piece of repetitive business is that their "secret" love affair is known all over the compound by telephone, by loudspeaker, etc. Yet even if we find them hypocrites, there is dispensation. It is war, after all. Frank, as the loudest voice for flag, country, and family, receives heavy ridicule. But just as often he looks so charmingly inept it is difficult to be angry with him (in a telephone conversation with Margaret he explains his desolation over her absence with, "the only thing that keeps me going are letters from my wife"). Our response to Margaret is more complex.

Margaret appears a victim of her own passions and delusions. The requisite argument in illicit affairs, that Frank will divorce his wife, seems unconvincing even to her. With such remarks as his cited above, how could she not know that a divorce will likely never happen? Of itself her sexual appetite is not in question. But when it overtakes her as she and Frank look over the quarters reserved for General McArthur in his expected visit, sex gets confused with adulation ("Big Mac," 1975). They enter the tent alone and comment approvingly on the decorations. Her admiration of the General's picture, draped in bunting as if enshrined, emphasizes her awe, her reverence for power. Finally, with an impassioned kiss she folds Frank over onto the General's bed; groping begins as the scene blacks out. The juxtaposition between her almost religious fervor and uncontrollable lust is hilarious, and deeply comic. It forces us to feel our way through relationships between power, sexuality, and, since Margaret is one, the nature of women.

What she lacks is Frank's bumbling charm to soften the irony of her conveniently setting aside her rigid code of proper military conduct, and, with it, her own professionalism as a career officer. (She is, after all, one version of the "new woman," portrayed more realistically in Mary Tyler Moore as an executive of a television station.) Only on occasion is she granted the immunity of understandable folly, and that when she is doing her job as a nurse. When she appears as the emotional woman, implications fly in all directions: hypocrisy; denial of a woman's right to enjoy sex as a man does, though she enjoys it anyway; toadying (in love as well as her job); the super patriot's thrill over power blending into orgasm; and an overall impression of her lack of control over her personal life. If in general $M^*A^*S^*H$ reflected growing public sentiment for greater freedom for women, it also expressed doubts about purity of intent and raised questions about the relationship between egoism and sex.[10]

Thus comedy does its job of exploring, pitting sympathy against sympathy, condoning against acceptance. (It could all be charted out as the relationship between our comic ethic and serious values.) True enough, the endings of episodes usually confirm then prevailing attitudes, or after investigation retreat into sure-fire put downs of authority. All in all $M^*A^*S^*H$ operates as subcomedy, and a good many of its later episodes drivel into soap opera. But as with Touchstone in *As You Like It*, counterstatement, an element of emotional dialectic, enriches our experience. One might even say sitcoms at their best require such an element because it is a sign of genuine responsiveness to the outlook of its audience—an outlook often riven with doubt, blurred by ambivalencies, itself groping its way through new and disturbing social changes. On the other hand, it is all too easy for the situation comedy to embody not what is actually transpiring in the feelings of its audience, but what is safe, accepted, and guaranteed to bolster ratings.

Whatever its more intense comic moments, semiotically the sitcom appears all but impoverished. It uses the medium of television in a highly conventional way. $M^*A^*S^*H$ is unusual in its range of camera work, including distance shots of the 4077th compound, hills surrounding it, and artful use of extreme close up, for instance, the framing of Margaret Houlihan's mouth alone as it carps unceasingly at Colonel Blake about lack of discipline in the unit. But even this series bends to the conventional, relying upon a basic six to eight foot distancing of viewers from the image, interspersed with close ups to reinforce a punch line or register an expression of narrative importance. That is typically the case even when the sitcom is shot "on location," or outside its usual living room or kitchen setting. For instance, in the *I Love Lucy* episode in the candy factory mentioned earlier, though there is ample possibility of distance shots, we are placed six to eight feet from the image. Close-ups only register facial expressions (Lucy's, Ethel's, the Supervisor's) to match the narrative or comic turns of the overall gag.

What is missing is as much a semiotic statement as what is visually present. The candy factory episode is an old theme: man against the machine. Compared to its larger scope in *Modern Times* or *À Nous La Liberté*, treatment of it in *Lucy* is a mere sketch. But all we know is what is presented *now*. And we are drawn into that immediate impression, literally placed by the camera as a member of a group—the family, crew at the office or operating room, or whatever. The other favorite shot, the close up, functions not only to heighten the effect of a gag, it mimics our silent participation in a conversation: we watch first this person, then that. And, of course, medium camera distance is often used to establish a lead-in, close up to reinforce the punch line.

All in all the use of the medium correlates with the general inclusion of audience in the transactional event of the situation comedy. What is lost by foregoing the larger scope film takes as its province is gained in focus and intensity—gained how much, lost how much? In its current state aesthetics does not provide ready answers.[11] No doubt the sitcom is semiotically vacuous, but, again, it is a socioaesthetic phenomenon, not a work of art in the usual sense. Conversely, the other major genre of television comedy, the variety show, is altogether more interesting in its use of the medium and, by ordinary standards, trivial in content.

Not surprisingly, the variety show is most amenable to humor. Amorphous, interspersed with musical or other entertainment, it is usually a pastiche of skits which may form a theme but need not. Like the cartoon strip it perpetuates a set of characters and even implies a symbolic "society" enabling viewers to bring prior acquaintance to each new show. Audiences tend to fasten attention on favored actors or actresses who operate, like the stand-up comic, through a repertoire of personae or fully realized dramatic characters. (The distinction is not hard and fast, but a persona is an aspect of the comedian, say the stage personality of a Phyllis Diller or Woody Allen, while the dramatic character is a created total personality, such as Lily Tomlin's Ernestine the telephone operator.) Personae disappear, replaced by new, more topical ones. Subject matter evolves continually. Other than the cameo artistry of the single skit, there is little pretense at literary or dramatic form. There is no "organic text," or even, in the usual sense, a work.

Taken all in all, series like *Monty Python* or *Saturday Night Live* are kin to farce in that they emphasize play at the expense of form and content. What they lack in dramatic sophistication they make up for with the advantages of humor, mainly freedom and responsivity to current, ephemeral concerns of their audience. At any moment the variety show flies into parody of well-known figures and thrusts at malevolencies or absurdities of our national life. Hence the genre seems satiric in aim, or at the least a form of social commentary. Indeed, its irony can be harsh, its humor wicked. But correction of man's vices and follies is not what the variety show is about. Entertainment is. As with farce, exposing absurdities is essentially a byproduct.

No less than the sitcom, the variety show works under constraining socioeconomic conditions. In addition to commercial pressures, it has obligations to its audience. Its first obligation, of course, is to be funny. But further, its subject matter is loosely bound by the prevailing values of a society or the segment of it a show targets. Directions are determined less by artistic effort than by shifting political events, styles, and fads. No matter, for the variety show aims primarily at play, ultimately with the medium itself. Typically its half hour entertainment is rapidly paced, visually alive with quick cuts, short skits, freeze frames, collapsing sets, and switches from live performance to film clips, or, in the *Monty Python* series, animation. The genre blithely traffics in stereotypes and awkward, flat figures quickly recognized as cartoons in themselves. These work partly as independent social commentary and partly as an element of continuity.

To keep play manageable the variety show needs some repetition of characters, of humorous or comic situations, and regular features. Such repeated business, or *shtick*, becomes expected, and "frames" viewer response. In *Laugh-In* (1968–73) there were the opening Cocktail Party, including the pie in the face or bucket of water over the head with "Sock it to me!"; the Flying Fickle Finger of Fate Awards; the decrepit old gentleman snuggling up to a spinsterish woman on a park bench, only to be clouted with her hand bag. In the *Monty Python* series it was the use of animation in the opening, or, at strategic points in the show, old black and white film clips of audiences in tumultuous applause; and use of familiar characters, such as the British Mum (a male actor in domestic drag), the nude organist, and John Cleese as the BBC news announcer, British Officer of the Regiment, or bowler-hatted banker of the city. All of these provided continuity and containment.

In its own way, then, the variety show faces irreconcilable demands; only the problem is less to restrain humor so that its effects will not overwhelm the essential "story" of the sitcom, and more how to provide a loose framework that will not unduly restrict the play of humor. *Saturday Night Live* (1975–80) followed *Laugh-In's* overall format of recurrent features—Ackroyd's and Martin's two "swinging" Czechoslovakian brothers, Gilda Radner's scratchy voiced Roseanne Roseannadanna, Jane Curtin's straight-faced news announcer, etc.—interspersed with music, including ridicule of musical fads. However, repetition was not the aim, and as the series went on (and as solid ratings accumulated) more creative effort was spent on the skits of the Not Ready For Prime-Time Players, the heart of the show's treatment of current topics. The advance in artistry over the often crude slapstick of *Laugh-In* was considerable.

One example will have to suffice, Don Corleone in a group therapy session (1976).[12] The Don is John Belushi's takeoff on the major figure of the popular film *The Godfather* (1972, directed by Francis Coppola), played by the husky-voiced Marlon Brando. The caricature is surface effect; so is mild ridicule of the therapist (Elliot Gould), who announces a different meeting time next week, and of the young woman who dominates the session with her chatter. As the Don leads off citing his troubles with the Batagglia family's moving in on his numbers, protection, and supply business, he lets slip that they also shot his son forty-six times. Ah-ha! The therapist picks it up immediately: Don Corleone is trying to deny something. His *real* anger is over the death of his son.

The Don admits that may be the case, which prompts the blonde young woman next to him (Laraine Newman) to urge him to get his feelings *out*, to *express* himself. She, we learn at length, had lived a smothered life in Encino, California until she found herself by recognizing her own inner feelings. Peppered with "I means" and "likes," accented with twiddling fingers, her account explains how she had become an airline attendant after coming to the realization that she had always loved PEOPLE! Don Corleone rises, and clutching at his chest, has a heart attack. As he staggers and falls, the blonde accuses him of avoiding his true feelings. The therapy session concludes with a reminder that they are all to meet at a time other than the regular one. They leave, stepping around the body of the Don.

Surface effects are clear: the spoof of the Don and parody of a bubble-brained flight attendant are like Hogarth's caricature of

Justice Wills in *The Bench*. But deeper "compositional elements" probably do not register in our consciousness. We catch the acute Freudian insight of the therapist's "Ah-ha!" and his censorious tone as he admonishes Don Corleone for hiding his true feelings about his son being shot forty-six times. But it is doubtful we make much of the nonparticipation of most of the group, a voiceless testimony to the therapist's controlling what should be an exercise in member involvement. Nor, with Laraine Newman's marvelous parody of the gushing blonde, do we notice that her having found her true self has nothing to do with the Don's problems. And, to judge from the unconcerned looking on of other members of the group, her account does not have anything to do with them either.

As with comedy in general, periphery of awareness counts. In this case it is the therapist's emphasizing twice that the meeting time is changed (more important than actual discussion of problems) and the largely passive, disinterested group, who, except for the blonde, say virtually nothing. Whether or not we are aware of the true target, we certainly *feel* the pipe wielding therapist's control of the session. His cold manipulation and the hollow gestures of the group are summed up in the lack of concern for the gasping Don Corleone and the stepping around his body as if he had never existed.

So, within the loose collection of items in a variety show genuine cameo artistry can occur. But for every well wrought episode of this kind there are five or six that are shapeless, frenetic slapstick, that is, pointless play. This is the quality that makes *Saturday Night Live* farcical. Why not *farce*? It was said earlier that farce is a mode that risks its own fictional, dramatic being by challenging the conventions of the medium itself. On the whole, *Saturday Night Live* plays within the confines of expected format. True, it is rapidly paced, uses quick cuts, voice-over, an occasional head through the wall of a stage set, and the like. But its skits are usually done with painstaking realism, as in the therapy session cited above, with camera distance the typical six to eight feet of the sitcom and close ups used to emphasize punch lines. On the whole, the show seldom realizes the full potential of television to play with it in the manner of true farce.

That is something that cannot be said of the *Monty Python* series. Perhaps of all variety shows since Ernie Kovacs's pioneering work in the 1950s and 1960s, *Monty Python* comes closest to semiotic mayhem, flipping over virtually every conventional response that watching television inculcates in us. Parody and social commentary are heavy elements, yet compared to the American variety show *Monty Python* is much freer within its overall format, the reiterative business that binds the series together. It is freer yet in play with the medium through use of old film clips, startling camera work, and animation.[13]

Though any authority figure will do, favorite Pythonian targets are the military, police, and politicians, e.g., a rehearsal of a conservative and union party broadcast, with a choreographer directing voice inflections and giving cues where dancers will come in and sing about rising prices, inflation, and unemployment. The upper class and "the establishment" are consistently ridiculed, as are historical figures or stereotypes recalling the days of the empire. The BBC and popular television in general are lampooned, the first for its conservative style, the second for its poor taste. In a reversal of the glittering give away show, a presenter calls people to blackmail them, showing snapshots or poorly done video accounts of a liaison with faces blacked out, while a superimposed caption quickly flashes the amount being extorted. But descriptions of individual skits misrepresent the movement within the overall format.

Occasionally a particular show will have a theme—war and militarism, art and art criticism, psychiatry, or ants—but even when that occurs, it is not binding. The theme is pornography in an opening skit involving a job agency in the times of the Tudors, only it is a front for a sleazy Soho bookstore.[14] The establishment is raided by Superintendent Gaskell of the Vice Squad, disguised as Sir Philip Sidney. But shop assistants and customers take him as the true nobleman, so, cut to "The Life of Sir Philip Sidney," with an Elizabethan setting and Gaskell–Sir Philip recounting how he thwarted the Harry Tony mob and sent them up for five years. Pornography enters again when Sir Philip, after the defeat of Spaniards, returns to find his wife reading "Gay Boys in Bondage," by William Shakespeare, and at the end of the show when a vicar is buying dirty books in a last shot of the bookstore's postcards. Captions credit members of the Python group with supplying interesting poses, heavy breathing, and so on. In between there are seven skits, including one on dead authorities who do not answer the question "Is there life after death?", that have nothing to do with the theme of pornography.

This movement, or jerking, from one subject to another by visual association (if any at all) gives the series a frenetic, disjointed quality that is its essential semiotic message. Sometimes mayhem is made part of a juxtaposition, as in the skit "Hell's

Grannies," where gray-headed ladies roam like teenage gangs, beating up innocent bystanders or roaring around on mopeds. But as often as not thematic point is oblique, as when police use a magic wand that makes criminals and illegally parked cars disappear. The sequence goes on with the wand gag, ending with policemen dancing around a burglar bound to an altar at Stonehenge; the image appears in a newspaper read by a Chief Constable.

> *Chief Constable.* Now this is the kind of thing that gives the police a bad name, sergeant.
> *Pull out further to reveal police sergeant in a long shimmering slim-fitting ladies evening gown, diamenté handbag and helmet.*
> *Sergeant.* I know, sir.
> *Intercom buzzer goes on desk.*
> *Chief Constable. (depressing knob)* Yes, Beryl?
> *Beryl. (male voice)* Attila the Hun to see you, sir.[15]

The magic wand gives no clear focus to ridicule. Do the police have magical powers? Doesn't the Chief Constable know how the Sergeant is dressed? In any event, though it provides a strong visual punch line, the Sergeant's appearance in an evening gown does not tie in with the magic wand. Attila (actually Mr. Norman Hun, who wants to give himself up for pillaging) has nothing at all to do with wand or the Sergeant in drag.

Along with abandoning narrative line, *Monty Python* plays with its own fictional credibility. A skit in which the Vercotti brothers try to sell protection to an army colonel so nothing mysterious will happen to his unit ends in Pirandelloesque stepping out of role. The Colonel orders the episode stopped because it is badly written, while other characters protest it is only because he couldn't think of a punch line.[16] Use of old film clips—in black and white set off from the show's color, and often speeded up—emphasizes the patent theatricality, or irreality. So do mix-ups in episodes, when a character from an earlier skit will appear incongruously in a later one. And so does the *Python's* play on their script. For example a pet shop owner says to an angry customer whose dead parrot cannot be replaced that he has a brother with a shop in Bolton who will find one for him. A caption appears: "A Similar Pet Shop in Bolton, Lancs." A door appears with a sign on it, "Similar Pet Shops Ltd."

Perhaps the most noticeable reminder that *Monty Python* is not to be taken as *mimesis* is use of animation. Even their animation—in the opening and at various unexpected moments during the show—is not the ordinary variety. It is often a compound of old photographs of mustachioed gentlemen with eyes glowing in darkened sockets, the top of their heads hinging open to sprout flowers and release butterflies, their mouths moving mechanically to utter words printed on ribbons. At any moment the image can be squashed by a huge foot descending from the top of the frame.[17] A Bobby opens his tunic to reveal a woman's figure, a terrifying, pneumatic Aardvark roams the land, a coy nude smiles at us from a tinted postcard. We are in a surrealistic world, or as one script direction reads:

> A bleak landscape. A large foot with a Victorian lady on top of it comes hopping past. A door in a building opens and the society members (real people, superimposed) run out, along the cartoon, and disappear, falling into nothingness. Cut to section of an oesophagus. The members (now animated cut-outs) fall down into a stomach where they are joined by various large vegetables. Pull back to show that this is a cutaway view of an Edwardian gentleman. He belches.[18]

The work of Terry Gilliam, the animator, could be placed with that of serious postmodernists; however, he studied with Harvey Kurtzman, creator of *Playboy's Little Annie Fanny*, and considers himself a cartoonist.

On the whole then, the sitcom and variety show resemble comedy and farce as they appear in other media. Socioeconomic conditions of broadcasting are more confining for the situation comedy than for its twin. The weakness that tempts the sitcom— its lapsing into humor and gags for their own sake—is a source of strength for the much more flexible variety show. With the variety show's commitment to humor, one seldom finds the well-rounded cameo artistry that can come in situation comedy episodes. Instead, there is a much more visually alive play with the medium in *Saturday Night Live* and, preeminently, *Monty Python*. Unfortunately, these seem to be the very qualities that automatically disqualify farcical television for serious study, just as the sitcom's open-ended form and responsivity to ephemeral interests of its audience do not fit our assumptions about what constitutes aesthetic achievement.

8

Contexts, Extensions

By way of opening and situating my subject in current theories of comedy, I maintained I had a modest purpose, understanding, as if understanding could be entirely free of interpretation. Inevitably one is led into larger contexts, for instance the issue of unity in *Henry IV Part 1*. I have tried to focus on the workings of comedy, avoiding for the most part critical discussion of particular works. Methodologically speaking, the effort has been costly. Anyone familiar with theories of comedy will likely feel the approach taken here is too tidy, rigid, and reductive. Issues of audience and text have been left unresolved. Questions abound, not the least of which is how this study might be applied.

Regarding the schematic nature of concepts I have presented, my diagrams can leave the impression that all one need do is chart the relationship between serious and comic values to unearth the "meaning" of comedy. To a large extent that is true of work in the Menandrine tradition, including current popular novels and films. But obviously variations on conventional form require adaptation of my approach, to Shaw's comedy, for instance.

Shaw writes wordy, discursive scripts, but he does not forego the theater's power to evoke emotion, nor comedy's to explore values.[1] In *Candida* the heroine's final rejection of the young poet Marchbanks has theatrical force because it comes in the crosscurrents of our feelings regarding Marchbanks, Morell, Candida, marriage, and romanticism. Shaw overturns theatrical conventions also, for instance the happy ending in Eliza's choice of Freddy instead of Higgins in *Pygmalion*. In *Caesar and Cleopatra* he plays with his audience's conception of history and expectations of formal dialogue, that is, both axes of "meaning" and of perceptual play apply to Shaw's work but to different degrees since he was constantly experimenting. Memorable for its debate between Don Juan and the Devil, the philosophical comedy *Man and Superman* has "realistic" characters—Tanner, Octavius, Ann—to whom we respond with mixtures of serious and comic values, whereas the allegorical nature of *Heartbreak House* dilutes our emotional involvement and heightens awareness of issues.

With a work like *Heartbreak House*, however, we are a ways from the Menandrine tradition, but then, there are a good many ludic works that have little or no connection with the mainstream of theatrical comedy, and are no less comic or satiric for that. One whole strand of contemporary writing is indebted to Comedy of the Absurd, ranging from Tom Stoppard's *Rosencrantz and Guildenstern Are Dead* to the fiction of Donald Barthelme or, less obviously, the work of Sam Shepard. To what extent, if any, does the methodology used here apply to "comedies" mixed in kind? As I have insisted, the breaking down of response into serious and comic elements is applicable to drama or literature (or film or television) which embodies "meaning" in character and action of at least a quasi-representational kind. Yet it is this mode of theatrical representation that many contemporary playwrights reject: its linear construction, cause and effect, psychologically consistent, coherent characters, language that conveys meaning, and, above all, separation between the comic and the serious.

What becomes important in discussion of this sort of hybrid comedy are not the underlying values of audience response (though they are not to be totally discounted), but, rather, perceptual play and use of the medium. For instance Shepard's *La Turista* (1967) plays with our customary theatrical expectations in the manner of Ionesco: a boy appears, acts unaccountably, talks in two or three voices, and answers a telephone that does not work but rings for him; the "plot" involves little more than Kent's, the hero's, trying to overcome diarrhea.[2] Though there are moments of sympathy for Kent, when the boy spits in his face or when he has an attack of the trots, and though we find him charmingly amusing as he struts about proclaiming victory over amoebic dysentery, by the end of act 2 he has ceased to be a recognizable realistic character. He has become "theatricalized" (or one could take the ending as a surrealistic projection of Kent's mind, a dream). He speaks a lengthy symbolic monologue from behind the audience, while the Mexican Doctor assumes the voice of a realistic American father figure trying to coax him back into the play. *La Turista* ends with Kent running onto stage and through an upstage wall, leaving a cut out silhouette that reminds one of the last frame of a Bugs Bunny cartoon—a desperate act of escape from father as well as the entrapment of theater.

By contrast, *Curse of the Starving Class* (1978)[3] has fewer "absurdist" elements than *La Turista*. People speak in different voices;

two cordial gangsters appear, like those of Pinter's *The Birthday Party*, and set off a bomb that apparently kills Emma, the daughter, by accident. Yet overall Shepard's characters, living in a littered house in a run-down avocado orchard, have the wholeness and scruffy charm of those of John Steinbeck's *Cannery Row.* The drunken, spendthrift father, who turns up after another long absence, sees himself as the put upon provider without whom the family would starve. (He brings a large bag of artichokes, along with a pile of dirty clothes.) Irresponsible though he is, he has a quick mind and a gift for language. We have mixed feelings about him, as we do for the loud, devious, and none too bright mother, Ella. So, while characters are sometimes slightly out of focus, and inconsistent, they are largely "realistic" and evoke our usual theatrical response. In the same way that analysis of values and emotional dialectic helps one to grasp comedy's contribution to *1 Henry IV*, it can help sort out our response to *Curse of the Starving Class*, at least to a point. For the play is not rollicking fun. Its final symbolic image of an eagle and cat locked in a death struggle from which neither can free itself has nothing comic about it.

One could go on with manifold forms comedy takes (the surrealism of Marcel Aymés stories, the satiric, fantastic novels of Kurt Vonnegut, or in painting the humor and grotesquerie of Breughel, the clowning of Dali) and no doubt the two axes of analysis described here would apply in varying degrees, would have to be modified, or might be wholly inappropriate. Yet the problem, it seems to me, is not to give a global accounting of each and every possibility comic artists might create (the search for an answer, a teleology). Rather, it is to articulate comic response in a useful way for a variety of works in different media, thereby showing how comedy works as an aesthetic mode—overall, in general. And, since choices must be made, why not choose the mainstream of our comic tradition for works that "mean," and "the other" of that tradition, farce, for those committed to perceptual play?

In the interests of communicating to a wide range of readers, I have kept to readily accessible media of expression such as theater, the novel, film, and television. What of other media not usually included in literary or dramatic study? If comedy is its own aesthetic mode, study of it should be applicable to these as well, for instance, music and dance. Except that one encounters in them the same fuzziness of conception that plagues literary analysis, the same uncertain methodology and slippery terms, and the same bias toward the serious. A look at both music and dance should indicate whether this study can apply to them—a glance, only to suggest where further work might lead.

Though they have certain affinities with drama as performing arts, music and dance have their own semioses and prompt the question, what is it the composer or choreographer plays *with*? The response is to some extent with representation, but mainly with aural and kinesthetic sensation. So with music, opera can be set aside as an essentially theatrical medium; virtually all that has been said of stage comedy applies to opera, give or take the need for recitative or aria. (If we had a number of very early comic opera interludes, skits, lampoons, or variety acts, probably what has been said of farce might apply to them, but by the mid-1700s *opera buffa* or in France *opera comique* had emerged as a fully developed theatrical genre.) It is the musical element of opera that defies explanation, just as orchestral music's various forms of play resist a full accounting of how they come about.

Comic expression in music is difficult to describe, much less analyze. Flat out parody or clowning with conventions is the least mysterious aspect of comic or humorous effect, and even it has its problems. Pretentious, serious, and outdated forms are an easy target for performers: in England Gerard Hoffnung's and in America Peter Schickele's awful renditions of classical scores; in popular music the great innovator of lampoon, Spike Jones; and in opera Anna Russell's takeoffs on Wagnerian sopranos. But what does one do with comic effect built into "serious" composition? Mozart took the conventions of his age to task in *The Musical Joke*, K.522. The piece sounds like a divertimento by a mediocre talent played by thorough incompetents, yet its satirizing is selective and the whole is well-crafted Mozartian music. That raises two questions: Is parody separable from the whole composition; what in music allows for raucous slapstick on the one hand and playful wit or irony on the other? These lead to the further issues of play and surface and deep effects in music.

Parody is an overt, directed, and recognizable game, one that can be quite subtle, but that is intended to mimic and is so acknowledged by listeners. Play is a more general phenomenon, a mode of musical existence. And, like play in the philosophical sense, in music it has a Janus-faced duality, its cheerful flippancy capable of turning into dark, grotesque effect. One is tempted to associate parody with surface gags—the obvious exaggerations of convention in *The Musical Joke*, Debussy's use of the Prelude to *Tristran und Isolde* in *Golliwog's Cake Walk*, and so on—while reserving deep effect for thoroughly musical play that has little or no reference to anything outside itself, for instance, Mozart's sly use of *opera buffa* melody at the end of his *String Quartet in G Major*, K.387. But that is not possible, unless one wants to ignore the problems implicit in such a distinction—no less than representation in music and the nature of our auditory response.

Whether music represents anything outside of its own being is still under debate,[4] yet to the ordinary listener Ferde Grofé's cloppings and ee-yaws in the *Grand Canyon Suite* "depict" donkeys, just as Gershwin imitates taxi horns in *An American in Paris*. These have a certain charm, as do the oboe playing Sasha the duck and bassoon playing Grandfather in *Peter and the Wolf*, but comic effect overall comes most often from play with our musical associations. Not that echoing or appropriating a musical element is in itself amusing. One can hardly accuse Beethoven of humor in using Mozart's *Quartet in A Major* in his own scherzo of the *A Minor String Quartet*, opus 132, or Copland, either, for using a Quaker song in *Appalachian Spring*. Juxtaposition, or the clashing together of two unlikely associations, is required, as in Verdi's use of the fugue to end *Falstaff*, self-mockery of a "learned" form producing irony. And, in turn, juxtaposition assumes that there *is* a repertoire of associations listeners bring to the experience of music. As in literature and drama, expectation must be in force for turns on it to occur.

No problem, one can say, with the more obvious clashings just cited, but the real tests are humor, wit, irony, whimsy, or playfulness in all its shades, with the composer's own flippancies with his structures—in other words, pure play with music. Two factors merge here, a range of structural play (upon expectation, with conventions, with the form itself), and gradation between and overlapping of conscious and unconscious response. The range of play on musical structures is endless, nuanced, and thus far not fully explained in terms of listener response. Strauss's *Till Eulenspiegel* and its merry, impudent style, or Dvořák's *Humoresque*, are at one end of a vast spectrum. At the other is Mozart's playfulness, when he is cheerfully playful, and such things as Schumann's sly reference to "La Marseillaise" in *Faschingsswank aus Wien* (the French national anthem was forbidden in Vienna). The strength composers give an echo is infinite in possibility, and always dependent upon its immediate context, e.g., the working of melody into a larger structure and interpretation in a specific performance. Or there need be no echo at all, only faint allusion.

Looking at the situation from the perspective of listener response—of the ordinary person, not of the musician or musicologist—what appears to happen is that there is a threshold of recognizability. A composer recreates a perceptible, familiar element as part of a movement, a melodic line, or distinctive instrumentation to juxtapose it with another, discordant one, or to couch it in a musical context whose associations do not admit the possibility of such an effect. (Juxtaposition is not the only device at work; music moves through time, and every assertion of a basic theme or style can be a lead-in.) Then there is deep play of which the listener may be only dimly cognizant, feels as "expression," or a "mood." So to speak, the listener is responding not to the lexicon of his or her experience, all of the "semantic meanings" of particular effects, but to the syntax of music itself, to melody, tempo or rhythm, harmonics, and other primal elements which are as beyond awareness as they are beyond articulation.[5]

There are, of course, listeners and listeners, and even among the musically illiterate one ear may pick up faint echoes or slant allusions another will miss entirely. Still, one might expect that there are common properties in listening such that Koestler's Gestaltist-cognitive paradigm of the joke could apply to music. After all, there has been considerable study of musical cognition, e.g., of our tendency to hear two notes as one, of pitch-streaming or grouping, of memory of a sequence of notes in terms of pitch interval allowing us to recognize transposition of a melodic theme into a new key.[6] Thus far, to my knowledge no one has attempted to apply this study to comic effect or play in music.

However generally, the concept of surface and deep response applies, but I presume no one would be rash enough to carry it over in toto onto music.[7] A more applicable notion is play—in its Janus-faced doublesidedness—though it goes under other names in musical literature, e.g., "irony."[8] The cheerful side of play is manifest in Papageno's song in *The Magic Flute*, a suddenly rising, high flute, a strong, shrill sound repeated and worked into the melodic line. It is not a "birdcall" like Beethoven's cuckoo in the *Sixth Symphony;* it is an avian voice that is musical in sound and substance, its playfulness generated from its startling appearance in the score. Or there is Mahler's use of "Frère Jacques" in the "Totenmarsch" of his *First Symphony,* where the effect is both flippant and somber. Play can get dark and chaotic, too. Ravel's *La Valse* begins innocently enough, dissects the form, and ends in a cacaphony suggesting a musical lunatic asylum. Or there is that inveterate player, Erik Satie. His titles are often cheerful one-liners—*Three pieces in the form of a pear, Memoirs of an amnesiac*—

but, musically considered, some of his compositions show play in its flippant, loony, and dark aspects.[9]

If extending this treatment of comedy into music presents difficulties, carrying it over to dance raises formidable obstacles. At least there is a precise "language" for music; our corresponding language for dance is largely impressionistic and lacks a widely accepted conceptual vocabulary. Insofar as dance is comic theater, one can discuss it with some ease, but when dance is *the* means of expression, we bump against a number of problems: its spatial/temporal existence, its semiotic language, the influence of music, and an audience's repertoire of kinesthetic significations and its expectations. Even with these difficulties, the two axes of play, with content or meaning and with perception, apply to dance roughly in the same way comedy works in representational and nonrepresentational art.

Though the distinction between the two kinds of art is reasonably clear in painting, it is fuzzy in dance. At any rate, as contrasted to Merce Cunningham's pure movement devoid of meaning, the dance equivalent of representational art is traditional ballet, related narrative and dramatic forms, or, in general, dance theater. That actual presentation is symbolic rather than "realistic" makes no difference. Dance confers phenomenological immediacy; its impact is "real." Dance theater is essentially a mixed mode yoking narrative and bodily movement, compromising both in a story interrupted by a *pas de deux*, the step then curtailed to fit dramatic need. Artistic direction reconciles this tension between dance and drama, but in ballet reconciliation has already taken place in the basic positions and moves, themselves derived from narrative or dramatic necessity. An audience learns the significations of ballet's repertoire of movements, just as it learns those of larger, choreographic elements—the stately procession, the scene of festivity, the exuberance of a series of *jétés*, and the like.

To the extent ballet is a "language,"[10] one could say it has an extensive "lexicon" assuring, for instance, that a pirouette usually connotes a frenetic, intensifying, outward mood. "Mood" is appropriate because for the most part significations are generalized emotional states: happy, disappointed, expectant, or sad as the case may be. Give or take specific interpretations of the dance movement, these states are matched with emotions arising in the course of dramatic action. While there is always an element of dance as pure movement—and the possibility of deep kinesthetic response, to be taken up later—ballet tends to traffic in surface signification, association, and symbolic suggestion. It is off these that the most obvious games are played. The very codifications of ballet's positions and the typically cool, controlled facial expressions of dancers invite mimicry.

Again, parody is instructive. Since the days of music hall and burlesque, the male dancer's tights and ballerina's slender figure have been targets, most recently in spoofing by the male Ballet de Trocadero de Monte Carlo. The group transcends slapstick effect of men dressed as women by supplying a relatively high level of dance. Their work includes single pieces such as the death of the Swan Queen, with slightly excessive rippling, winglike movements of his/her arms and moulting feathers coming loose to drift to the stage with a dying fall. Our attention is caught by the "Prince" in his too full wig, or the muscular "Swan Queen" on point, but there is peripheral action, a running, often subtle exaggeration of typical routines and choreography that probably only a balletomane notices at the moment. As with music, one encounters the reciprocal connection between consciousness and deep and surface effect. How conscious one's reaction is to parodic choreographic patterns obviously depends on familiarity with ballet, but it is also influenced by the degree of exaggeration. Assuming a casual respondent (our groundling again), what is inherent in dance that can produce deep comic effect?

The answer is simple, and dauntingly complex: dance operates upon our unconscious perceptual structurings of experience, as Klee did in *Revolution of the Viaducts,* only in this case what are involved are all the ups and downs, sideways movements, comings toward, goings from, trajectories, spatial relationships, and so on that make up our primal kinesthetic "world." We know little enough about this kinesthetic realm from the dancer's and choreographer's point of view, even less about its nature and how it works in audience response. Various attempts have been made to describe movement in this context; among the best known is Rudolf von Laban's.[11] Laban sees the dancer's movements as contained in an icosahedron, which affords "corners" or points of reference for describing virtually any motion vertically, laterally, and diagonally. He further analyzes quality of movement by space, time, weight, and flow, maintaining that certain combinations of these (direct or indirect space, sudden or sustained time, etc.) correspond to psychological states. His description works, though the connections between movement and audience response tend to be generalized, emphasizing stereotypical steps and routines.[12]

No doubt a full semiotic of the kinesthetics of dance will come in the distant future.[13] For now we do know motion evokes feelings. Something moving toward us does not "mean" anything. If it is moving slowly, it is slightly disturbing, perhaps vaguely confrontational as it draws near since it is entering our sphere of sensation. If the thing approaches slowly, we can digest the phenomenon. If it approaches rapidly, with little or no time to accommodate it in our perceptual sphere, it becomes threatening. (That is why we feel foolish when hiking on a forest path as we duck from a low hanging twig.) Movement away evokes feeling as well: rapid movement connotes transience, instability; slow movement suggests diminution, loss.[14]

In the larger configurations of dance, any of these motions can be a lead-in. A slowly receding figure in the distance conveys a sense of, perhaps, rueful awareness of the fleetingness of love; suddenly he clicks his heels, throws his cap in the air—freedom at last! The punch line would register consciously, the lead-in likely would not. Similarly, with a male and female dancing together we are aware of gestural signals and bodily attitudes, and certainly facial expressions, but are probably not conscious of spatial relationship, the architecture of the total dance movement.[15] This relationship can connote equivalence (each dancer mirroring the other), complementarity (one facilitating the other's movements), opposition (the opposite of facilitation), conflict (radical asymmetry, resistance to mutual movement), or many other shades of tension or cooperation. The moment passes quickly and is enmeshed in the larger movements of choreography; we sense its implications, but are probably not cognizant of them. The potential for play is obvious: surface messages of endearment can be juxtaposed with an underlying antagonism, or the reverse. Gestural and other signals can be in tune with the "messages" of movement in space—say an overall impression of decisive opposition—to provide a lead-in for a sudden turn, the two dancers seizing each other in an embrace.

Like play in comedy overall, choreographers' twists on our kinesthetic perception result in a wide range of effects, from the parodic, flip dance gags of David Gordon's Pick Up Company to the quiet humor of Balanchine in *Concerto Barocco*, from the comically sad *Epitaphs* by Paul Taylor (the work parallels *Waiting for Godot*) to the absurd, bittersweet *Untitled* of the Pilobolus group.[16] Quite in the usual sense of play, however, dance's turns on expectation, juggling of spatial and temporal patterns, and jolting of our perceptual framework tend toward farce, phenomenologically and in manner of performance.[17] Regarding the latter, clowning, slapstick, *buffo*, mime, or what theater people loosely call *commedia dell'arte* style, are essentially forms of dance. That is most apparent in the work of silent film comedians. Body language was their primary form of communication, and with Chaplin it approached dance both in the slap footed walk and twirling cane of his tramp persona and the choreographed clownery of action, for instance, in his epic boxing match with Mack Swain in *The Champion*.

All of which is not to reduce comic effect in dance to a kick in the pants. The point is that both "serious" dance and slapstick— clearly related in the comic work of groups like Momix or The Pick Up Company—are entwined in the primal regions of response where comedy and seriousness are undifferentiated. Seen from the point of view of perceptual play, dance may finally resolve itself into Merce Cunningham's pure and abstract movement devoid of dramatic meaning. Our primal kinesthetic world has no "meaning" other than its phenomenological presence. No doubt that explains why it is largely beyond the reach of consciousness and why our conceptual language for it remains imprecise.

The intent of these excursions into music and dance was to show how this treatment might apply to "other" kinds of esthetic expression traditionally separated from literature, drama, and the plastic arts. Were there space, film animation could be included, as well as hybrid forms such as opera (a whole section could be spent on Don Giovanni's duet with Leporelo before the statue of the Commandant), but now the more important matter is extension. In what ways can the approach used here be useful?

Minimally, this description of comedy offers a groundwork for formal, structural analysis. The workings of comedy are no more mysterious than those of the sentence or of compositional elements of a painting. These workings can be taken as a syntactical account, of local effects or of the supra-language of comedy. In the latter case one would be producing a semiotic "structural poetics" similar, say, to that of Yuri Lotman.[18] The joke and juxtaposition are kernels capable of being transformed into larger structures and by rules almost as predictable, if not as quantifiable, as those of a generative grammar. But structural or semiotic study would likely exclude just that element which is of compelling interest, involvement of perceptual habits, emotions, and values in our interaction with comedy.

Including these would provide the basis for a full "rhetoric" of comedy (as in Wayne Booth's *Rhetoric of Fiction*), a project partly begun by Alice Rayner.[19] While Rayner's paradigm of *utile et dulce* tends to limit comedy to argument, her attention to the values underlying response suggests wider application to more than a few periods of theater, genres, playwrights, and nationalities, or to more than one medium. Whatever approach one takes, among forms of persuasion, "emotional dialectic," as I call it, is a powerful configuration of response. Furthermore, it works two ways, illuminating what an audience experiences and what the outlook of the artist is in a particular case.

The same configuration should interest the social historian. One can apply the distinction between comic ethic and moral or social values diachronically across a period.[20] Admittedly, many comedies would have to be examined, and account taken of the influence of popular or coterie audience. Particular attention would be given to endings. The argument is that comic values— wit, cleverness, success versus dullness, stupidity, and failure— are cultural invariables. They are then constants in a simple calculus that isolates exactly the drifts and eddies of opinion that are otherwise difficult to substantiate. (At what point does a father's authority become tyrannical, or a young woman's wit invitational?) This presupposes that the comedy studied *does* traffic in serious issues; for that reason farce would be less revealing than works in the Menandrine tradition.

Contemporary comedy is an even more reliable guide to popular opinion, analysis of undercurrents of response more exact than it can be for the historian. That is because analysis is on solider methodological grounds, and subject matter is more accessible. Unlike, say, estimates of audience reaction to Molière's comedies, the popularity of particular films or a television series is known through earnings or ratings, occasionally by surveys. The general situation applies: explorative comedy registers ambivalence, comedy of attack shows rejection of certain values, and subcomedy registers wide public acceptance. For instance, the film *9 to 5* (1980, director Colin Higgins) is something of a milestone in the progress of women's rights in the United States. Its very stereotypes—sensitive, capable women suppressed by a bullying martinet of a boss—show popular sentiment. So does its alignment of comic values: the boss is the utter loser, the women winners. Like most subcomedy *9 to 5* may be aesthetically meager, but it reflects audience feelings quite accurately.

Much more interesting, culturally as well as aesthetically, is comedy which explores attitudes through emotional dialectic. It is as rare as it has ever been. But it need not be a whole work; it can appear as a secondary element, in various intensities, indicating rather minute turns in public feeling. Paul Mazursky in *Bob & Carol & Ted & Alice* (1970) pokes fun at the self-realization fad of the Esalen Institute and similar movements in California of the late 1960s. But in their quest for selfhood Bob and Carol are charming nitwits. Sympathy and ridicule collide, reflecting some ambivalence and, further, generating deeper feeling on our part than if the characters had been negatively portrayed. Grasping the exact force and counterforce of ridicule at a given moment and collectively throughout a film can turn up sometimes exquisite articulation of emotions.

In *When Harry Met Sally* . . . (1989, writer Nora Ephron, director Rob Reiner), over lunch the hero and heroine are discussing faked orgasms. When Harry asserts that a man knows when a woman is playacting, Sally disagrees and exemplifies with a slowly building, loudly dramatized, moaning "orgasm." The camera shifts from his face to hers, but also picks up the puzzled expressions of onlookers in the crowded restaurant, including those of two middle-aged women. Sally's outrageous demonstration is funny enough, with Harry's uncomfortable glances at others, but these are just a lead-in. The episode ends with one of the middle-aged women saying to a waiter (as she nods at Sally), "I'll have what she's having." The punch line works because the woman had been merely there, in the background; our attention had been fastened on Sally's performance and its effect on Harry.

The episode is rich in emotional undercurrents. Primarily, there is ridicule of Harry's masculine smugness, which must be overcome if love is ever to flourish. But the ridicule is mitigated by our sympathy for his embarrassement at Sally's dramatic display. Sally, on the other hand, is the comic winner, hands down. However, she has gotten so carried away in her need to win the argument that she has forgotten protocols of public behavior; to a much lesser degree than Harry, she still looks the fool. That is, if Harry has an inflated ego, so has she to some extent. Ridicule works in two directions, or three if we count the middle-aged woman, giving depth to our involvement and fine tuning interaction between pride, the matter of orgasm, proprieties of public display, and, by way of the middle-aged woman, female sexuality. Which predominates? Essentially the episode is about egos, but all depends upon emotional undercurrents throughout the whole film.

Of course, the episode is also a stunning piece of comic writing and directing. Close-ups, mainly of Harry's embarrassed smiles, keep our attention narrowly focused; medium range shots are dominated by Sally's moaning performance, but include a great deal of peripheral material: nods, vaguely interested or puzzled faces, the bustle and chatter of a restaurant at lunchtime, and quietly inserted, the middle-aged woman who is to provide the brief, powerful punch line. As with jokes, the finer skill is in careful design of the lead-in, which keeps us diverted and seems to end with Sally's smile of victory at having made her point. Even that is a diversion, the more so because it is exactly what we would expect at that moment. All of which brings us to the other major concept used here, perceptual play.

It is assumed that criticism in various fields can use knowledge of the workings of comedy, its techniques and artistry. (That could also apply to aesthetics, which has not paid much attention to the ludic arts and, indeed, seems to have studiously avoided them.[21]) But perhaps the most interesting aspect of play with perception concerns farce. What has been said here could add a footnote to the work of Albert Bermel or Anthony Caputi,[22] and, with reservations, to Bakhtin's "History of Laughter" prefacing his study of Rabelais.[23] If so, I would be delighted. The fact is, we understand the "other" of our comic tradition imperfectly and appreciate it even less.

On the other hand, it has to be admitted that farce is not easy to discuss. It is not a text, even one read by a theatrically imaginative reader. Above all, farce is *event*. It happens, and with a phenomenological impact our conceptual language cannot quite capture. It is all very well to say with Heidegger that "art is the setting-in-work of truth," or with Shklovsky that the purpose of art is to make "the stone *stony*," but that leaves us some distance from articulating the actual experience, the registering on consciousness. Wittgenstein pointed out a major epistemological problem: We cannot account for mental phenomena by reference to ourselves alone or in terms of our own private language.[24] Logically, language is communal, and so, I suggest, are our perceptual processes. As if these were not enough, cognitive science (and who else should know?) has yet to accommodate in its paradigms of mind what are called propositional attitudes, i.e., belief, desire, fear, and hope, the emotional dimension of experience phenomenological accounts of aesthetic experience can scarcely avoid.[25]

Given these and other methodological pitfalls, the study of farce and slapstick is still exciting, chiefly because it forces us to confront art as experience, an idea we have not fully assimilated. Parallels between the work of *Monty Python* and current practice in "serious" art—beyond the obvious, Terry Gilliam's animation—

may seem unlikely, but the group's jolting the very structures of perception is consonant with avant-garde and postmodernist practice. However defined, and definition is still underway, postmodernist art has features that apply to farce as well. It uses parody extensively, delights in mixing "codes," particularly those of elitist art museums and belletristic criticism, and denies the *objet d'art*, or object-content, in favor of art as performative act, e.g., John Cage's musical "happenings," Carolee Scheenmann's *Interior Scrolls*, dance by Yvonne Rainer, David Ansin's "talk-poetry," or predecessors such as Duchamp, Magritte, and Vautier.[26] In other words, postmodernism is committed to play, with established forms, with banal, mundane, and commercial things, with the very idea of art itself.[27] Like theater before it (Pirandello's "anti-illusionism," the antitheater of Artaud, Beckett, Ionesco, etc.) postmodernist art and literature seeks to redefine its ontology as contingency, instability, and undecidability. The dislocation, or relocation, of esthetic activity now underway is what *farceurs* have been engaged in for a long while.

This kinship between farce and radical artistic practice is not coincidental. It was foreshadowed by Dadaists and by Theater of the Absurd's use of slapstick in its assault on the audience, and legitimized to an extent in Jacques Derrida, a philosophical *farceur* (or Nietzschean Overman, depending upon one's point of view). Farce now enjoys a congenial climate because it is compatible with powerful intellectual movements. Dislocation, displacement, and deconstruction are expressions of a profound shift away from a metaphysics no longer credited and toward an acceptance of play as an authentic mode of being—the freeplay of quanta in a meaningless universe, the squigglings of qualia in the mind, the celebration, rather than the exorcising, of the irrational in humanity. In short, farce may no longer be the "other" but at the heart of comedy, and human being as well.

If so, what gives farce or perceptual play in general, such status? At the risk of echoing Nietzsche, I have to say farcical play does appear to have, if not a *telos*, a place in the scheme of things. As I suggested discussing Falstaff's mind flipping over the word "counterfeit," play is intimately connected with creativity. While theorists in the field have been sneaking up on the connection, e.g., Albert Rothenberg and his "Janusian thinking" as a feature of genuinely creative work,[28] they have not arrived at full appreciation of how play, in its most intense and value free mode, is an essential condition of the creative act.

Witness Albert Einstein's answers to the question put to him by Jacques Hadamard, a psychologist, as to how the scientist came up with his brilliant conceptions.[29] (These were the days before rumors that Mrs. Einstein had invented relativity.) Einstein responded with great deliberateness in five steps, A through E. In his quarter page or so describing the stages of inception, he speaks of "psychical entities" or thought blobs which precede assignment of words or mathematical symbols. These entities come together in "rather vague play," and this "combinatory play seems to be the essential feature in productive thought." The entities, now referred to as images, are visual, and some "are of a muscular type," that is, palpable, physical. After a laborious search for words, a second stage is reached, when "the mentioned associative play" can be called up at will. By this time the "play with the mentioned elements" is analogous to certain logical connections, and we are into invention and problem formulation.

One cannot push the notion too far, but play appears to be coexistent with inception—not invention, not problem solving, but that vaguely associative and disperse movement of quanta in the mind even before they assume recognizable shapes or names. Some would reduce creativity to problem solving;[30] only, who formulates the problems in the first place? Common experience and intuition tell us that creativity begins not with given A, given B, but with "what if?"—what if the molecular shape of DNA were a double helix, or the landscape behind Mona Lisa were not continuous in line, left slightly skewed in perspective? That the mind in a state of inception is chaotic as well as playful in the ordinary sense is not surprising. Play destabilizes, puts us at risk, but does creativity occur without either condition?

However interesting as a line of inquiry, I am not implying a direct correlation or "empathic" connection between creativity and farce and comedy, particularly since the net result of our experiencing their play is usually a heightened, excited emotional state, that is, unless we are a playwright or film maker we do not leave a good stage play or film with our creative impulses energized. What has happened, overall, is that we have been put in touch with a primal condition of being seldom experienced in our ordinary lives in the intensity comedy, and especially farce, provide. There has been excitement, exultation of the mind at play, the spontaneous flow of its pointless, excess energies, and the release of laughter. And, even if only on reflection, there is the appeal of artifice—more felt than thought, true, yet of great value as aesthetic experience. For the predisposed, comedy and farce may stimulate creative thinking—indirectly, later, and in a particular medium—but these are, in any case, part of the education of the sensibility all art affords.

These, then, are some of the ways of understanding comedy's operations and how our participation in them fits into larger contexts of interpretation. But I may not be the most reliable source on the matter. I find comedy alone sufficient for a life's study, perhaps because there is no other experience I know of which celebrates so completely and in itself our being, our noble, loony humanity.

Notes

Chapter 1. Groundings, Groundlings

1. Jeffrey H. Goldstein and Paul E. McGhee, eds., *The Psychology of Humor: Theoretical Perspectives and Empirical Issues* (New York and London: Academic Press, 1972), pp. 3–39.

2. See Paul McGhee and Jeffrey H. Goldstein, eds., *Handbook of Humor Research*, 2 vols. (New York and Berlin: Springer, 1983); Holland on laughter, n. 41 below; and essays by Morreall, et al. in *The Philosophy of Laughter and Humor*, ed. John Morreall (Albany: State University of New York Press, 1987).

3. *Poetics* 5.1; Horace, *Satires, Epistles, and Ars Poetica*, trans. H. R. Fairclough, Loeb Classical Library (Cambridge: Harvard University Press, 1929), pp. 478–79, 11.333–46; Henri Bergson, *Laughter, an Essay on the Meaning of the Comic*, trans. Cloudesley Brereton and Fred Rothwell (1911; reprint, New York: Macmillan, 1917); Susanne K. Langer, *Feeling and Form, a Theory of Art* (New York: Charles Scribner's Sons, 1953), pp. 326–50; Northrop Frye, *Anatomy of Criticism* (Princeton: Princeton University Press, 1957), pp. 163–86; C. L. Barber, *Shakespeare's Festive Comedy* (Princeton: Princeton University Press, 1959). Selections from these are also to be found in *Theories of Comedy*, ed. Paul Lauter (New York: Doubleday, 1964) and Robert W. Corrigan, ed., *Comedy: Meaning and Form*, 2d ed. (New York: Harper and Row, 1981), both key anthologies. I indicate only major theorists, but the generality holds. For surveys of theories of comedy, see Gurewitch, *Irrational Vision*, below, pp. 13–82; Heilman, *Ways of the World*, n. 5 below, pp. 254–78; and Maurice Charney, *Comedy High and Low* (New York: Oxford University Press, 1978), pp. 179–90.

4. Morton Gurewitch, *Comedy, the Irrational Vision* (Ithaca and London: Cornell University Press, 1975).

5. Robert Heilman, *The Ways of the World* (Seattle and London: University of Washington Press, 1978).

6. Alice Rayner, *Comic Persuasion: Moral Structure in British Comedy from Shakespeare to Stoppard* (Berkeley and Los Angeles: University of California Press, 1987). Rayner is something of an exception, as discussed further on.

7. *Aristotle on Comedy* (Berkeley and Los Angeles: University of California Press, 1984).

8. Elder Olson, *Theory of Comedy* (Bloomington and London: University of Indiana Press, 1968).

9. From selection in Lauter, *Theories*, n. 3 above, p. 453.

10. Q.v. Lauter, *Theories*, pp. 446–47, 424–31; Ernst Kris in *Psychoanalytic Explorations in Art* (New York: International University Press, 1952), pp. 204–39, extends Freud's concepts into aesthetics.

11. *The Life of the Drama* (New York: Atheneum, 1964), pp. 219–56, esp. pp. 227–31, extracted in Corrigan, above.

12. Morton Gurewitch, *Irrational Vision*, pp. 49–59, passim. Gurewitch's own

categories of comedy are satire, humor, farce, and irony, all depending upon treatment of folly (p. 9); these are not derived from Freud.

13. For problems of response, see Una Chaudhuri, "The Spectator in Drama/ Drama in the Spectator," *Modern Drama* 27 (1984): 281–98 and Stanton B. Garner, Jr., *The Absent Voice: Narrative Comprehension in Theater* (Urbana and Chicago: University of Illinois Press, 1989), pp. xiv–xvii, 3–12, and esp. 176–77, n. 13. (Unfortunately Garner does not address comedy and ties response to narrative structuring, a higher level of experience than I am pursuing here. Closer to that is Wolfgang Iser's application of Helmuth Plessner's theories in "Counter-Sensical Comedy and Audience Response in Beckett's *Waiting for Godot*," *Bucknell Review* 26 [1981]: 130–89, esp. 139–45.) Problems are avoided by rejecting the idea of the audience altogether. Herbert Blau finds a generalized audience of participants, celebrants, viewers, and voyeurs, but it is an abstraction realized only in particular performances; see *The Audience* (Baltimore and London: The Johns Hopkins University Press, 1990). Yet critics who discuss comedy assume audiences exist and respond in certain ways. E.g., David Richman finds Shakespeare's comedies "make audiences experience pain in the midst of laughter" and experience "wonder," or an "amazed hush": *Laughter, Pain, and Wonder: Shakespeare's Comedies and the Audience in the Theater* (Newark, London, and Toronto: University of Delaware Press, 1990), pp. 16–17. I would side with Richman—"the audience" is a legitimate conception—but with full awareness of its methodological problems.

14. See note 3 above. Charney's coverage of comic practice—not response— is similar to my own, but our theoretical approaches are so different that citing where we agree or disagree would consume pages of notes.

15. Heilman, *Ways of the World*, p. 252.

16. Rayner, *Comic Persuasion*, pp. 6, 49. Her version of audience values is discussed later, with my own views; here the point is that for her comedy is essentially argument, manifest in "utopian" and "dystopian" modes of expression.

17. William F. Gruber, *Comic Theaters: Studies in Performance and Audience Response* (Athens: University of Georgia Press, 1986), p. 82. Gruber is alert to involvement of an audience with the play. However, he leans heavily in the direction of the actor, and, compared to Garner, *Absent Voice*, skirts the question of what kind of sentience is responding. So with Scott C. Shershow in *Laughing Matters: The Paradox of Comedy* (Amherst: University of Massachusetts Press, 1986), where paradox tends to become disembodied from actual response.

18. Cited n. 3. Reference is to theories of comedy; there are critical approaches that are not compatible with my views, e.g., deconstructionist readings in general, primarily because of different underlying assumptions about audience and text.

19. Johan Huizinga, *Homo Ludens: A Study of the Play Element in Culture* (1939; reprint, Boston: Beacon Press, 1950).

20. Mihai Spariosu, *Literature, Mimesis and Play: Essays in Literary Theory* (Tübingen: Gunter Narr, 1982), pp. 13–52, and *Dionysus Reborn: Play and the Aesthetic Dimension in Modern Philosophical and Scientific Discourse* (Ithaca and London: Cornell University Press, 1989). For quick consultation on key points I include citation of the more compact *Literature*.

21. Freidrich von Schiller, "Letters on the Aesthetical Education of Man," esp. XIV and XV, in *Complete Works* (New York: Collier, 1902), vol. 8. See Spariosu, *Literature*, pp. 23–25; *Dionysus*, pp. 53–65.

22. Lawrence Hinman, "Nietzsche's Philosophy of Play," *Philosophy Today* 18 (1974): 106–24.

23. On Nietzsche, Spariosu, *Literature,* pp. 25–26; Spariosu, *Dionysus,* pp. 68–100.

24. Hans-Georg Gadamer, *Truth and Method* (1960; reprint, New York: Seabury Press, 1975).

25. Richard Macksey and Eugenio Donato, eds., *The Structuralist Controversy: The Languages of Criticism and the Sciences of Man* (Baltimore and London: The Johns Hopkins University Press, 1972), pp. 264–65; Spariosu cites this lecture as a key statement (*Dionysus,* p. 155) and places Derrida in the context of the thought of Nietzsche, Heidegger, and Deleuze; I include Lavinas, Derrida's mentor, as an influence.

26. Play for Spariosu is the reemergence of prerational thought—the Dionysus reborn of his title—a view with which most would agree; whether play is a form of power manifest in *agon* as a cosmic principle is open to question.

27. Roger Caillois, Meyer Barash trans., *Man, Play, and Games* (1958; New York: Schocken, 1979).

28. For general scope see J. Bruner et al., eds, *Play—Its Role in Development and Evolution* (New York: Basic Books, 1976); Spariosu, *Literature,* pp. 29–40 and *Dionysus,* Part II, pp. 165f; Michael J. Ellis, *Why People Play* (Englewood Cliffs, N.J.: Prentice-Hall, 1973). For child development, Susanna Millar, *The Psychology of Play* (Baltimore: Penguin, 1968) and Jean Piaget, *Play, Dreams, and Imitation in Childhood,* trans. C. Gattegno and F. M. Hodgson (New York: Norton, 1951). For science, Paul Feyerabend, *Against Method* (New York: Humanities Press, 1975). Manfred Eigen and Ruthild Winkler have attempted integration of work in disparate fields (art, science, music, etc.) around the concept of play and game, emphasizing the latter, most recently in *Laws of the Game: How the Principles of Nature Govern Chance,* trans. Robert Kimber and Rita Kimber. (New York: Harper and Row, 1983). Spariosu cites others, *Dionysus,* pp. 202–3, n. 25, n. 26. For play and game in literature and related fields, see James A. G. Marino's "An Annotated Bibliography of Play and Literature," *Canadian Review of Comparative Literature* 12 (1985): 306–58.

29. For instance, see in Richard Kearney, *The Wake of the Imagination* (London: Hutchinson, 1988), pp. 252–53, 366–67 and Jeffrey Nealon, "Samuel Beckett and the Postmodern: Language Games, Play in *Waiting for Godot,*" *Modern Drama,* 31 (1988): 520–28.

30. Harold C. Goddard, *The Meaning of Shakespeare* (Chicago: University of Chicago Press, 1957), pp. 183–85. For other literary discussions, see Marino's bibliography, above.

31. Dennis Huston, *Shakespeare's Comedies of Play* (New York: Columbia University Press, 1981).

32. Eugen Fink, *Speil als Weltsymbol* (1960) is the major work; I use *Oase des Glücks: Gedanken zu einer Ontologie des Speils* (Freiburg: Karl Albert, 1957), a portion of which is translated as "The Ontology of Play," *Philosophy Today* 18 (1974): 147–61. References are to this translation.

33. I have to disagree; comedy often plays *with* meaning.

34. Spariosu contrasts this "play within reason" to the prerational view of play as violent, unconstrained, and arbitrary (*Dionysus,* p. 22).

35. Applied to comedy, the essential difference is between unstructured and structured play. Philosophically, that is a gross oversimplification; there are many varieties of play/game. Spariosu uses Wittgenstein's notion of "family resem-

blance" to deal with them (*Dionysus,* pp. 3–4), but comes up with some distant kin in his clusters.

36. Peter Hutchinson, *Games Authors Play* (London and New York: Methuen, 1983).

37. I refer to what psychologists call the "percept," occuring at the moment sensory response begins to have significance. As Rudolf Arnheim puts it, sensory perception is not limited to sensation; perception "must look for structure. In fact, perception *is* the discovery of structure," and all perception is symbolic; since structural qualities are generalities, we perceive "individual appearances as *kinds* of things, *kinds* of behavior" ("Art as Therapy," in *New Essays on the Psychology of Art* [Berkeley and Los Angeles: University of California Press, 1986], p. 253).

38. Hutchinson in *Games Authors Play* uses the adjective "playful," but many of the games he cites are not inherently "gamey" or "fun," e.g., allegory, allusion, ambiguity, montage and collage, myth, prefiguration, and symbols. Tricks used by comedians are also used by artists for serious purposes, including nonsense (e.g., Lucky's Jaberwockyan display of "thinking" in *Waiting for Godot*).

39. Aaron Gurewitsch, *The Field of Consciousness* (1952; Pittsburgh: Duquesne University Press, 1964) is the major work; here I paraphrase Lester Embree, ed., *Marginal Consciousness* (Athens, Ohio and London: Ohio University Press, 1982), esp. pp. 39–51. Norman F. Dixon has a similar conception in *Preconscious Processing* (Chichester and New York: John Wiley and Sons, 1981), pp. 9–19 and 223–60. Rolf von Eckartsberg surveys other notions of the conscious/unconscious/semiconscious mind in "Maps of the Mind: The Cartography of Consciousness," in *Metaphors of Consciousness,* eds. Ronald S. Valle and Rolf von Eckartsberg (New York and London: Plenum, 1981), pp. 21–93.

40. Ellen J. Langer, *Mindfulness* (Reading, Mass.: Addison-Wesley, 1990), pp. 9–57. Reference is to immediate response, of which Garner says, "the patterning activities of human consciousness are rendered particularly difficult during perception's initial encounters with an esthetic object" (*Absent Voice,* n. 13, p. 9). For research see D. E. Berlyne, *Aesthetics and Psychobiology* (New York: Meredith Corp., 1971), p. 112.

41. Such as those surveyed by Norman N. Holland in early chapters of *Laughing: A Psychology of Humor* (Ithaca and London: Cornell University Press, 1982); also, see Morreall, n. 2 above.

42. Hans Robert Jauss, *Aesthetic Experience and Literary Hermeneutics,* trans. Michael Shaw (1977; reprint, Minneapolis: University of Minnesota Press, 1982), pp. 123–34, 189–200.

43. Reception (reader response) theory is reviewed by Robert C. Holub, *Reception Theory, a Critical Introduction* (London and New York: Methuen, 1984); Temma F. Berg, "Psychologies of Reading," in *Tracing Literary Theory,* ed. Joseph Natoli (Urbana and Chicago: University of Illinois Press, 1987), pp. 248–77; and Shlomith Rimmon-Kenan, *Narrative Fiction: Contemporary Poetics* (London and New York: Methuen, 1983).

44. Norman Holland, "The New Paradigm: Subjective or Transitive?" *New Literary History* 7 (1976): 335–46 and *The Dynamics of Literary Response* (New York: Oxford University Press, 1968).

45. David Bleich, *Subjective Criticism* (Baltimore: The Johns Hopkins University Press, 1978).

46. Wolfgang Iser, *The Implied Reader: Patterns of Communication in Prose Fiction from Bunyan to Beckett* (Baltimore: The Johns Hopkins University Press, 1974),

pp. 274–94 and *The Act of Reading: A Theory of Aesthetic Response* (Baltimore: The Johns Hopkins University Press, 1978), pp. 34–35, passim; for Fish's objections, "Why No One's Afraid of Wolfgang Iser," *Diacritics* 11 (1981): 2–13, and for an evaluation of Fish's alternative, the "interpretive community," see Chaudhuri, n. 13 above, 285.

47. Pointed out by Holub, *Reception*, p. 85 and Berg, "Psychologies," pp. 260–61. Gregory Columb gives a fuller appraisal, and comparison with Umberto Eco's "Model Reader," in "The Semiotic Study of Literary Works," in Natoli, *Tracing*, pp. 340–43. Marco De Marinis has the same difficulty of textual control of the "model spectator" in theater: "Dramaturgy of the Spectator," trans. Paul Dwyer, *Drama Review* 31 (1987): 100–14.

48. Maurice Merleau-Ponty, *Phenomenology of Perception*, trans. Colin Smith (1945; reprint, London: Routledge and Kegan Paul, 1962).

49. Martin Heidegger, *Poetry, Language, Thought*, trans. and introd. Albert Hofstadter (New York: Harper and Row, 1975), pp. 39, 71f. The translation is an amalgam of parts of works.

50. Victor Shklovsky, "Art as Technique," in *Russian Formalist Criticism*, eds. L. T. Lemon and M. J. Reis (Lincoln: University of Nebraska Press, 1965), p. 12; Bert O. States, *Great Reckonings in Little Rooms: On the Phenomenology of Theater* (Berkeley and Los Angeles: University of California Press, 1985).

51. Bernard Beckerman, *Dynamics of Drama: Theory and Method of Analysis* (New York: Knopf, 1970), pp. 137–44, 151f.

52. Sondra H. Fraleigh, *Dance and the Lived Body, a Descriptive Aesthetics* (Pittsburgh, Pa.: University of Pittsburgh Press, 1987), 221f.

53. Bruce Wilshire, *Role Playing and Identity: The Limits of Theatre as Metaphor* (Bloomington and London: Indiana University Press, 1982).

54. Paul Ricouer, "The Question of the Subject: The Challenge of Semiology," in *The Conflict of Interpretation: Essays in Hermeneutics*, ed. Don Ihde (Evanston, Ill.: Northwestern University Press, 1974), p. 237. Part of the "challenge of semiology" in Ricouer's view is applied to the "challenge of psychoanalysis."

55. Umberto Eco, *A Theory of Semiotics* (Bloomington and London: Indiana University Press, 1979), pp. 68–72. (So with De Marinis: his "Model Spectator" is a "hypothetical construct," a part of "a theoretical metalanguage": "Dramaturgy," 102.)

56. A. J. Greimas and J. Courtés, *Semiotics and Language: An Analytical Dictionary* (Bloomington and London: Indiana University Press, 1982), pp. 254–55.

57. Roland Barthes, *S/Z*, trans. Richard Miller (1970; reprint, New York: Hill and Wang, 1974), pp. 16–20, passim.

58. Keir Elam, *The Semiotics of Theatre and Drama* (London and New York: Methuen, 1980).

59. Umberto Eco, *The Role of the Reader: Explorations in the Semiotics of Texts* (Bloomington and London: Indiana University Press, 1979), pp. 200–60. For a more sympathetic assessment of Eco, see Gregory Columb, *Tracing*, n. 44 above, pp. 335–40.

60. Harold Garfinkel, "Studies of the Routine Grounds of Everyday Activities," in *Studies in Social Interaction*, ed. David Sudnow (New York: Free Press. 1972), p. 29.

61. Donald A. Norman, *The Psychology of Everday Things* (New York: Basic Books, 1988), pp. 114–27, 225–26; his concern is with *things*, rather than mind, but he posits an unconscious network of mental patterns (pp. 116–17). Cf. Ellen J. Langer, *Mindfulness*, n. 40 above.

62. Rudolf Arnheim, *Art and Visual Perception*, rev. ed. (Berkeley and Los Angeles: University of California Press, 1974); E. H. Gombrich, *Art and Illusion* (1960; Princeton: Princeton University Press, 1969).

63. E.g., as reported by Vicki Bruce and Patrick Green, *Visual Perception: Physiology, Psychology and Ecology* (London: Lawrence Erlbaum, 1985).

Chapter 2. Operations of the Art of Comedy

1. In perusing a painting, say, time is a factor, as are education, background in art, etc. M. Godkewitsch still maintains that "correlates of humor can depend upon quantifiable, manipulable, structural properties of simple verbal stimulus patterns alone"; in other words, we respond pretty much alike at a primary level of perception ("Correlates of Humor: Verbal and Nonverbal Aesthetic Reactions as Functions of Semantic Distance Within Adjective-Noun Pairs," in *Studies in the New Experimental Aesthetics: Steps Toward an Objective Psychology of Aesthetic Appreciation*, ed. D. E. Berlyne [Washington, D.C.: Hemisphere, 1974], p. 302). Cross-cultural study of perceptual patterning in aesthetic response—Ugandans and Canadians—shows a strong correlation between complexity and "looking-time," or, again, the suggestion that human beings all pretty much perceive alike at first exposure (D.E. Berlyne, *Studies in*, p. 327 and chap. 12). Consciousness and unconsciousness will be taken up further on, but it should be stressed that the distinction between my "semisomnambulent state" and full awareness can imply binary difference—not the case at all. Rudolf Arnheim's version of the difference is intuition versus intellection. Rather than two modes he sees a continuum, from the "thinking" of visual perception, which operates by Gestaltist field processes occurring rapidly and "below the level of consiousness," to the analytical thinking of conscious attention, e.g., in finding a meaningful organization when one is not implicit in sensation ("The Double-Edged Mind," in *New Essays*, cited chap. 1, n. 37, pp. 13–30).

2. Deep/surface should not be equated with Chomskyan or generative grammar. The problem, recognized by Arnheim and others, is that the linguistic paradigm fits the visual arts awkwardly. The notion of deep/surface will be worked out in terms of each medium as it is encountered. It will be maintained that the only firm distinction between deep and surface is conscious recognition. Because deep structures of perception are givens of our culture we are largely unaware of them, whereas they would be glaringly obvious to, say, the Eskimo or the Melanesian.

3. Arthur Koestler, *The Act of Creation* (London: Hutchinson, 1964), pp. 30–42.

4. A number are examined by Walter Nash, *The Language of Humor* (London and New York: Longman, 1985); Keir Elam gives a more copious treatment including rhetorical as well as grammatical forms in *Shakespeare's Universe of Discourse: Language Games in the Comedies* (Cambridge: Cambridge University Press, 1984).

5. Henry Fielding, *The History of Tom Jones, A Foundling*, Book 5, chap. 5. Here and for well-known works hereafter no text citation is given unless there is a reason, e.g., line numbering of *Henry IV, Part 1* varies from text to text. Editions of works not widely known will be given. Relevant criticism will be cited only for works or artists discussed at some length.

6. The term "discrepancy of awareness" is Bertrand Evans's, *Shakespeare's Comedies* (Oxford: Clarendon Press, 1960).

7. Esp. for the unreliable narrator, see Wayne Booth, *The Rhetoric of Fiction* (Chicago: University of Chicago Press, 1961), p. 211f.

8. The relationship between our "real" and fictional worlds is complex, as shown by Thomas G. Pavel, *Fictional Worlds* (Cambridge: Harvard University Press, 1986). Kendall L. Walton in *Mimesis as Make-Believe* (Cambridge: Harvard University Press, 1990), pp. 63–67, passim, sees a fictional world as a network of propositions, rational or not, which we accept as make-believe; it is insulated from our real world. It is only provisionally insulated from unconscious configurations of our psychically "actual" worlds, however—the ones that intrude upon make-believe when an artist asks us to accept wholly improbable, inconceivable actions. (See Pavel, "Salient Worlds," *Fictional Worlds*, p. 43f).

Chapter 3. The "Meanings" of Comedy

1. Gilbert Norwood gives a traditional view in *Greek Comedy* (London: Methuen, 1931), pp. 13–37 (Old Comedy), 37–57 (Middle), and 58–71 (New); or, see Margarete Bieber, *The History of the Greek and Roman Theater* (Princeton: Princeton University Press, 1961), pp. 36–50, 87–107.

2. There are signs, however, of increasing interest in and appreciation for farce and slapstick, e.g., Anthony Caputi's learned history, *Buffo: The Genius of Vulgar Comedy* (Detroit: Wayne State University Press, 1978) and Albert Bermel's *Farce: A History from Aristophanes to Woody Allen* (New York: Simon and Schuster, 1982).

3. "Bundle" is vague, but these kinds of emotions—in philosophy "propositional attitudes"—still elude satisfactory explanation. (The term, from Bertrand Russell, is both a convenient formulation and an escape from having to articulate mental processes, according to William Bechtel, *Philosophy of Mind, an Overview for Cognitive Science* [Hillsdale, N.J. and London: Lawrence Erlbaum, 1988], pp. 47–50).

4. Alice Rayner's version is that there is a "comic impulse" which often collides with moral values (*Comic Persuasion*, chap. 1, n. 6, pp. 9–11), and it can evoke a "double response" (p. 59). Our minds run parallel—or ran; I used the concept first in my dissertation on Jacobean comedy, University of California, Berkeley, 1963. The difference is that I see "double response" operating in all comedy to some degree and I give the concept considerably more methodological weight than she does.

5. *The Odd Couple* and *Barefoot in the Park* are in *The Comedy of Neil Simon*, introd. Neil Simon (New York: Equinox, 1971). Simon has received little critical attention. Robert K. Johnson, agreeing with Walter Kerr, finds the ending of *The Odd Couple* "doesn't work" (as the happy ending of *Barefoot* does); however, the play is so good overall it "easily overrides its third-act weaknesses" (*Neil Simon* [Boston: Twayne, 1983], pp. 20–22). Edythe M. McGovern at least recognizes the undercurrents operating and praises Simon for finding a "middle course" between extremes of attitude, in *Not-So-Simple Neil Simon, a Critical Study* (Van Nuys, Calif.: Perivale Press, 1978), p. 61.

6. Robert Hunting summarizes opinions in *Jonathan Swift*, rev. ed. (Boston: Twayne, 1989), pp. 116–18.

7. The strand of existentialism in the novel has been noted frequently, e.g., Jan Solomon, "The Structure of *Catch-22*," *Critique* 9 (1967): 46–57; for recent discussion of humor, chaos, and their bearing on the novel overall, see Robert

Merrill, "The Structure and Meaning of *Catch-22*," *Studies in American Fiction* 14 (1986): 139–52.

8. On the ending: David H. Richter, *Fable's End: Completeness and Closure in Rhetorical Fiction* (Chicago: University of Chicago Press, 1974), pp. 136–65 and David M. Craig, "Closure Resisted: Style and Form in Joseph Heller's Novels," *Centennial Review* 30 (1986): 238–50; Craig sees Heller as resisting closure, or stasis, and the ending of *Catch-22* as "opening outward" (250).

Chapter 4. Modes of Comedy: "Meaning"

1. Robert B. Heilman, for example, finds a great many "meanings" under the rubrics flight, challenge, conciliation—attitudes toward the world expressed in comedy—with each broken down into subtypes; *The Ways of the World* (Seattle and London: University of Washington Press, 1978), pp. 68–85. Alice Rayner in *Comic Persuasion* finds an equally wide range of "meanings." Centering comedy in play does not negate or foreclose either typology, or any theory for that matter.

2. Not the most appreciative view of satire. For a corrective, see the work of David Worcester, James Sutherland, Robert C. Elliot, as well as Gilbert Highet, *The Anatomy of Satire* (Princeton: Princeton University Press. 1960), Alvin B. Kernan, *The Cankered Muse* and *The Plot of Satire* (New Haven: Yale University Press, 1965 [both]). See esp. *Plot*, pp. 187–211, where Kernan contrasts comedy and satire: they are different in their "spirit" and "worlds," but not in aesthetic being. Leon Guilhamet contrasts the two, with comedy showing what is "benign or of no concern at all," whereas satire reinterprets the ridiculous in an ethical light, finding harm and evil in it—*Satire and the Transformation of Genre* (Philadelphia: University of Pennsylvania Press, 1987), p. 8. Few critics in the field would agree with my description of satire, and not only because it is generalized.

3. Text is the Arden, rev. ed., edited by Agnes Latham. *As You Like It* (London: Methuen, 1975).

4. Shakespeareans might disagree with this emphasis, but they recognize a disquieting note in the pastoral world of Arden. C. L. Barber sees Touchstone as a realistic counterbalance to the play's romanticism (*Shakespeare's Festive Comedy*, chap. 1, n. 3 above, pp. 232–39); Ralph Berry goes further, and rather overstates the case: "Touchstone in his relationships advances a standard by which we are invited to measure all other relationships in the play"—*Shakespeare's Comedies: Explorations in Form* (Princeton: Princeton University Press, 1972), p. 187; J. A. Bryant, Jr. goes to another extreme, finding Jaques the key to "finding the true potential for comedy in Lodge's *Rosalynde*": *Shakespeare and the Uses of Comedy* (Lexington: University Press of Kentucky, 1986), p. 164.

5. Most commentators do not find the spoof and playfulness in the conclusion I do. Anne Barton sees it as showing Shakespeare's "faith in comic resolutions," a "triumph of form," "displaying only a flicker of unease" in "'As You Like It' and 'Twelfth Night': Shakespeare's Sense of an Ending," *Shakespearian Comedy*, Stratford-Upon-Avon Studies, 14 (London: Edward Arnold, 1972), pp. 170–71. One way to account for a "flicker of unease" is to treat the ending as a masque, a switch in mode, as Latham does in the Arden edition, above, pp. xxi–xxiii. On the whole, however, critics tend to take the ending straightforwardly, e.g., Bryant, above, finds it suitably symbolic (pp. 157–58); in a feminist reading Susan Carlson finds the ending doubly serious, a conventional conclusion and an entrapment of women in marriage in "Women in *As You Like It*," *Essays in Literature* 14 (1987): 165–67.

6. On Mammon and Tribulation, see Myrddin Jones, "Sir Epicure Mammon: A Study in 'Spiritual Fornication,'" *Renaissance Quarterly* 22 (1969): 233–42 and Robert M. Schuler, "Jonson's Alchemists, Epicureans, and Puritans," *Medieval and Renaissance Drama in England* 2 (1985): 171–208.

7. Ben Jonson, *The Complete Plays of Ben Jonson*, vol. 3, ed. G. A. Wilkes (Oxford: Clarendon Press, 1982), 3.2.20–26. Citations are to this edition.

8. Regarding the ending, Lovewit's character and its moral (lately theatrical) implications have drawn considerable attention. As R. V. Holdsworth notes, if Jonson had followed the conventions of New Comedy, Surly, not Lovewit, would be the play's hero and would tie up action—introd. to *"Every Man in His Humour" and "The Alchemist": A Casebook* (London: Macmillan, 1978), p. 27. But Surly loses as a game player. There is general consensus that Lovewit runs against expectations of a morally appropriate ending, e.g., Judd Arnold, "Lovewit's Triumph and Jonsonian Morality," *Criticism* 11 (1969): 151–66, sees Lovewit as "cavalierly aloof," an "intellectual aristocrat" who wins out over the masses of fools (166); Robert N. Watson, *Ben Jonson's Parodic Strategy: Literary Imperialism in the Comedies* (Cambridge: Harvard University Press, 1987), pp. 132–36, emphasizes Lovewit's ironic detachment and awareness of the game he is involved in. Near my own view is Carol A. Carr's in "Play's the Thing: A Study of Games in *The Alchemist*," *Colby Library Quarterly* 18 (1982): 113–25, except that she sees moral purpose in Lovewit's games, i.e., they "reveal in microsom the corruption of the larger world" (125), and, in general, takes game, not play in the fullest sense, as Jonson's concern.

9. Citations are to Niccolò Machiavelli, *The Comedies of Machiavelli*, ed. and trans. David Sices and James B. Atkinson (Hanover and London: University Press of New England, 1985), pp. 153–275. No line numbers are given.

10. Also, critics have connected the play to *Il Principe*, or Machiavelli's declined fortunes about 1518, e.g., Franco Tonelli, "Machiavelli's *Mandragola* and the Signs of Power," in *Drama, Sex and Politics*, Themes in Drama 7, ed. James Redmond (Cambridge: Cambridge University Press, 1985), pp. 35–54. But it takes some wrenching of Callimaco's character to have him a comic Prince winning out over fortune, and a diminution of Ligurio as the brains of the enterprise.

11. Like Joseph A. Barber, I see Callimaco as a juvenile idiot: "The Irony of Lucrezia: Machiavelli's *Donna di virtù*." *Studies in Philology* 82 (1985): 450–59. The other key figure, Lucrezia, partly determines our feelings about Callimaco. Unlike Barber (457–58), I find Lucrezia not in control of things until the last scene, a theatrical enigma. Ronald Martinez clears up some of the mystery about her, and the play's connection with political thinking, by relating her to Livy's Rape of Lucretia, so that Lucrezia becomes both *Fortuna* and *Natura*—"The Pharmacy of Machiavelli: Roman Lucretia in *Mandragola*," *Renaissance Drama* 14 (1983): 1–47, esp. 39–41.

12. James B. Atkinson, introd. to *Comedies*, contrasts the ending with that of Terrence's *Andria*, which reaffirms the Roman social ethic and stability of the family, whereas Machiavelli's does no such thing (pp. 18–19). But, says Atkinson, if the triumph of wrong is taken literally, Machiavelli will have failed (p. 19). To prevent this outcome, the playwright uses satire and farce, which presumes that Machiavelli had moralistic intentions and that satire and farce will urge the audience "to scrutinize the nature of the social fabric formed at the play's end" (p. 21). Both assumptions are dubious.

13. For *Importance* in relation to Victorian society, see Epifanio San Juan, Jr.'s *The Art of Oscar Wilde* (Princeton: Princeton University Press, 1967), pp. 180–97.

14. San Juan rather gives up on the play's aesthetic nature: "It would be folly to analyze this masterpiece—most critics have simply contented themselves with fuzzy impressions" (p. 180), a statement that applies, by and large, to this day. And some few critics have panned *Importance*, e.g., Shaw's well-known description of the play as immature, inhuman, and mechanical (which should be paired, as Bermel does, with Shaw's praise of Wilde as "our only thorough playwright . . . plays with everything: with wit, with philosophy, with drama . . . with the whole theater": Review of *An Ideal Husband*, cited in *Farce*, chap. 3, n. 2 above, p. 125). For recent discussions see Donald H. Ericksen, *Oscar Wilde* (Boston: Twayne, 1977), pp. 145–52, and Peter Raby, *Oscar Wilde* (Cambridge: Cambridge University Press, 1988), pp. 120–31.

Chapter 5. Modes of Comedy: Perceptual Play

1. And sometimes not even then. E.g., Albert Bermel sees the plot devices Wilde parodies as trite, that is, taken seriously by the playwright: *Farce* (New York: Simon and Schuster, 1982), p. 124. Farce need not be slapstick in style; its heart is play with conventions and audience mindset, including the expectation that the work will make sense.

2. The major characters of *Bloom County* are "summarized" in *Penguin Dreams and Stranger Things* (Boston and Toronto: Little, Brown and Company, 1985), pp. 5–10, which also shows some of the thematic clusters of the strip.

3. For the group and their "comic genetics," see Robert Wilmut, *From Fringe to Flying Circus: Celebrating a Unique Generation of Comedy, 1960–1980* (London: Eyre-Methuen, 1980). Other sources given below.

4. As one might expect, *Blazing Saddles* has not been the hit with critics that it was with audiences. James Monaco wrote that with it Brooks "found his niche," and took "its superficial structure for his next three films . . . all essentially sophormoric": *American Film Now* (New York and London: New American Library, 1979), pp. 237–38. The writer in *Films in Review* 25 (March 1974): 182–183 praised Brooks as a "comic genius." Another reviewer granted that the film would be a commercial success, but felt it a shame Brooks "still doesn't know how to harness his stable of gags into something more than an updated Abbot and Costello farce"—*Variety Film Reviews, 1907–1980*, 16 vols. (New York and London: Garland, 1983), vol. 13 (13 Feb. 1974).

5. For another point of view, see Thomas G. Nollet, "Tom Sharpe and the Satire of Racism: Caricature and Farce in *Riotous Assembly*," *Studies in Contemporary Satire* 15 (1988): 11–19.

6. References are to paperback edition (London: Pan Books, 1973).

7. References are to paperback edition (New York: Bantam, 1977). The novel has not attracted much critical attention. For correspondence with Prigogine's "dissipative structures," Physics, and Zen see Mark Siegel, "The Meaning of Meaning in the Novels of Tom Robbins," *Mosaic* 14 (1981): 119–31.

8. Beverly Gross takes characters as more "fictionally real" than I do and finds "in an overstructured world only the misfit [e.g., Sissy or Chink] is free"— "Misfits: Tom Robbins's *Even Cowgirls Get the Blues*," *North Dakota Quarterly* 50 (Summer, 1982): 36.

9. It is odd that I exclude Rabelais and Sterne, but Bakhtin has studied the first from a carnival, if not play, perspective (see chap. 8, n. 23 below), and

Tristram Shandy as play has been discussed most capably by Spariosu, *Literature, Mimesis and Play* (Tübingen: Gunter Narr, 1982), pp. 92–105.

Chapter 6. Comic/Serious, Serious/Comic

1. "Death of a Toad" from *Ceremony and Other Poems* (New York: Harcourt, Brace and World, 1948), p. 40 by Richard Wilbur, copyright 1950 and renewed 1978 by Richard Wilbur, reprinted by permission of Harcourt Brace Jovanovich, Inc.

2. Samuel Beckett, *Waiting for Godot* (New York: Grove, 1954), p. 39; Ruby Cohn examines comic effect in *Samuel Beckett: The Comic Gamut* (New Brunswick, N.J.: Rutgers University Press, 1962), pp. 208–25; work on comic aspects of Beckett's theater is surveyed by Richard Keller Simon, "Beckett, Comedy, and the Critics: A Study of Two Contexts," in *Beckett Translating/Translating Beckett*, ed. Alan W. Friedman, et al. (University Park and London: Pennsylvania State University Press, 1987), pp. 85–86. See also Ewa Hryniewicz, "*Waiting for Godot*: Beckett's *Homo Ludens*," *Arizona Quarterly* 42 (1986): 261–70, mainly concerning language play; and of more methodological interest, Wolfgang Iser, "Counter-Sensical Comedy and Audience Response in Beckett's *Waiting for Godot*," *Bucknell Review* 26 (1981): 139–89, esp. 139–45.

3. John Millington Synge, *Playboy of the Western World*, in *J. M. Synge, Collected Works* (London: Oxford University Press, 1968), vol. 4, bk. 2: act 3, p. 147. The editor, Ann Saddlemyer, does not give line numbers. For commentary, see Donna Gerstenberger, *John Millington Synge*, rev. ed. (Boston: Twayne, 1990), pp. 67–84. She emphasizes the play's tragic aspects, rather dismissing comedy, "which draws man smaller than life, ridiculous in his pursuit of some inflated notion, and reconciled at last to the necessities of society" (p. 74). In general critics have somehow overlooked Synge's subtitle, "A Comedy in Three Acts."

4. Gerstenberger, pp. 75–79, does not agree. Randolph Parker in "Gaming in the Gap: Language and Liminality in *Playboy of the Western World*," *Theatre Journal* 37 (1985): 65–85, finds "liminality," or a lacuna between two psychic states, as a gap between our "real" outer world and that of the play (78). In any event, Synge adopts a strategy calculated to confuse the audience (77). In other words, Synge plays a joke on us. Or as Edward Hirsch sees it, "comic language and farce continually challenge the play's empirical conventions, and vice versa"; the play is "problematic precisely because it insistently creates a way of responding to it which it then contradicts": "The Gallous Story and the Dirty Deed: The Two Playboys," *Modern Drama* 26 (1983): 97.

5. William Butler Yeats, "J. M. Synge and the Ireland of His Time," in *Essays and Introductions* (London: Macmillan, 1961), p. 337.

6. Since Irving Ribner's rejection of E. M. W. Tillyard's thesis explaining how Bolingbroke-Henry could break the bloodline and still be legitimate ruler—*The English History Play in the Age of Shakespeare* (Princeton: Princeton University Press, 1957), pp. 157–77—there has been a small industry in debunking the notion that Shakespeare was influenced by the idea of Providence. Shakespeare's view came to be seen as ambivalent, probing; that translated into a reevaluation of King Henry. M. M. Reese in *The Cease of Majesty: A Study of Shakespeare's History Plays* (New York: St. Martin's Press, 1961) initiated a movement questioning the motives, if not villainizing the character, of Bolingbroke-Henry. Barbara J. Baines gives a more balanced view in "Kingship of the Silent King: A Study of Shakespeare's Bolingbroke," *English Studies* 61 (1980): 24–36.

7. Robert Ornstein, *A Kingdom for a Stage: The Achievement of Shakespeare's History Plays* (Cambridge: Harvard University Press, 1972), p. 126. Ornstein's comment still applies.

8. James Calderwood, *Metadrama in Shakespeare's Henriad* (Berkeley and Los Angeles: University of California Press, 1979), pp. 68–87. Calderwood rather waffles on conception of audience: we have a Pirandelloesque awareness but again we do not, depending on whether the text is read, experienced as theater, or both.

9. Edward Pechter, "Falsifying Men's Hopes: The Ending of '1 Henry IV,'" *Modern Language Quarterly* 41 (1980): 211–30, discussed below.

10. Elizabeth Freund, "Strategies of Inconclusiveness in *Henry IV, Part 1*," in *Shakesperean Comedy*, ed. Maurice Charney (New York: New York Literary Forum, 1980), pp. 207–16. She draws upon Richard A. Lanham's *The Motives of Eloquence: Literary Rhetoric in the Renaissance* (New Haven and London: Yale University Press, 1976), e.g., *1 Henry IV* is ambivalent: history is fixed in time, and operates by one reality, while rhetorical reality—primarily in Hal and Falstaff—is in the real time of drama, and always in flux; the two orders of existence contend (*Motives*, pp. 208–9). For Freund, too, comedy is associated with *homo rhetoricus*, freeplay, liberated artifice, and "dramatic reality" as opposed to history, mimesis, and fixity. Hence, for *1 Henry IV* "the single, unequivocal recognition permitted is that disjunctive equivocation is total and unrelenting" (p. 214)—one of the more relentless descriptions of the play.

11. William Shakespeare, *Henry IV, Part 1*, The Oxford Shakespeare (Oxford: Clarendon Press, 1987), pp. 37–41.

12. Text used is the Oxford, above. On Hal, see introduction, pp. 59–64; Bevington also summarizes major interpretations of Falstaff and sees the tavern as a "play world" that must be rejected as battle approaches (pp. 56–58).

13. Shakespeareans do not agree. On the "play extempore," see Waldo F. Mc Neir, "Structure and Theme in the First Tavern Scene of *Henry IV, Part One*," in *Essays on Shakespeare*, ed. Gordon A. Smith (University Park and London: Pennsylvania State University Press, 1965), pp. 67–83; Richard L. McGuire, "The Play-within-the-play in *1 Henry IV*," *Shakespeare Quarterly* 18 (1967): 47–52; Paul A. Gottschalk, "Hal and the 'Play Extempore' in *1 Henry IV*," *Tennessee Studies in Language and Literature* 15 (1974): 605–14, who sees Falstaff as existing in his own childlike world where all is reduced to play. Even Gottschalk, however, emphasizes the underlying seriousness of the episode and its foreshadowing of what is to come.

14. Pechter in "Falsifying Men's Hopes," cited n. 9, sees the ending as both "closural effect" and frustration of our expectations as audience when Falstaff rises with "Embowelled?" (I would agree). Hence, with an intermingling of Calderwood's "metatheater," Pechter sees *Part 1* as "abandoning its own purposes," or redefining them "as the mood fits" (228; I do not agree). Still, there is an "irresolute resolution" that fits the meanings of the play (230). For Freund, cited n. 10, the "irresolute resolution" confirms her thesis that mimesis and form should be thrown out in favor of taking *1 Henry IV*'s disjointedness as its mode of existence.

15. See Bernard Spivack, *Shakespeare and the Allegory of Evil* (New York: Columbia University Press, 1958), pp. 87–91, 203–4, and on Iago, pp. 3–22. Related is Willard Farnham's *The Shakespearian Grotesque: Its Genesis and Transformations* (Oxford: Clarendon Press, 1971), pp. 47–96.

16. For rule by power, or Machiavelli's *raison d'état*, see Moody E. Prior, *The*

Drama of Power: Studies in Shakespeare's History Plays (Evanston, Ill.: Northwestern University Press, 1973), pp. 220–21; on *1 Henry IV*, pp. 183–218, and on Boling-broke-Henry, pp. 219–48.

Chapter 7. Humor/Comedy, Television

1. Reference is not to postmodernist theory or practice, but to traditional aesthetics, e.g., Roger Scruton, *The Aesthetic Understanding* (New York and London: Methuen, 1983), pp. 15–16, and B. R. Tilghman, *But Is It Art? The Value of Art and the Temptation of Theory* (Oxford: Blackwell, 1986), pp. 84–87.

2. I touch upon postmodernism and the "open-ended" work or "happening" later on. For now, see Umberto Eco, *The Open Work*, trans. Anna Cancogni, introd. David Robey (1962–68; reprint, Cambridge: Harvard University Press, 1989), pp. 1–23. Eco has in mind musical pieces by Karlheinz Stockhausen and Henri Pousseur that are "fields of possibilities" in performance, Mallarmé's *Livre*, an unfinished "work in movement," or *Finnegans Wake*, which, though finished, doubles back to its beginning.

3. See David Grote, *The End of Comedy: The Sit-Com and the Comedic Tradition* (Hamden, Connecticut: Archon, 1983), esp. chap. 3, "The New Comedy of American Television," pp. 57–105.

4. Not even an "open work" in Eco's sense, above; such a work is *designed*, not as the product of chance (*Open*, p. 116), e.g., Antonioni's *L'Avventura*. The sitcom is strongly influenced by audience whim and eventualities in national life, although its episodes are structured narrative that can be altered as need arises.

5. This outlook has been dominated by the family, often as a microcosm of society; see Ella Taylor, *Prime-Time Families: Television Culture in Postwar America* (Berkeley and Los Angeles: University of California Press, 1990).

6. Taylor gives a fuller account, pp. 66–77.

7. See Pierre Machery, *A Theory of Literary Production*, trans. Geoffrey Wall (1966; reprint, London: Routledge and Kegan Paul, 1978); Fredric Jameson, *The Political Unconscious: Narrative as a Socially Symbolic Act* (Ithaca and London: Cornell University Press, 1981); Terry Eagleton, *Marxism and Literary Critique* (Berkeley and Los Angeles: University of California Press, 1976).

8. See Taylor, *Prime Time*, pp. 127–30.

9. Richard Hooker, *M*A*S*H* (New York: Pocket Books, 1969), pp. 115–23.

10. For instance, in "House Arrest" (1975) a visiting Colonel Reese, the most decorated nurse in the army, tries to seduce Major Frank Burns, and when caught by Margaret Houlihan yells "rape!" rather than admitting her intent and her failure.

11. In *The Open Work*, n. 2 above, Eco discusses television but emphasizes live coverage of events, praising spontaneity and improvisation, which can contribute to a performance that is an "organic whole" (p. 113; the analogy is the jazz session). He does not take up television comedy.

12. From *The Best of John Belushi*, Warner Home Video (Hollywood: Warner, 1985).

13. George Perry, in *The Life of Python* (Boston and Toronto: Little Brown, 1983) gives a lively account of the show overall, emphasizing its visual components.

14. Episode 36, *The Complete Monty Python's Flying Circus: All the Words* (New York: Pantheon, 1989), 2:180–93.

15. Episode 13, *All the Words*, 2:172–73.
16. Episode 8, *All the Words*, 1:105.
17. For samples of animation, see Perry, *Life*, p. 79, passim; the foot is a takeoff on that of Cupid in Bronzino's *Venus and Cupid*.
18. Episode 18, *All the Words*, 1:239.

Chapter 8. Contexts, Extensions

1. On Shaw's comedy overall, see *George Bernard Shaw*, Modern Critical Views, ed. Harold Bloom (New York, New Haven, and Philadelphia: Chelsea House, 1987).

2. In *Sam Shepard, Seven Plays*, introd. Richard Gilman (New York: Bantam, 1981); on *La Turista* see Linda Hart, *Sam Shepard's Metaphorical Stages* (New York and London: Greenwood, 1987), pp. 36–44. For influence of absurd theater on Shepard (*Godot* on *Cowboys #2*), Susan Brienza, "Sam No. 2: Shepard Plays Beckett with an American Accent," in *Beckett Translating/Translating Beckett*, ed. Alan W. Friedman et al. (University Park and London: Pennsylvania State University Press, 1987), pp. 181–95. Gilman argues that the influence was minimal compared to rock music, the "happenings" of Cage and Rauschenberg, western films, etc., *Seven Plays*, pp. xiii–xvi.

3. In *Seven Plays*; for commentary, see Hart, *Stages*, above, pp. 68–75.

4. Peter Kivy recites the arguments for and against in *Sound and Semblance: Reflections on Musical Representation* (Princeton: Princeton University Press, 1984).

5. Rudolf Arnheim describes elements of this syntax—e.g., effects of deviation from the tonal base, associations of melancholy with the minor mode, of vigor with the major—in "Perceptual Dynamics in Musical Expression," in *New Essays on the Psychology of Art* (Berkeley and Los Angeles: University of California Press, 1986), pp. 214–27.

6. For instance, John A. Sloboda, *The Musical Mind: The Cognitive Psychology of Music*, Oxford Psychology Series No. 5 (Oxford: Clarendon Press, 1985).

7. Sloboda moves in that direction by adapting a Chomskyan model of deep/surface grammar to the concepts of Heinrich Schenker, for whom surface effects are variations on deep structure or *Ursatz*, e.g., in the tonic triad as creation and resolution of tension (*Musical Mind*, pp. 10–23). However, he does not apply it to comic effect in music. Alan M. Perlman and Daniel Greenblatt find deep structures of jazz in underlying harmonies, as expressed by chord symbols, and surface effect in the lexicon of "licks" and melodic line—"Miles Davis Meets Noam Chomsky: Some Observations on Jazz Improvisation and Language Structure," in *The Sign in Music and Literature*, ed. Wendy Steiner (Austin and London: University of Texas Press, 1981), pp. 169–83. For other approaches, see Robert West, Peter Howell, and Ian Cross, "Modelling Perceived Musical Structure," in *Musical Structure and Cognition*, ed. Peter Howell, et al. (London and New York: Academic Press, 1985), pp. 21–52.

8. See Jean-Pierre Barricelli, "Romantic Irony in Music," in *Melopoesis: Approaches to the Study of Literature and Music* (New York and London: New York University Press, 1988), pp. 155–67.

9. Or so it seemed to traditionalists, who allowed only the neoclassic *Socrate* (1918) to be a "serious" composition. In *Erik Satie* (Boston: Twayne, 1988), Alan M. Gillmor argues that Satie was a *fumiste*, or practical joker, in the tradition of Rabelais, Alphonse Allais, and Alfred Jarry (p. xii).

10. Even with so highly codified a form as ballet, there is disagreement over whether dance is analogous to language. Mary Wigman believed so in *The Language of Dance*, trans. Walter Sorell (1963; reprint, Middletown, Conn.: Wesleyan University Press, 1966). Of late theorists have rejected a correlation between dance and spoken or written language, e.g., Sondra Horton Fraleigh, *Dance and the Lived Body, a Descriptive Aesthetics* (Pittsburgh, Pa.: University of Pittsburgh Press, 1987), pp. 71–73, and Susan Leigh Foster, *Reading Dance: Bodies and Subjects in Contemporary American Dance* (Berkeley and Los Angeles: University of California Press, 1986), pp. 88–97. Foster speaks of "vocabularies" and "syntaxes" but bases her concept on Roman Jakobson, with an admixture of Kenneth Burke's "four master tropes" and Roland Barthes, among others.

11. Rudolf von Laban, *The Mastery of Movement* (London: Macdonald and Evans, 1960); *Choreutics* (London: Macdonald and Evans, 1968).

12. Foster gives a fuller description (*Reading Dance*, pp. 77–78); she notes of Laban's connections, as "stereotypic as these correspondences are, they exemplify the prevalent cultural experience of matching observable qualities of movement with attributes of personality [in the dancer]" (p. 78).

13. For recent work, and difficulties, see Judith Lynne Hanna, "Toward Semantic Analysis of Movement Behavior: Concepts and Problems," *Semiotica* 25 (1979): 77–110, esp. "Dance Semiotics: A Processual Model," 83.

14. These kinds of evocations of feeling are considered by Michael McCloskey, "Naive Theories of Motion," in *Mental Models*, ed. Dedre Gentner and Albert L. Stevens (London: Lawrence Erlbaum, 1983), pp. 299–324; for more dance oriented discussion, see Maxine Sheets, *The Phenomenology of Dance* (Madison: University of Wisconsin Press, 1966), pp. 54–56, 123–24.

15. Elements of this architecture are described by Doris Humphrey in *The Art of Making Dances* (New York: Holt, Rinehart and Winston, 1959), chaps. 6–10, as aspects of "Design"; for connotations I give below, see Fraleigh, *Dance and Lived Body*, "Moving as Two," 198–99f, which I paraphrase. These elements are "deep" compared to hand gestures, say, but I am no more sure than anthropologists about the dividing line, or zone, between deep and surface. Drid Williams, "Deep Structures of the Dance," *Yearbook of Symbolic Anthropology* 1 (1978): 211–30, applies Chomsky and comes up with seven transformational rules (215). But for the problems with deep/surface, see introduction, *Society and the Dance: The Social Anthropology of Process and Performance*, ed. Paul Spencer (Cambridge: Cambridge University Press, 1985), pp. 35–38. With Spencer I see deep structure as not consciously perceived by members of a culture and doubt the efficacy of a linguistic model applied to dance.

16. Pilobolus and *Untitled* are described by Deborah Jowitt, *Time and the Dance Image* (New York: William Morrow, 1988), pp. 361–65; she also discusses two related groups: Alwin Nikolais's and the Mummenschanz.

17. Dance theorists do not use "farce" in the sense I do, but they recognize the effect of reversing or flipping expectations over; Humphrey refers to it as "broken form," or dance's version of the nonsequitur, "a haven for comedy" that can also produce the dark effect of "satire or madness—any irrational state" (*Art of Making*, pp. 145–55).

18. Yuri Lotman, *The Structure of the Artistic Text*, trans. Ronald Vroon (1970; Ann Arbor: University of Michigan Press, 1977).

19. See *Comic Persuasion*, discussed in chap. 1; for a compendium of possible "tropes," see Peter Hutchinson, *Games Authors Play* (London and New York, Methuen, 1983), Part II. Actual application of the concepts here could be en-

riched by, say, Austin's and Searle's "speech act" theory or Wittgenstein's language-as-game, as in Keir Elam's *Shakespeare's Universe of Discourse: Language Games in the Comedies* (Cambridge: Cambridge University Press, 1984).

20. Results could augment concepts in the history of ideas, or help support inferences drawn from "hard data" along the lines of the *Les Annales* school, e.g., LeRoy Ladurie's use of archives and journals in *Montaillou* and *Carnival in Romans*. Much depends upon the number of comedies analyzed and the researcher's ability to spot when a gag is being pulled off; catching shades of humor and irony is more difficult than recognizing a joke.

21. Among the few exceptions in recent discussion, Roger Scruton takes on the subject of laughter, if not comedy, in *The Aesthetic Understanding* (London and New York: Methuen, 1983), pp. 153–65. Also, see *The Philosophy of Laughter and Humor*, ed. John Morreall (Albany: State University of New York Press, 1987), e.g., Mike W. Martin, "Humor and Aesthetic Enjoyment of Incongruity," pp. 172–86. Relying mainly on Bermel, below, Stuart E. Baker does a literary, aesthetic study in *Georges Feydeau and the Aesthetics of Farce* (Ann Arbor, Mich.: UMI Research Press, 1981). A subfield that has been concerned with at least humorous response is "psychological esthetics," q.v. *Studies in the New Experimental Aesthetics: Steps Toward an Objective Psychology of Aesthetic Appreciation*, ed. D. E. Berlyne (Washington, D.C.: Hemisphere, 1974), esp. Godkewitsch, pp. 279–304; and Koestler, *Act of Creation*, cited chap. 2, n. 3.

22. Bermel's *Farce: A History from Aristophanes to Woody Allen* (New York: Simon and Schuster, 1982) is copious and appreciative of the art, but, as the author admits, not a theoretical statement; in *Buffo: The Genius of Vulgar Comedy* (Detroit: Wayne State University Press, 1978) Caputi restricts himself, unfortunately, to the history of Italian low comedy.

23. Mikhail Bakhtin, *Rabelais and His World*, trans. Hélène Iswolsky (1965; Cambridge: MIT Press, 1968). The reservations are his image of common folk as a sort of ur-proletariat and his notion that when staged as farce the "carnival spirit," and its upside down, inside out illogic, are eviscerated to become bourgeois entertainment. Caputi, above, has shown the transfer of the Saturnalia and other festive rites onto stage without loss of gross appeal or vitality.

24. Ludwig Wittgenstein, *Philosophical Investigations*, trans. G.E.M. Anscombe (1953; Oxford: Blackwell, 1968), sections 243–403 (or slightly earlier), discussed in *The Private Language Argument*, ed. with introd. by John V. Canfield (New York and London: Garland, 1986).

25. For propositional attitudes, see Jay L. Garfield, *Belief in Psychology: A Study in the Ontology of Mind* (Cambridge: MIT Press, 1988); following E. C. Tolman, Garfield moves away from physiology and toward "sciences such as semantics, sociology, perceptual optics, and ecology" as fundamental to understanding psychology (p. 153). In *The Rationality of Emotion* (Cambridge: MIT Press, 1990), Ronald de Sousa sees emotions as a kind of perception, as having dramatic structure, and as mediating between reason and beliefs, desires, and so on. By and large cognitive science is still tied to models of the mind that tend to exclude emotions.

26. For Cage, Scheenmann, et al., see Henry M. Sayre, *The Object of Performance: The American Avant-Garde since 1970* (Chicago and London: University of Chicago Press, 1989), who deals with rejection of art as an object in favor of art as a happening; see also *The Anti-Aesthetic: Essays on Postmodern Culture*, ed. Hal Foster (Port Townsend, Washington: Bay Press, 1983). Richard Kearney in *The Wake of the Imagination: Ideas of Creativity in Western Culture* (London: Hutchinson,

1988) places the work of Duchamp, Magritte by way of Foucault, and Vautier in the overall context of ideas and literature; pp. 269–71, 332–35, or in general, chap. 8, "Postmodern Culture: Apocalypse Now?" pp. 299–358.

27. Criticism lags behind practice. "Play" has been most often used adjectivally, loosely, e.g. by Eco when he writes that the reader "abandons himself to the free play of reactions that the work provokes in him" and that "the free play of associations" becomes an integral part of the work (*Open Work*, chap. 7, n. 2, above, p. 103). However, Kearney uses "play" nominally throughout chap. 7 of *Wake*, "The Parodic Imagination [of postmodernist thinking]," pp. 251–98, esp. in reference to Barthes, pp. 274–77, and Derrida, p. 289. That is to say, "play" is emerging as a concept particularly applicable to postmodernism; Spariosu's work will likely spur its use.

28. Albert Rothenberg, *The Emerging Goddess: The Creative Process in Art, Science, and Other Fields* (Chicago and London: University of Chicago Press, 1979); Rothenberg's "Janusian" or "split" thinking could be seen as one pattern resulting from cognitive probing and exploration, or play, q.v. Greta G. Fein, "Pretend Play: Creativity and Consciousness," in *Curiosity, Imagination, and Play: On the Development of Spontaneous Cognition*, ed. Dietmar Gorlitz and Joachim F. Wohlwill (Hillsdale, N.J. and London: Laurence Erlbaum, 1987), pp. 281–304.

29. Albert Einstein, "Letter to Jacques Hadamard," in *The Creative Process, A Symposium*, ed. with introd. by Brewster Ghiselin (1952; reprint, Berkeley and Los Angeles: University of California Press, 1985), pp. 32–33.

30. E.g., Robert W. Weisberg, *Creativity, Genius and Other Myths* (New York: W. H. Freeman, 1986), mentioned because the rationalist explanation of creativity still has considerable influence in the field.

Bibliography

Aristotle. *Aristotle's Theory of Poetry and Fine Art with a Critical Text and Translation of the Poetics*. Translation and commentary by S. H. Butcher. 4th ed. London: Macmillan and Company, Ltd., 1932.

Arnheim, Rudolf. *Art and Visual Perception*. Rev. ed. Berkeley and Los Angeles: University of California Press, 1974.

———. *New Essays on the Psychology of Art*. Berkeley and Los Angeles: University of California Press, 1986.

Arnold, Judd. "Lovewit's Triumph and Jonsonian Morality." *Criticism* 11 (1969): 151–66.

Baines, Barbara J. "Kingship of the Silent King: A Study of Shakespeare's Bolingbroke." *English Studies* 61 (1980): 24–36.

Baker, Stuart E. *Georges Feydeau and the Aesthetics of Farce*. Ann Arbor, Mich.: UMI Research Press, 1981.

Bakhtin, Mikhail. *Rabelais and His World*. Translated by Hélène Iswolsky. Cambridge: MIT Press, 1968.

Barber, C. L. *Shakespeare's Festive Comedy: A Study of Dramatic From and Its Relation to Social Custom*. Princeton: Princeton University Press, 1959.

Barber, Joseph A. "The Irony of Lucrezia: Machiavelli's *Donna di virtù*." *Studies in Philology* 82 (1985): 450–59.

Barricelli, Jean-Pierre. *Melopoesis: Approaches to the Study of Literature and Music*. New York and London: New York University Press, 1988.

Barthes, Roland. *S/Z*. Translated by Richard Miller. New York: Hill and Wang, 1974.

Barton, Anne. "'As You Like It' and 'Twelfth Night': Shakespeare's Sense of an Ending." *Shakespearian Comedy*. Stratford-Upon-Avon Studies, 14, edited by John Russell Brown and Bernard Harris, 160–80. London: Edward Arnold, 1972.

Bechtel, William. *Philosophy of Mind, an Overview for Cognitive Science*. Hillsdale, N.J. and London: Lawrence Erlbaum, 1988.

Beckerman, Bernard. *Dynamics of Drama: Theory and Method of Analysis*. New York: Knopf, 1970.

Beckett, Samuel. *Waiting for Godot*. New York: Grove, 1954.

Beluschi, John. *The Best of John Beluschi*. Hollywood: Warner Brothers Video, 1985.

Bentley, Eric. *The Life of the Drama*. New York: Athaneum, 1964.

Berg, Temma F. "Psychologies of Reading." In *Tracing Literary Theory*, edited by Joseph Natoli, 248–77. Urbana and Chicago: University of Illinois Press, 1987.

Bergson, Henri. *Laughter, an Essay on the Meaning of the Comic*. Translated by Cloudesley Brereton and Fred Rothwell. New York: Macmillan, 1917.

Berlyne, D. E. *Aesthetics and Psychobiology.* New York: Meredith Corp., 1971.

————, ed. *Studies in the New Experimental Aesthetics: Steps Toward an Objective Psychology of Aesthetic Appreciation.* Washington, D.C.: Hemisphere, 1974.

Bermel, Albert. *Farce: A History from Aristophanes to Woody Allen.* New York: Simon and Schuster, 1982.

Berry, Ralph. *Shakespeare's Comedies: Explorations in Form.* Princeton: Princeton University Press, 1972.

Bieber, Margarete. *The History of the Greek and Roman Theater.* Princeton: Princeton University Press, 1961.

Blau, Herbert. *The Audience.* Baltimore and London: The Johns Hopkins University Press, 1990.

Bleich, David. *Subjective Criticism.* Baltimore: The Johns Hopkins University Press, 1978.

Bloom, Harold, ed. *George Bernard Shaw.* Modern Critical Views. New York, New Haven, and Philadelphia: Chelsea House, 1987.

Booth, Wayne. *The Rhetoric of Fiction.* Chicago: University of Chicago Press, 1961.

Breathed, Berke. *Penguin Dreams and Stranger Things.* Boston and Toronto: Little, Brown and Company, 1985.

Brienza, Susan. "Sam No. 2: Shepard Plays Beckett with an American Accent." In *Beckett Translating/Translating Beckett,* edited by Alan W. Freidman, Charles Rossman, and Dina Sherzer, 181–95. University Park and London: Pennsylvania University Press, 1987.

Brooks, Mel. *Blazing Saddles.* Hollywood: Warner Brothers, 1974.

Bruce, Vicki, and Patrick Green. *Visual Perception: Physiology, Psychology and Ecology.* London: Lawrence Erlbaum, 1985.

Bruner, Jerome, Alison Jolly, and Kathy Sylva, eds. *Play—Its Role in Development and Evolution.* New York: Basic Books, 1976.

Bryant, J. A., Jr. *Shakespeare and the Uses of Comedy.* Lexington: University Press of Kentucky, 1986.

Caillois, Roger. *Man, Play, and Games.* Translated by Meyer Barash. New York: Schocken, 1979.

Calderwood, James. *Metadrama in Shakespeare's Henriad.* Berkeley and Los Angeles: University of California Press, 1979.

Canfield, John V., ed. *The Private Language Argument.* New York and London: Garland, 1986.

Caputi, Anthony. *Buffo: The Genius of Vulgar Comedy.* Detroit: Wayne State University Press, 1978.

Carlson, Susan. "Women in *As You Like It.*" *Essays in Literature* 14 (1987): 151–69.

Carr, Carol A. "Play's the Thing: A Study of Games in *The Alchemist.*" *Colby Library Quarterly* 18 (1982): 113–25.

Charney, Maurice. *Comedy High and Low: An Introduction to the Experience of Comedy.* New York: Oxford University Press, 1978.

Chaudhuri, Una. "The Spectator in Drama/Drama in the Spectator." *Modern Drama* 27 (1984): 281–98.

Cohn, Ruby. *Samuel Beckett: The Comic Gamut.* New Brunswick, N.J.: Rutgers University Press, 1962.

Columb, Gregory. "The Semiotic Study of Literary Works." In *Tracing Literary*

Theory, edited by Joseph Natoli, 306–49. Urbana and Chicago: University of Illinois Press, 1987.

Corrigan, Robert W., ed. *Comedy: Meaning and Form*. 2d ed. New York: Harper and Row, 1981.

Craig, David M. "Closure Resisted: Style and Form in Joseph Heller's Novels." *Centennial Review* 30 (1986): 238–50.

De Marinis, Marco. "Dramaturgy of the Spectator." Translated by Paul Dwyer. *Drama Review* 31 (1987): 100–14.

Derrida, Jaques. "Structure, Sign, and Play in the Discourse of the Human Sciences." In *The Structuralist Controversy: The Languages of Criticism and the Sciences of Man*, edited by Richard Macksey and Eugenio Donato, 247–65. Baltimore and London: The Johns Hopkins University Press, 1972.

De Sousa, Ronald. *The Rationality of Emotion*. Cambridge: MIT Press, 1990.

Dixon, Norman F. *Preconscious Processing*. Chichester and New York: John Wiley and Sons, 1981.

Eagleton, Terry. *Marxism and Literary Critique*. Berkeley and Los Angeles: University of California Press, 1976.

Eckartsberg, Rolf von. "Maps of the Mind: The Cartography of Consciousness." In *Metaphors of Consciousness*, edited by Ronald S. Valle and Rolf von Eckartsberg, 21–93. New York and London: Plenum, 1981.

Eco, Umberto. *The Role of the Reader: Explorations in the Semiotics of Texts*. Bloomington and London: Indiana University Press, 1979.

———. *A Theory of Semiotics*. Bloomington and London: Indiana University Press, 1979.

———. *The Open Work*. Translated by Anna Cancogni, introduction by David Robey. Cambridge: Harvard University Press, 1989.

Eigen, Manfred, and Ruthild Winkler. *Laws of the Game: How the Principles of Nature Govern Chance*. Translated by Robert Kimber and Rita Kimber. New York: Harper and Row, 1983.

Einstein, Albert. "Letter to Jacques Hademard." In *The Creative Process: A Symposium*. Edited with introduction by Brewster Ghiselin, 32–33. 1952; reprint. Berkeley and Los Angeles: University of California Press, 1985.

Elam, Keir. *The Semiotics of Theatre and Drama*. London and New York: Methuen, 1980.

———. *Shakespeare's Universe of Discourse: Language Games in the Comedies*. Cambridge: Cambridge University Press, 1984.

Ericksen, Donald H. *Oscar Wilde*. Boston: Twayne, 1977.

Evans, Bertrand. *Shakespeare's Comedies*. Oxford: Clarendon Press, 1960.

Farnham, Willard. *The Shakespearian Grotesque: Its Genesis and Transformations*. Oxford: Clarendon Press, 1971.

Fein, Greta G. "Pretend Play: Creativity and Consciousness." In *Curiosity, Imagination, and Play: On the Development of Spontaneous Cognition*, edited by Dietmar Gorlitz and Joachim F. Wohlwill, 281–304. Hillsdale, N.J. and London: Lawrence Erlbaum, 1987.

Feyerabend, Paul. *Against Method*. New York: Humanities Press, 1975.

Fielding, Henry. *The History of Tom Jones, a Foundling*. Introduction by George Sherburn. New York: Random House, 1950.

Fink, Eugen. "The Ontology of Play." Translation by Sister Delphine Kolker. *Philosophy Today* 18 (1974): 147–61.

Fish, Stanley. "Why No One's Afraid of Wolfgang Iser." *Diacritics* 11 (1981): 2–13.

Foster, Hal, ed. *The Anti-Aesthetic: Essays on Postmodern Culture.* Port Townsend, Wash.: Bay Press, 1983.

Foster, Susan Leigh. *Reading Dance: Bodies and Subjects in Contemporary American Dance.* Berkeley and Los Angeles: University of California Press, 1986.

Fraleigh, Sondra H. *Dance and the Lived Body, a Descriptive Aethetics.* Pittsburgh: University of Pittsburgh Press, 1987.

Freund, Elizabeth. "Strategies of Inconclusiveness in *Henry IV, Part 1.*" In *Shakespearean Comedy,* edited by Maurice Charney, 207–16. New York: New York Literary Forum, 1980.

Frye, Northrop. *Anatomy of Criticism.* Princeton: Princeton University Press, 1957.

Gadamer, Hans-Georg. *Truth and Method.* Edited by Garrett Barden and John Cumming. New York: Seabury Press, 1975.

Garfield, Jay L. *Belief in Psychology: A Study of the Ontology of Mind.* Cambridge: MIT Press, 1988.

Garfinkel, Harold. "Studies of the Routine Grounds of Everyday Activities." In *Studies in Social Interaction,* edited by David Sudnow, 1–30. New York: Free Press, 1972.

Garner, Stanton B., Jr. *The Absent Voice: Narrative Comprehension in Theater.* Urbana and Chicago: University of Illinois Press, 1989.

Gerstenberger, Donna. *John Millington Synge.* Rev. ed. Boston: Twayne, 1990.

Gillmor, Alan M. *Erik Satie.* Boston: Twayne, 1988.

Goddard, Harold C. *The Meaning of Shakespeare.* Chicago: University of Chicago Press, 1957.

Godkewitsch, M. "Correlates of Humor: Verbal and Nonverbal Aesthetic Reactions as Functions of Semantic Distance Within Adjective-Noun Pairs." In *Studies in the New Experimental Aesthetics: Steps toward an Objective Psychology of Aesthetic Appreciation,* edited by D. E. Berlyne, 279–304. Washington, D.C.: Hemisphere, 1974.

Gombrich, E. H. *Art and Illusion.* Reprint. Princeton: Princeton University Press, 1969.

Gottschalk, Paul A. "Hal and the 'Play Extempore' in 1 Henry IV." *Tennessee Studies in Language and Literature* 15 (1974): 605–14.

Greimas, A. J., and J. Courtés. *Semiotics and Language: An Analytical Dictionary.* Bloomington and London: Indiana University Press, 1982.

Gross, Beverly. "Misfits: Tom Robbins' *Even Cowgirls Get the Blues.*" *North Dakota Quarterly* 50 (Summer 1982): 36–51.

Grote, David. *The End of Comedy: The Sit-Com and the Comedic Tradition.* Hamden, Conn.: Archon, 1983.

Gruber, William F. *Comic Theaters: Studies in Performance and Audience Response.* Athens: University of Georgia Press, 1986.

Guilhamet, Leon. *Satire and the Transformation of Genre.* Philadelphia: University of Pennsylvania Press, 1987.

Gurewitch, Morton. *Comedy, the Irrational Vision*. Ithaca and London: Cornell University Press, 1975.

Gurewitsch, Aaron. *Marginal Consciousness*, edited by Lester Embree. Athens, Ohio and London: Ohio University Press, 1982.

Hanna, Judith Lynne. "Toward Semantic Analysis of Movement Behavior: Concepts and Problems." *Semiotica* 25 (1979): 77–110.

Hart, Linda. *Sam Shepard's Metaphorical Stages*. New York and London: Greenwood, 1987.

Heidegger, Martin. *Poetry, Language, Thought*. Translated, compiled, and with introduction by Albert Hofstadter. New York: Harper and Row, 1975.

Heilman, Robert B. *The Ways of the World: Comedy and Society*. Seattle and London: University of Washington Press, 1978.

Highet, Gilbert. *The Anatomy of Satire*. Princeton: Princeton University Press, 1960.

Hinman, Lawrence. "Nietzsche's Philosophy of Play." *Philosophy Today* 18 (1974): 106–24.

Hirsch, Edward. "The Gallous Story and the Dirty Deed: The Two Playboys." *Modern Drama* 26 (1983): 85–102.

Holdsworth, R. V. *"Every Man in His Humour" and "The Alchemist": A Casebook*. London: Macmillan, 1978.

Holland, Norman. *The Dynamics of Literary Response*. New York: Oxford University Press, 1968.

———. "The New Paradigm: Subjective or Transitive?" *New Literary History* 7 (1976): 335–46.

———. *Laughing: A Psychology of Humor*. Ithaca and London: Cornell University Press, 1982.

Holub, Robert C. *Reception Theory, a Critical Introduction*. London and New York: Methuen, 1984.

Hooker, Richard. *M*A*S*H*. New York: Pocket Books, 1969.

Horace. *Satires, Epistles, and Ars poetica*. Translated by H. R. Fairclough. Loeb Classical Library. Cambridge: Harvard University Press, 1929.

Hryniewicz, Ewa. "*Waiting for Godot:* Beckett's Homo Ludens." *Arizona Quarterly* 42 (1986): 261–70.

Huizinga, Johan. *Homo Ludens: A Study of the Play Element in Culture*. Boston: Beacon Press, 1950.

Humphrey, Doris. *The Art of Making Dances*. New York: Holt, Rinehart and Winston, 1959.

Hunting, Robert. *Jonathan Swift*. Rev. ed. Boston: Twayne, 1989.

Huston, Dennis. *Shakespeare's Comedies of Play*. New York: Columbia University Press, 1981.

Hutchinson, Peter. *Games Authors Play*. London and New York: Methuen, 1983.

Iser, Wolfgang. *The Implied Reader: Patterns of Communication in Prose Fiction from Bunyan to Beckett*. Baltimore: The Johns Hopkins University Press, 1974.

———. *The Act of Reading: A Theory of Aesthetic Response*. Baltimore: The Johns Hopkins University Press, 1978.

———. "Counter-Sensical Comedy and Audience Response in Beckett's *Waiting for Godot*." *Bucknell Review* 26 (1981): 139–89.

Jameson, Frederick. *The Political Unconscious: Narrative as a Socially Symbolic Act.* Ithaca and London: Cornell University Press, 1981.

Janko, Richard. *Aristotle on Comedy.* Berkeley and Los Angeles: University of California Press, 1984.

Jauss, Hans Robert. *Aesthetic Experience and Literary Hermeneutics.* Translated by Michael Shaw. Minneapolis: University of Minnesota Press, 1982.

Johnson, Robert K. *Neil Simon.* Boston: Twayne, 1983.

Jones, Myrddin. "Sir Epicure Mammon: A Study in 'Spiritual Fornication'." *Renaissance Quarterly* 22 (1969): 233–42.

Jonson, Ben. *The Complete Plays of Ben Jonson.* Edited by G. A. Wilkes. 4 vols. Oxford: Clarendon Press, 1981–1982.

Jowitt, Deborah. *Time and the Dance Image.* New York: William Morrow, 1988.

Kearney, Richard. *The Wake of the Imagination: Ideas of Creativity in Western Culture.* London: Hutchinson, 1988.

Keith-Spiegel, Patricia. "Early Conceptions of Humor: Varieties and Issues." In *The Psychology of Humor: Theoretical Perspectives and Empirical Issues,* edited by Jeffrey H. Goldstein and Paul E. McGhee, 3–39. New York and London: Academic Press, 1972.

Kernan, Alvin B. *The Cankered Muse.* New Haven: Yale University Press, 1965.

————. *The Plot of Satire.* New Haven: Yale University Press, 1965.

Kivy, Peter. *Sound and Semblance: Reflections on Musical Representation.* Princeton: Princeton University Press, 1984.

Koestler, Arthur. *The Act of Creation.* London: Hutchinson. 1964.

Kris, Ernst. *Psychoanalytic Explorations in Art.* New York: International University Press, 1952.

Laban, Rudolf von. *The Mastery of Movement.* London: Macdonald and Evans, 1960.

————. *Choreutics.* London: Macdonald and Evans, 1968.

Langer, Ellen J. *Mindfulness.* Reading, Mass.: Addison-Wesley, 1990.

Langer, Susanne K. *Feeling and Form, a Theory of Art.* New York: Charles Scribner's Sons, 1953.

Lanham, Richard A. *The Motives of Eloquence: Literary Rhetoric in the Renaissance.* New Haven and London: Yale University Press, 1976.

Lauter, Paul, ed. *Theories of Comedy.* New York: Doubleday, 1964.

Lotman, Yuri, *The Structure of the Artistic Text.* Translated by Ronald Vroon. Ann Arbor: University of Michigan Press, 1977.

McCloskey, Michael. "Naive Theories of Motion." In *Mental Models,* edited by Dedre Gentner and Albert L. Stevens, 299–324. London: Lawrence Erlbaum, 1983.

McGhee, Paul and Jeffrey H. Goldstein, eds. *Handbook of Humor Research.* 2 vols. New York and Berlin: Springer, 1983.

McGovern, Edythe M. *Not-So-Simple Neil Simon, a Critical Study.* Van Nuys, Calif.: Perivale Press, 1978.

McGuire, Richard L. "The Play-within-the-play in *1 Henry IV." Shakespeare Quarterly* 18 (1967): 47–52.

McNeir, Waldo F. "Structure and Theme in the First Tavern Scene of *Henry IV,*

Part One." In *Essays on Shakespeare,* edited by Gordon A. Smith, 67–83. University Park and London: Pennsylvania State University Press, 1965.

Machery, Paul. *A Theory of Literary Production.* Translated by Geoffrey Wall. London: Routledge and Kegan Paul, 1978.

Machiavelli, Niccolò. *The Comedies of Machiavelli.* Edited and translated by David Sices and James B. Atkinson. Hanover, N.H. and London: University Press of New England, 1985.

Marino, James A. G. "An Annotated Bibliography of Play and Literature." *Canadian Review of Comparative Literature* 12 (1985): 306–58.

Martin, Mike W. "Humor and Aesthetic Enjoyment of Incongruity." In *The Philosophy of Laughter and Humor,* edited by John Morreall, 172–86. Albany: State University of New York Press, 1987.

Martinez, Ronald. "The Pharmacy of Machiavelli: Roman Lucretia in *Mandragola."* *Renaissance Drama* 14 (1983): 1–47.

Merleau-Ponty, Maurice. *Phenomenology of Perception.* Translated by Colin Smith. London: Routledge and Kegan Paul, 1962.

Merrill, Robert. "The Structure and Meaning of *Catch-22."* *Studies in American Fiction* 14 (1986): 139–52.

Millar, Susanna. *The Psychology of Play.* Baltimore: Penguin, 1968.

Monaco, James. *American Film Now.* New York and London: New American Library, 1979.

Nash, Walter. *The Language of Humor.* London and New York: Longman, 1985.

Nealon, Jeffrey. "Samuel Beckett and the Postmodern: Language Games, Play in *Waiting for Godot."* *Modern Drama* 31 (1988): 520–28.

Nollet, Thomas G. "Tom Sharpe and the Satire of Racism: Caricature and Farce in *Riotous Assembly."* *Studies in Contemporary Satire* 15 (1988): 11–19.

Norman, Donald A. *The Psychology of Everyday Things.* New York: Basic Books, 1988.

Norwood, Gilbert. *Greek Comedy.* London: Methuen, 1931.

Olson, Elder. *The Theory of Comedy.* Bloomington and London: University of Indiana Press, 1968.

Ornstein, Robert. *A Kingdom for a Stage: The Achievement of Shakespeare's History Plays.* Cambridge: Harvard University Press, 1972.

Parker, Randolph. "Gaming in the Gap: Language and Liminality in *Playboy of the Western World."* *Theatre Journal* 37 (1985): 65–85.

Pavel, Thomas G. *Fictional Worlds.* Cambridge: Harvard University Press, 1986.

Pechter, Edward. "Falsifying Men's Hopes: The Ending of '1 Henry IV'." *Modern Language Quarterly* 41 (1980): 211–30.

Perlman, Alan M., and Daniel Greenblatt. "Miles Davis Meets Naom Chomsky: Some Observations on Jazz Improvisation and Language Structure." In *The Sign in Music and Literature,* edited by Wendy Steiner, 169–83. Austin and London: University of Texas Press, 1981.

Perry, George. *The Life of Python.* Boston and Toronto: Little Brown, 1983.

Piaget, Jean. *Play, Dreams, and Imitation in Childhood.* Translated by C. Gattegno and F. M. Hodgson. New York: Norton, 1951.

Prior, Moody E. *The Drama of Power: Studies in Shakespeare's History Plays.* Evanston, Ill.: Northwestern University Press, 1973.

Python, Monty. *The Complete Monty Python's Flying Circus: All the Words.* 2 vols. New York: Pantheon, 1989.

Raby, Peter. *Oscar Wilde.* Cambridge: Cambridge University Press, 1988.

Rayner, Alice. *Comic Persuasion: Moral Structure in British Comedy From Shakespeare to Stoppard.* Berkeley and Los Angeles: University of California Press, 1987.

Reese, H. M. *The Cease of Majesty: A Study of Shakespeare's History Plays.* New York: St. Martin's Press, 1961.

Review of *Blazing Saddles,* by Mel Brooks. *Films in Review* 25 (March 1974): 182–83.

———. *Variety Film Reviews, 1907–1980.* Vol. 13, 13 February 1974. New York and London: Garland, 1983.

Ribner, Irving. *The English History Play in the Age of Shakespeare.* Princeton: Princeton University Press, 1957.

Richman, David. *Laughter, Pain, and Wonder: Shakespeare's Comedies and the Audience in the Theater.* Newark, London, and Toronto: University of Delaware Press, 1990.

Richter, David H. *Fable's End: Completeness and Closure in Rhetorical Fiction.* Chicago: University of Chicago Press, 1974.

Ricouer, Paul. "The Question of Subject: The Challenge of Semiology." In *The Conflict of Interpretation: Essays in Hermeneutics.* Translated by Kathleen McLaughlin and edited by Don Ihde, 236–66. Evanston, Ill.: Northwestern University Press, 1974.

Rimmon-Kenan, Shlomith. *Narrative Fiction: Contemporary Poetics.* London and New York: Methuen, 1983.

Robbins, Tom. *Even Cowgirls Get the Blues.* New York: Bantam, 1977.

Rothenberg, Albert. *The Emerging Goddess: The Creative Process in Art, Science, and Other Fields.* Chicago and London: University of Chicago Press, 1979.

San Juan, Epifanio, Jr. *The Art of Oscar Wilde.* Princeton: Princeton University Press, 1967.

Sayre, Henry M. *The Object of Performance: The American Avant-Garde since 1970.* Chicago and London: University of Chicago Press, 1989.

Schiller, Friedrich von. "Letters on the Aesthetical Education of Man." *Complete Works of Freidrich Schiller.* 8 vols. [No translator given.] New York: Collier, 1902.

Schuler, Robert M. "Jonson's Alchemists, Epicureans, and Puritans." *Medieval and Renaissance Drama in England* 2 (1985): 171–208.

Scruton, Roger. *The Aesthetic Understanding.* New York and London: Methuen, 1983.

Shklovsky, Victor. "Art as Technique." In *Russian Formalist Criticism,* edited by L. T. Lemon and M. J. Reis, 3–24. Lincoln: University of Nebraska Press, 1965.

Shakespeare, William. *As You Like It.* Arden Edition, rev. Edited by Ann Latham. London: Methuen, 1975.

———. *Henry IV, Part 1.* The Oxford Shakespeare. Edited by David Bevington. Oxford: Clarendon Press, 1987.

Sharpe, Tom. *Riotous Assembly.* London: Pan Books, 1973.

Shaw, George Bernard. *Review of "An Ideal Husband," by Oscar Wilde.* In *Theatres in the Nineties,* 1:9. Vol. 24 of *Works of George Bernard Shaw.* 36 vols. London: Constable and Company Ltd., 1932.

Sheets, Maxine. *The Phenomenology of Dance.* Madison: University of Wisconsin Press, 1966.

Shepard, Sam. *Sam Shepard, Seven Plays.* Introduction by Richard Gilman. New York: Bantam, 1981.

Shershow, Scott C. *Laughing Matters: The Paradox of Comedy.* Amherst: University of Massachusetts Press, 1986.

Siegel, Mark. "The Meaning of Meaning in the Novels of Tom Robbins." *Mosaic* 14 (1981): 119–31.

Simon, Neil. *The Comedy of Neil Simon.* Introduction by Neil Simon. New York: Equinox, 1971.

Simon, Richard Keller. "Beckett, Comedy, and the Critics: A Study of Two Contexts." In *Beckett Translating/Translating Beckett,* edited by Alan W. Freidman, Charles Rossman, and Dina Sherzer, 85–94. University Park and London: Pennsylvania State University Press, 1987.

Sloboda, John A. *The Musical Mind: The Cognitive Psychology of Music.* Oxford Psychology Series Number 5. Oxford: Clarendon Press, 1985.

Solomon, Jan. "The Structure of Catch-22." *Critique* 9 (1967): 46–57.

Spariosu, Mihai. *Literature, Mimesis and Play.* Tübingen: Gunter Narr, 1982.

———. *Dionysus Reborn: Play and the Aesthetic Dimension in Modern Philosophical and Scientific Discourse.* Ithaca and London: Cornell University Press, 1989.

Spencer, Paul, ed. *The Social Anthropology of Process and Performance.* Cambridge: Cambridge University Press, 1985.

Spivack, Bernard. *Shakespeare and the Allegory of Evil.* New York: Columbia University Press, 1958.

States. Bert O. *Great Reckonings in Little Rooms: On the Phenomenology of Theater.* Berkeley and Los Angeles: University of California Press, 1985.

Synge, John Millington. *J. M. Synge, Collected Works.* Edited by Robin Skelton. 4 vols. London: Oxford University Press, 1968.

Taylor, Ella. *Prime-Time Families: Television Culture in Postwar America.* Berkeley and Los Angeles: University of California Press, 1990.

Tilghman, B. R. *But Is It Art? The Value of Art and the Temptation of Theory.* Oxford: Blackwell, 1986.

Tonelli, Franco. "Machiavelli's *Mandragola* and the Signs of Power." *Drama, Sex and Politics.* Themes in Drama 7, edited by James Redmond, 35–54. Cambridge: Cambridge University Press, 1985.

Walton, Kendall L. *Mimesis as Make-Believe: On the Foundations of the Representational Arts.* Cambridge: Harvard University Press, 1990.

Watson, Robert N. *Ben Jonson's Parodic Strategy: Literary Imperialism in the Comedies.* Cambridge: Harvard University Press, 1987.

Weisberg, Robert W. *Creativity, Genius and Other Myths.* New York: W. H. Freeman, 1986.

West, Robert, Peter Howell, and Ian Cross. "Modelling Perceived Musical Structure." In *Musical Structure and Cognition,* edited by Peter Howell, Ian Cross, and Robert West, 21–52. London and New York: Academic Press, 1985.

Wigman, Mary. *The Language of Dance.* Translated by Walter Sorell. Middletown, Conn.: Wesleyan University Press, 1966.

Wilbur, Richard. *Ceremony and Other Poems.* New York: Harcourt, Brace and World, 1948.

Williams, Drid. "Deep Structures of the Dance." *Yearbook of Symbolic Anthropology* 1 (1978): 211–30.

Wilmut, Robert. *From Fringe to Flying Circus: Celebrating a Unique Generation of Comedy, 1960–1980.* London: Eyre-Methuen, 1980.

Wilshire, Bruce. *Role Playing and Identity: The Limits of Theatre as Metaphor.* Bloomington and London: Indiana University Press, 1982.

Wittgenstein, Ludwig. *Philosophical Investigations.* Translated by G.E.M. Anscombe. Oxford: Blackwell, 1968.

Yeats, William Butler. *Essays and Introductions.* London: Macmillan, 1961.

Index

197